Chicken Soup for the Soul

Just Us Girls

101 Stories about Friendship for Women of All Ages

Jack Canfield, Mark Victor Hansen & Amy Newmark

Chicken Soup for the Soul Publishing, LLC
Cos Cob, CT

Chicken Soup

www.chickensoup.com

for the Soul

Contents

❶
~The New Friend Project~

❷
~My Group~

❸
~She Knows~

❹
~Down the Block~

❺
~It Works~

❻

~Taking the Plunge~

❼

~Second Looks~

8

~Adventures with the Girls~

9

~Distant and Close~

10

~The Write Stuff~

⓫

~Relative Friends~

Chapter
1

Just Us Girls

The New Friend Project

Wanted: Mom Friends

Are we not like two volumes of one book?
~Marceline Desbordes-Valmore

For me, the early days of motherhood were isolating. I had quit a rewarding job to become a stay-at-home mom, and while I loved being with my six-month-old son, what I missed most was adult conversation. Every day, I pounced on my husband, Dwayne, the moment he came home from work, anxious to hear news from the outside world. We both knew I needed to make "mom friends." But how?

Although I often took Ethan with me on errands, shopping at the grocery store didn't exactly provide a chance to make a new friend. Ethan was content to smile at the other customers and look at the brightly colored displays, but I wasn't. "We need to find something better to do," I told him.

Surprisingly, the solution was just a few miles away.

"I want to pick up a few things at the library. Let's all go," Dwayne said on one of his days off. He didn't need to ask twice. I loved to read, but hadn't had much time or energy since Ethan was born. Perhaps a good book would lift my spirits.

After choosing a novel, I decided to venture past the adult department. The children's area looked inviting, and with Ethan in the stroller I felt qualified to take a closer look. A decorated wall displayed schedules of activities for children of all ages, even babies. I picked up one and noted an upcoming playgroup for babies and toddlers. I doubted I would know anyone there, but it had to beat sitting at home.

The next week I gathered my courage, and Ethan and I headed to the library. "We're going to go play, and we'll have a great time," I said to him, partly to convince myself. "Da, da, da," he babbled in agreement.

The library's community room was filled with a play kitchen, a small ball pit, lots of toys for babies and toddlers, and half a dozen moms and their children, none of whom looked familiar. Uh oh.

"Welcome to playgroup. I'm Misty, the playgroup coordinator," said a smiling woman about my age. "How old is your baby? What's his name?" she asked, her friendliness instantly putting me at ease. Misty introduced me to the other moms, and we began chatting about our children's milestones, their favorite baby foods, and their sleep schedules while the babies and toddlers played around us. I left the playgroup feeling energized and excited about these potential new friendships.

After that first playgroup, Ethan and I rarely missed a date. As he grew, I added "Tot Time" and preschool "Story Time" activities to our schedule. And when his younger sister and brother were born, our calendar filled up even more. Together we've learned about gardening, met small animals from the local zoo, played math and alphabet games, and most importantly, we've all made new friends.

I'm grateful for the moms I've met at the library. We share similar backgrounds and interests, and with children in the same age group, we can offer each other a sympathetic ear and advice. To help pass the time when our children were younger, we met at a different park each week during the summer so they could play and we could chat. Nowadays, my friends and I get together for dinner or shopping without the kids so we can enjoy each other's uninterrupted company. And we still attend lots of library activities with our children.

I'm still amazed how one small act of bravery made such a huge difference in my level of happiness. Go ahead and strike up a conversation with the mom at the next park bench. Seek out other moms at your church or your child's school and start your own playgroup or book club. And don't forget to check for activities at your local library. You just may meet some lifelong friends.

~Melissa Zifzal

From Gym Friend to Real Friend

Why not go out on a limb? Isn't that where the fruit is?
~Frank Scully

I have been going to the gym for years, hoping to keep my body strong and my bones straight. My mother had severe osteoporosis and I was determined to do all I could to prevent that from happening to me. So I worked out—hard.

On this particular day, I was pressing through my twentieth pushup with a metal weight perched on the middle of my back, feeling every muscle complain, when I heard a woman's voice say, "I don't like this." At least I wasn't the only one who found working out at the gym trying. When I finished, I looked up and saw a familiar face, a woman who had been going to the gym regularly like me. She was doing sumo squats. We complained to each other about how hard the exercises were today. Our trainer ignored us, as usual.

She finished her workout and left while I was just at the beginning of mine. Our trainings frequently overlapped so we had the chance to talk while we sweated. We were always glad to see each other as gym friends but had never made an attempt to get together outside of the gym.

Later that week, as she was leaving and I was coming in, I said on a whim, "Would you like to meet for lunch some day?"

She seemed pleasantly surprised.

"Sure," she said.

We made a date for the following Friday after our workouts. She would do some errands and come back for me after I was done.

"Great!" I said, and we went our separate ways.

As the date drew closer, though, I wondered what we would talk about.

On the day we were supposed to get together, our trainer handed me a note. It was an apology. My gym friend was called in to work and wouldn't be able to meet me. I thanked him for the message, stuffed it in my purse, and went on with my training. But it made me a little edgy. Had I been too pushy? We had never really chatted about anything substantial. Would it be embarrassing for both of us? Had she thought about our meeting and decided it was a bad idea after all?

When we met again she was the one to bring up our getting together. So we made another date. This time she stayed on the tread-mill while I exercised and waited for me. We left together and went to a local restaurant in the same shopping center. It was an unusually warm winter day so we ordered and brought our plates outside.

As we settled down we looked at each other across the table and before we knew it we were halfway through our meals and deep into conversation. We learned more about each other as we ate our salads than we had discovered in all the years during our workouts. We found that we had similar philosophies and interests. We talked about family and travels and whatever else popped into our minds. Almost two hours passed before we decided we had better move on.

We had parked our cars side by side without even knowing it.

"I decided," she said, "that I only want to be friends with some-one who speaks to my heart."

Then she smiled warmly and I knew she meant me. And I knew that I now had a girlfriend who would be part of my life in and outside of the gym.

~Ferida Wolff

Wild Bouquet of Friends

A friend is one of the nicest things you can have,
and one of the best things you can be.
~Douglas Pagels

Michelle dropped into my life just when I needed her. Like manna from heaven. Five of my seven closest friends had moved in the past year. I just knew if I stood on the end of my drive, waving goodbye to a sweetheart sister one more time, my heart would break.

Enter Michelle. I met her at church, and she was a master at making friends. Her husband had been in the Navy. And his civilian job brought many transfers, too. Moving was a way of life for her, and she rose to the challenge.

"Want to come over for lunch today?" Michelle asked.

We were scraping glue from eight-foot tables. Day one of Vacation Bible School and the craft room had gone wild.

"Today?" I asked.

I barely knew Michelle. She'd been around church for a while, but our paths hadn't crossed. Until VBS.

"Sure," she said. "I'll make pizza. The kids can play."

Michelle had three young sons and a daughter. I had three young sons, too. Sounded like a good fit. But I was tired and the morning had been full.

"C'mon" she said, as if tapping my thoughts. "I'll make you an iced tea. I have a nice porch and we can sit."

Sold.

My sons and I went to Michelle's that day, and it took about ten minutes for us to feel like we'd all been friends for a hundred years. Michelle had that way about her. And by the time the boys and I loaded into our van and headed home, I felt as though I'd been given a sweet gift. Michelle eased some of the hurt of those relocated friendships.

And I didn't even have to try to find her.

The next day at Bible school, Michelle was waiting by the door. "I need to get groceries tonight," she said. "Want to come?"

I thought of my cupboards at home. Mother Hubbard for sure. But I'd never gone for groceries with a friend. Seemed like a solo task to me. "Together?" I asked.

"Of course," she said. "Another friend is going to go, too. But there's plenty of room in the Land Rover."

I agreed. And when Michelle picked me up that evening, I was surprised. Her other friend was much younger. Single. I wondered where Michelle had met her and what we'd have in common. I expected a thirty-something mama, like me.

But the evening was a delight.

It was fun to meet someone new and to hear about a life that was so different from mine.

And such was life with Michelle. As I got to know her better, I got to know many others, too. Michelle was different from anyone I'd ever met. And she had a lot of friends. Older friends. Friends in their twenties. Single. Married. Friends with no children. Friends with a half-dozen kids. I'd always played things safe, choosing friends who were just like me, but Michelle reached far. She had friends who were working through divorces and addictions. She was a friend even to some who were hard to befriend.

And I was in awe of her. She'd more than filled a void in my life. And I learned from watching her love.

Then came a sad day. The day she told me she was going to move.

"It's a transfer," she said. "But it will be good for my family. I know we'll meet others who could use a new friend."

But what about me? I wondered. Another friend. Moving away. Maybe it wasn't worth it, getting so deep into someone's life. Who would take her place? Who would be my friend?

The weeks rolled by and Michelle's home became a maze of cardboard boxes. I helped her pack her life, and it felt as though I were packing my own heart. Then came moving day. Once again I stood on the end of the drive. Michelle's children waved like wild and mine waved back hard. I kicked a few pebbles with the tip of my shoe as her white truck became smaller and disappeared.

Gone. Another friend.

The next few days were hard and quiet. Michelle was a pursuer. An inviter. An initiator. With her gone, the phone seemed quiet. I missed her smile. Her warmth. The way her kitchen was a haven for women of all walks of life.

Then one afternoon my boys and I were playing outside. Their laughter rose above the high squeal of the swings. But I didn't feel like laughing. I was lonely for a friend.

And that's when I saw the young mother.

She was walking down the sidewalk, newborn babe strapped to her chest. Her bright red ponytail bobbed high on her head. Two young boys ran in front of her, darting off the sidewalk and back on. She was young. Very young.

I pushed gently on my little son's back. His swing flew high. The mother was just about in front of our house. I pushed again. My little guy cheered. The little parade moved closer, this mother so much younger than me.

And I thought of Michelle.

"C'mon, guys," I said. I pulled on the chains and gently stopped their swings. "There's a mama and some boys coming down the block. Let's go over and say hello."

My sons raced forward, filled with the anticipation of a new friend. I moved forward, too, recognizing that desire in my own heart.

"Hi," I said when we reached the sidewalk. "Nice day for a walk."

That young mother and I chatted in the afternoon sun, and in time, she became one of my very close friends. But my friendships didn't stop there. I began to stretch out. Look beyond my own age, life stage, and circumstance. Before too long I had older friends. Friends without children. Single friends. Friends whose lives were very different from mine.

And the blessing was sweet.

I still miss Michelle. But I know she's reaching others, spreading joy, providing a shoulder, loving and teaching others how to love. And I sometimes wish she hadn't moved.

But this special lady left me with the very best parting gift—the ability to see the beauty in a wild bouquet of friends.

~Shawnelle Eliasen

4

Friends of Susan Society

Remember, you don't need a certain number of friends,
just a number of friends you can be certain of.
~Author Unknown

When Susan — my best friend of thirty years — died, three of her friends and I got together with her daughter to organize a memorial service in her honor. For a week, we turned our grief into lists — lists of things to do, food and whatnot to buy, people to call and e-mail.

The memorial turned out even better than we had hoped, complete with Susan's favorite foods and a slide show that reflected all aspects of her life, from childhood to adulthood, from family to work. After the crowd departed, and her daughter went home, the four organizers sat down for a recap and chat.

Although we all knew Susan, and had met each other on several social occasions, none of us were close. Still reeling from the void in my life that Susan's death had caused, I came up with a suggestion. "Let's keep in touch. Maybe we can go for dinner in a couple of weeks. Sort of a Friends of Susan Society." The three women nodded.

Work kept me busy during the week, keeping my mind off my grief. Evenings and weekends were much harder. Sunday mornings in particular, when Susan and I used to go out for breakfast and a walk, now stretched long and bleak. One of the women and I e-mailed a couple of times, but the other two were busy with family and travel. Several months passed before one of the busier women suggested meeting for dinner.

I arrived at the restaurant first and waited for the others, a little nervous. Slightly younger, and the only one still working, I was also much lower down on the educational pecking order than they had been, a substitute teacher rather than a principal or high-level school board position.

I felt as if I were back in grade school, trying to make friends with kids in my class I knew by sight but had never really talked to. I wiped my palms on my pants, took a deep breath, and pasted a smile on my face.

I needn't have worried. We had a delightful evening and they never made me feel anything other than included. Many of our conversations began, "Remember when Susan did...?" Or, "Let me tell you a funny story about Susan." Or, "I was thinking about Susan the other day and..." We traded stories about Susan's inability to organize anything, her love of travel and hiking, her culinary experiments, the way you knew she was really angry when her voice got very soft. It was almost as if she were there with us, laughing in the background.

At the end of the evening, we promised to get together again, but one woman was off to Europe for two months, a second took care of her grandkids three days a week, a third had a retired husband and daughter with serious health issues.

By the time I got home the glow of the evening had dulled. Something felt off. For the next two days I thought about it—nice women, nice evening, nice conversation—what could be wrong? But I still couldn't shake the feeling that all the "nice" in the world didn't quite add up.

I needed to talk to someone, so I called a friend who knew about the evening.

"How did it go?" Mavis asked.

"Okay."

"Just okay? You were looking forward to having dinner with these women. I know you were hoping to make some new friends. What happened?"

I tried to untangle my thoughts. "It was a really nice dinner. We traded Susan stories and talked a bit about what we were doing, but..." Still not sure, I hesitated.

"But what?"

"But it was still all about Susan," I blurted out. "I wanted to make new friends, but these were... they were old friends, but they were Susan's old friends, not mine. Apart from all having known Susan, we don't really have any interests in common. I guess I was looking for an instant Susan clone to take over being my best friend. Dumb, I know."

"Not dumb. It's tough to lose a best friend. Wanting to turn people who knew her into your friends is simply a way of keeping her alive, if only by proxy."

I sighed. "Too bad it doesn't work."

"What are you going to do?"

I took a moment to think. "I do need to make more friends, but it should be about me, not Susan. There's a teacher I know slightly at work who seems very nice. Maybe it's time to try yoga again. I'm sure I could meet a couple of people there." I paused as more ideas came to my head. "And the women in my book club. There's no reason we couldn't do things outside book club nights. Like go to a movie or out for coffee."

Mavis laughed. "Sounds like the Friends of Susan Society will need a new name—the Friends of Harriet Society. Just move slowly. Friendships take time and effort to build but..."

"...the right ones are worth the effort," I completed. "Mavis?"

"Yes?"

"Thanks for being my friend."

~Harriet Cooper

Time to Say Goodbye

No person is your friend who demands your silence,
or denies your right to grow.
~Alice Walker

I'd just returned from our regular monthly lunch date. As usual, my friend and I had exchanged the latest news, relished the gossip about other friends' breakups, and laughed until our make-up ran. But driving home, I began to feel as I had the last several times.

It started like a wisp, a feather across my mind, and quickly heightened. What irked me so much?

I went to my journal. It always gave me answers.

Warming up, I started writing about the basics to help get me started—the phone call for a day that fit both our schedules, the big discussion the night before. "What do you feel like? Chinese? Italian? Decadent Deli?" Giggling, we chose Decadent—two kids skipping healthy diet school.

Then I described the restaurant. Arriving first, I had time to look around. The booth was roomy, upholstery past its prime. On the table sat the perennial bowl of sour pickles, with little pieces of garlic bobbing in the brine. The plastic-covered menu, three feet tall, promised anything your heart desired. Smiling hello, the gravel-voiced waitress asked if I were alone. From her collar hung a giant wilting cloth gardenia.

Continuing to write, I felt a small nervousness, an excitement that always told me I was getting closer to the truth.

As I studied the menu, my friend rushed in, breathless and flushed. We screamed and hugged. She slid into the booth opposite me and immediately started talking.

"The traffic! This idiot in front of me for six miles! Couldn't make up his mind. Where did he learn to drive, Jupiter? Kept weaving in and out, the jerk!"

I wondered why she didn't pass him or take another route.

She kept talking, interrupted only by the waitress taking our orders for overstuffed pastrami sandwiches and diet sodas.

I kept writing, trusting the moving pen. Reliving our visit, I found, as always, the answers coming.

She lived, I saw, in a state of chronic indignation. Everything—from the curl of the napkins to the highway driver to how others raised children—was cause for her righteous anger.

As she talked, the frown between her eyebrows deepened, and her lips moved like a sped-up cartoon. Her outrage was punctuated by hand motions that alternately clutched the air and flattened in open-palmed incredulity at humankind's folly.

She jumped from one thing to another with quirky logic: shopping on the Internet revealed the stupidity of retailers. Restaurant pasta less than al dente was a sin punishable by leaving the waiter two quarters. The supermarket checkers' sluggishness proved the regression of human evolution and threatened our entire civilization.

After almost an hour, she wound down, sandwich untouched. Now, I thought, I could talk, finally sharing meaningful bits of my life and the news about mutual friends. That was when I knew she would listen and nod in understanding. And we'd laugh with full abandon like we used to.

But instead our conversation reminded her to deplore something else. And she was off again, eyes popping, voice strident in irate virtue.

In the past, sometimes I'd sympathized with her constant diatribes and even joined in. But then I'd come home with a headache, and, despite my lunch indulgence, not at all nourished. Today, I now saw, was no different.

When it was time to leave, we kissed and promised to call.

As I kept writing, the picture grew clearer. I'd really known for a long time but didn't want to admit it. She'd been a friend so many years, and we used to have such fun. But the truths scribbled out in my journal couldn't be denied.

It was time to say goodbye.

~Noelle Sterne

Riding the Road to Friendship

When I see an adult on a bicycle,
I do not despair for the future of the human race.
~H.G. Wells

I was a Northern newcomer to a Southern adult community. I knew no one and was feeling very out of place and lonesome. I wanted desperately to make new friends.

Day after day, I saw groups of cyclers riding throughout the community and beyond the gates. Dressed in black Spandex riding shorts, brightly colored biking shirts, gloves and helmets, they appeared to be having a great time together. I looked longingly at them as they rode in pace lines of eight to twelve riders.

I knew how to ride a bike, but couldn't imagine myself ever accomplishing the level of riding I saw. I read an article in the community newspaper inviting those interested in biking to join a beginner's cycling group. It is not like me to join something where I know no one, but I pushed myself to attend an organizational meeting. I immediately began chatting with two women and we committed to our first group ride taking place later in the week.

Twelve men and women ventured out on our first eight-mile ride. We slowly pedaled in a long line through the quiet streets of our community. We began to meet three times a week, and steadily increased our distance and speed. Stopping for refreshments became the norm and we soon adopted our mantra, "We bike for food." As we sat chatting over coffee, strong friendships began to form. Many of us found we had other interests in common and began exploring them together.

Now, comfortable with several members of the cycling club, I decided to attend a few of their social events, a luncheon, a fifties party, and a holiday gathering. There, I met more folks. Men from the cycling group brought their wives to the social events and wives brought their non-cycling partners. Out of these gatherings grew a small dinner group and again my circle expanded. More opportunities for new friendships opened up when our club members planned a few overnight cycling trips in conjunction with other clubs from various parts of the state.

All of these new friendships were made possible by taking that first step outside my comfort zone. I now ride fifty to 100 miles a week, have improved my health, and have more friends than I ever imagined. Taking that first step and trying something new opened up a whole new world of fun and friendships for me.

~Mary Grant Dempsey

The Marriage Class

Success in marriage does not come merely through finding the right mate,
but through being the right mate.
~Barnett R. Brickner

"We're starting a new class that will improve your marriage," Pastor Bob announced from the pulpit one Sunday. "The sign-up sheet is coming around."

My husband Eric shot me a hopeful look. A look that clearly said, "We're not doing that, right?"

My return glance said, "Don't you think we should? It would be good for us."

His hand found mine. "I thought you were happy," he whispered.

I squeezed his fingers and said, "I am. But I want to take this class."

"But we're already so busy. Do you think we have time in our schedule for one more thing?" Eric was right about that. We had five children, the youngest one just five months old, and our time was already stretched extremely thin. But still, something told me to join this class.

I shrugged. "I just want to do this."

Eric nodded and when the sign-up sheet came around, he wrote our names on it.

The first night of the class, each couple had to stand up in front of the others and share a little bit about themselves. Because our church is large and holds two services each Sunday, I had never met many of the other people in the class.

One couple stood up to share about themselves. "We had a baby last October," the wife said. Eric smiled at me. Our own little Nathan was the same age.

Another couple shared the ages and genders of their children, and they matched up perfectly with our other kids. Major play date potential there.

And several couples shared that they were on their second marriages, just like Eric and me. Each spouse had brought children from their first marriage into the new family and they were in the process of blending everybody together, just like we were.

At the break time, Eric and I found ourselves chatting with one of those blended couples. They are a "yours, mine, and ours" family just like Eric and me. As we talked, I felt a connection with the wife and asked if she'd like to get together some time. She smiled and looked relieved that I'd asked.

"That sounds like fun," she said. "Especially since we have so much in common."

In the car on the way home from church, I told Eric how glad I was that we had joined the class.

"Am I that bad of a husband?" he said with a grin. "Are we on the rocks already?"

I laughed and patted his hand. "No, you're a great husband—terrific, in fact. But the truth is that I've been lonely since I moved here."

Eric's eyebrows shot up. "Lonely? We have five kids and you are always saying you never have a moment to yourself. 'I can't even go to the bathroom by myself,'" he whined, imitating me.

"Not that kind of lonely," I said. "Like lonely for girlfriends, people I have things in common with." When Eric and I had married, I moved two hundred miles away from my hometown. This meant leaving my family, my teaching job, and all of my friends. And while I know it was the right decision, I often missed those people. Especially my mom.

Eric squeezed my hand. "I know moving was hard on you. And you're right, this class might be the perfect chance to make some new friends."

I began to list all of the women I had found interesting. People I'd like to get to know better. Like the lady who had a baby the same age as mine, and the women who were in blended families. These ladies were second wives—a tough gig—and they were probably stepmoms too, a challenge in its own right. I had so much in common with these ladies and in that moment, I knew why something had prompted me to take the marriage class.

It wasn't for my marriage. Not really. It was more to meet these women who had similar life experiences to mine. To make friends with them and support each other. To have someone to meet for coffee. Maybe provide a listening ear. Or even a shoulder to cry on.

I hadn't taken the time to make new friends in my new town. And that was a big mistake. But I plan to fix it very soon.

Every Sunday night, when my marriage class meets, I'll not only be growing closer to my husband. I'll be growing closer to some new girlfriends.

~Diane Stark

Out of the Labyrinth

A single rose can be my garden... a single friend, my world.
~Leo Buscaglia

When we moved to Canada, I left behind a lifetime of friends and the eternal Texas summer. My definition of winter was the weeks between Thanksgiving and New Year's. After we packed up the plastic evergreen garlands and twinkling lights on January 2nd I just assumed it was summer again.

Then I moved to Montreal, where winter lasts between four and five months of the year. During the first real winter of my life, staring out my living room window at the snow at the end of March, I felt like I was on the surface of the moon, far away from everyone I loved. I was a new mom in a new city. I didn't know many people, and I didn't have any friends except for my husband, who was at work, and my baby, who'd just learned to crawl.

One day, tired of being shut in, I decided to visit a yarn shop. I thought a hobby would give me something to enjoy and offer a way to meet new people. Knitting seemed like a good choice in a place where winter lasted so much of the year.

I Googled directions, got ready, bundled up my daughter, and headed outside. It took me a while to find the place the first time. I eventually found the right street, but then passed by the yarn shop on the corner. Just as I might have passed by it a second time, I noticed an appliqué quilt in a corner window that said "Ariadne Knits."

Inside, a woman sat knitting on a canvas sofa. As it turns out, her name was Molly Ann, not Ariadne. After I came in that first time, stomped the snow off my boots, and took them off by the door, Molly Ann immediately invited me to sit down on her sofa while she made me a cup of warm tea. It felt like I'd stumbled into her living room instead of a shop. The radio was playing The Beatles. The space was bright and cheery. My daughter had fallen asleep during our walk from the metro to the store.

I was so grateful to sit quietly and drink some tea. Molly Ann was easy to talk to, like a good therapist or minister or girlfriend. We just started chatting. I asked about the shop's name. She told me that Ariadne is a woman from Greek mythology who gave a hero named Theseus a ball of yarn before he entered the labyrinth of a monster called the Minotaur. That way, Theseus could unwind the yarn as he went in and follow the strand back out after he slew the Minotaur.

The whole afternoon passed by. Molly Ann held my daughter for a few minutes, led me through a maze of shelves stacked with skeins, and helped me pick out yarn for a little baby cardigan.

"Do you really think I can knit a sweater?" I asked doubtfully as I followed her back to the cozy sitting area. The task sounded impossibly difficult.

"Sure you can," she told me. She offered to help me if I ran into any trouble.

I came back the next day, apologizing as she untangled the yarn.

"No worries," Molly Ann said, quickly fixing my mistake. She told me, in her honest straightforward style, that my daughter and I could come back at any time and stay as long as we liked.

I started going to the shop regularly once or twice a week. The snow melted. Spring came, then summer. My daughter learned how to walk and began saying her first words. Molly Ann always looked happy to see us come through the shop door. She kept a basket of toys next to the sofa and put the sharp needles out of reach.

Gradually, Molly Ann and I became friends. We got together outside the shop. We shared stories. We got to know each other. She watched over my daughter when my husband and I looked like we needed a night out. When I got pregnant a second time, Molly Ann let my toddler spend a few afternoons at the shop while I went to my doctor's appointments.

Just after I delivered my second baby, Molly Ann decided, after a lot of soul searching and thoughtful deliberation, to close Ariadne. The yarn shop was taking up too much of her time, and she just realized that she'd be happier doing something different with her life. She wanted knitting to be a pleasure, not a job. She held a sale and a closing party.

As we left the store that final night, I felt a wave of nostalgia. Yet even though the appliqué quilt was taken down from the window, I have Molly Ann as a friend for all seasons. We've helped each other untangle the strands in our lives and escape from our personal labyrinths. Sometimes, I've discovered, even after you've faced the monster inside, it takes another person to help you see your way back to the sunlight.

At overwhelming and vulnerable moments as a young mother in a strange new city, when I felt lonely and homesick and trapped, Molly Ann kept me from unraveling. She became my girlfriend and she knew just what to do. She made me a warm cup of tea and sat down to listen.

~Mitali Ruths

Leave the Door Open

The better part of one's life consists of his friendships.
~Abraham Lincoln

atching my parents walk to their car after help-ing me move into my dorm room, I was already feeling homesick. Most people don't leave home and go away for school at the age of fourteen, but there I was, out in the parking lot, waving goodbye to my mom and dad as tears started flowing down my cheeks.

My mom stopped and rushed over to give me one more hug, but she and I both knew there wasn't anything more she could do for me. It was too late to change my mind and go to my local high school closer to home. Too late to gather up all my things and jump into the comfort of my parents' car (and arms). It had been my decision to go to this school that my dad had once attended, and there was no turning back.

Boarding school is often thought of either as a place for delin-quent children or an expensive, preppy, all-girls or all-boys school akin to *The Facts of Life* television show. My high school was called a prep school, but it provided nothing like Blair, Natalie, Tootie and Jo's experience. It was a small religious school. We didn't wear uniforms and while my dormitory floor was all-girls, the school was co-ed. We also had a much younger version of Mrs. Garrett.

I quickly walked back into my dorm room, making sure all my tears were dried first. While fourteen years old is young enough to need a mom's shoulder to cry on, it's definitely too old to let anyone witness it.

My roommate wasn't in our room at the time. Earlier I had seen her with a group of girls already fitting in and making friends, whereas I was very quiet and didn't know a soul. I couldn't imagine going up to a group of girls and asking if I could join them. The excitement that filled the air on move-in day only meant heartache for me, as I longed to be included but was too shy to go into the hall and mingle.

Having no clue what I was supposed to do next, I felt alone on a floor filled with freshman girls. I pulled out my desk chair and sat down. Grabbing a pen and paper, I really had no intention of writing anything, but I honestly couldn't think of anything else to do.

Feeling the tears about to make an unwelcome appearance again, I was glad my desk faced the wall—gray and bleak though it was. I could hear giggling girls trotting back and forth down the hall past my room. It took all my might not to close the door, knowing that doing so would eliminate all chances of making a friend.

Just then two heads peeked into my doorway—my roommate, Becky, followed by a bubbly girl named Holly who said, "All the girls are going downstairs into the Student Union. Want to come?" I sprang up faster than I thought physically possible. Feeling an overwhelming sense of relief, I said, "Sure," and quickly joined my new friends. As Holly, Becky, and I walked down the hall, recruiting more girls to head to the basement lounge with us, I immediately knew I was going to be okay. Maybe more than okay.

For four hours I found myself talking and listening, telling stories and laughing with this group that had expanded to about twenty-five girls and boys. We were embarking on a four-year journey together that would equal what most people first experience in their college years. Not only did we share rooms, bathrooms, and three meals a day, we also shared clothes, shoes, late night talks, and the occasional fun of sneaking out after "lights out."

Living together beginning at age fourteen made us quickly become more than just new friends. Growing up together, we became a family. I'm eagerly anticipating a family reunion of sorts this summer at our twenty-year high school reunion. My "new" friends have since become my old friends and without a doubt will remain my forever girlfriends.

~Deanne Haines

Chapter 2

Just Us Girls

My Group

A Cup of Friendship

It is not so much our friends' help that helps us,
as the confidence of their help.
~Epicurus

The morning started with a bustle of lunches, shoe searches, backpack stuffing, and a swift run to two different bus stops. It was the first time both kids were in school every day, although the younger one only until 12:17 p.m. It was also the first school year of my pseudo single motherhood.

How does a person become a "pseudo" single parent? My husband had taken a job in a different state, two and a half hours from our home, in June of that year. It was unclear if this was going to be a long-term or short-term assignment. We decided as a couple that until it became more clear where this job was going, he would live away during the workweek and return on the weekends. Thus far, it had been a very long summer of entertaining and transporting our ten-year-old daughter and five-year-old son. The kids missed their dad during the week. They became annoyed with their nagging mother. It was not easy for my husband being away, but being the only parent five days a week was not exactly a walk in the park for me either. It was a challenging time for all of us.

The saving grace was that September was finally here. School was back in session. I would have from 8:30 a.m. until the kindergarten bus dropped my son off at 12:17 p.m. all to myself. Dizzy from the possibilities, and fully aware that general upkeep of the house needed to be factored in, I was pleased to have some "me time," such a rare and valuable commodity.

The second Tuesday of the school year, my friend Julie, whom I had met in a mother's group a few years prior, invited me to meet her for coffee. Julie had a regular standing coffee date with a group of women at a local coffee house. I had a list a mile long of things I needed to get done, but Julie said I would enjoy the break and the company. Since I was a free woman until 12:17 p.m., I agreed to meet for a quick cup of coffee. I figured it would be nice to talk with adults for a while, and the chance of them asking me to help them do math homework was pretty slim.

I arrived at the coffee house, parked, ordered my coffee, and joined the partially formed group of women at a large table. Julie said, "I think you have met some of these gals before." Then introduced me to everyone with a quick biography.

What she did not mention was that this hour and a half every Tuesday was going to make a huge difference in my life. She never mentioned that each of these women seated around this table was going to touch my heart and become someone I couldn't imagine not knowing or caring about. Coffee time is playfully described as "group therapy" by all of us. As a group, we have solved many of life's problems. We have recommended doctors, plumbers, babysitters, and countless other services to each other. We have laughed at the silliness of kids, spouses, boyfriends, parents, and pets. We have cried, in public mind you, over heartbreak and other life events. We have also laughed so obnoxiously loud that the rest of the patrons in the coffee house have gone silent and stared.

Not since I was in college have I had such a wonderfully supportive group of friends. Somehow, after I got married, got a job, and had kids, in the hectic shuffle of juggling everything, I lost sight of the value of having girl friends. There was a void in my life that I was not fully aware of until I made time to connect with other women like me, over a cup of coffee. It is always good to know that Tuesday coffee is just a few days away to help get some input and perspective on life's challenges.

The sincerity and honesty of my coffee ladies make them different from any female friends I have ever known. As a younger person, I was never secure enough to speak my mind. But through living and learning, I have found that true friendship is not based solely on good times, laughter, and making everyone feel good. True friendship is having someone to cry with, listen without judgment, offer wisdom, or just empathize when times get tough. It makes the good times even more joyful.

Sharing all of this over a simple cup of coffee is more precious than gold.

~Allison Potter

Girls Rule

Being a woman is a terribly difficult task,
since it consists principally in dealing with men.
~Joseph Conrad

I said no. No way. I didn't want to join. Why would I? It was a car club, for heaven sakes. And I had no interest in cars. As long as I could put the key in the ignition and the car would take me where I wanted to go, I was fine. I didn't want to know any more. My husband and my son, on the other hand, love cars. Corvettes, to be exact. They know how everything works and what every part is called. They read articles about Corvettes and they talk about cars all of the time. They had heard about a Corvette Club in our area and they wanted to join. That's fine... but leave me out of it. I had no interest.

My husband and our son did join the local club and went to meetings. They had a great time. I did not join or go with them. Why should I? But my husband could be very persuasive. He told me that he had met some very nice people and he asked that I come to one meeting with him just to check it out. We all know that marriage is about compromise, so I agreed to go. Besides, it meant I didn't have to cook dinner that night.

The room was full of people—both men and women. I was prepared to be bored, but much to my surprise, these people were not talking about cars. They were talking about the arrangements for going wine tasting in two weeks. Now, that got my attention. Yes, we would be taking our cars. But we'd be using those cars to get to the winery and go wine tasting. We signed up to go. And we had such a fun time.

The next thing they talked about was a brunch run to a wonderful restaurant right at the beach. When the sign-up sheet came around I grabbed the pen out of my husband's hand and signed our names in big bold letters. Wow, this car club thing was much better than I had anticipated! It was a very social club and we didn't spend much time talking about cars at all.

Time went on and we did more and more things with the Corvette Club. I became quite active in the club, even taking a board position, and became very close to a small group of women within the club. We did lots of things together outside of club events and had a wonderful time. We gave each other nicknames—I was Blue Barb. My friend was Red Barb. Not really difficult to understand... our names are Barbara and she has a red car. You can now figure out how I got my name. The nicknames of the other girls were just as silly.

Red Barb called me one day. The club was having elections and all of the board positions were open and needed to be filled. She asked if I would run for president. Me? President? Of a car club? Really? She had to be kidding... but she was serious. I thought about it and decided that it wasn't such a bad idea after all. But I needed my girlfriends around me. I started with Red Barb. If she would be my vice president then I would agree to be president. I contacted my other close Corvette Club friends and "persuaded" them to each run for a board position. I told them we would have fun together. We were a complete slate of officers filling every board position. We ran. And we were all elected! We were now the board of the Corvette Club.

The day my board and I were installed as officers of the club went down in Corvette Club history. Not only was a woman now in charge of the club, but each and every board position was filled by a woman. At the installation meeting, my daughter-in-law brought jeweled crowns to present to me and to all of my new board members. We wore them proudly as we glittered in the sun!

The changes we brought about were not at all subtle. After all, we were an all-female board in charge of a car club. My first official duty was to make a motion that we change the focus of the Corvette Club away from cars and make it into a Shopping Club. Some of the longtime members were not amused. Old fuddy-duddies! We didn't really make that change official, but we had fun pretending that we were serious. We pulled way back on the number of car shows and car museums we went to and started going to many more wineries, to nice restaurants, and even to high tea presented at a nearby hotel. We dressed up for some of our runs too—something a male president would never have stood for. The things we did became more girly, but one thing remained the same. We always drove in our Corvettes wherever we went—and wow, did they look beautiful. So did we!

My girlfriends and I worked hard together and worked well together. Our friendships grew and became stronger. And I went from not wanting anything to do with the club to becoming president. Who could have predicted that? I held the office of president for three years. And all of my girlfriends kept their positions too. We had such fun working together. We planned many activities—day runs for wine tasting, brunch, or dinner, museum trips to keep the guys happy, even overnight runs that have taken us completely across the United States and back. We have seen a lot of this amazing and diverse country. And the car club I had no interest in brought me a great group of girlfriends. Plus, everyone must have liked having a woman president in a male-dominated hobby because when it came time to elect a new board, the next president was a woman too!

~Barbara LoMonaco

The Swill Gang

*Friendship is a treasured gift, and every time I talk with you
I feel as if I'm getting richer and richer.*
~Author Unknown

The phone rang one Friday night when, as a single parent of four, I had just settled into my green rocker for another night of TV watching. It was a woman named Sunny calling from Valdosta, Georgia.

"I just read something you wrote in *Single Parent Magazine* and I have to talk to you. I'm a single parent too and sometimes I just don't know if I can make it on my own. I thought it would help to talk to someone else who's raising children alone."

We talked for an hour and Sunny continued to call every couple of weeks. We commiserated with each other because that year, 1989, was the worst year of my life.

It was the year the man I'd dated for ten months suddenly moved to Oklahoma to start a new career. It was the year my ex-husband, Harold, died of leukemia, not long after he married his girlfriend the day our divorce was final. Our nine-year-old son Andrew was devastated by his father's death but I was too angry at Harold about the divorce to even know how to grieve.

1989 was the year my oldest daughter, Jeanne, got caught in the middle of the California earthquake and I lived through nightmarish days wondering if she was safe. Jeanne was only twenty at the time and I thought she should have stayed in nice, safe Wisconsin for college, rather than taking off to explore life on the edge of the continent.

1989 was the year my eighteen-year-old daughter, Julia, graduated from high school and decided to spend the summer before college testing my sense of "loving motherhood." We hollered and picked at each other all summer. I'm not sure if the thought of leaving home for the first time to go to college had her befuddled or if I just couldn't get used to the idea of first Harold, then Jeanne, and now Julia leaving us. Many nights that year my family room felt like an empty auditorium as I sat alone with the TV set.

A few months later Sunny told me she wanted to move back to the northern part of the U.S. (her original home) so I invited her to Milwaukee for a weekend to attend a conference for single people. She stayed for a week and bought a house while she was here. She kept calling me her best friend even though I was wallowing too deep in my own miseries to be anybody's "best" anything.

I desperately wanted to find Sunny a few other friends, so after she made the move with her two young daughters, I decided to gather some of my female friends to meet her. I called every woman I knew. Friends from church, work, and the neighborhood. Women I met over the years through other people. Mothers of my children's friends. A couple from my writer's group.

I was nervous about inviting them to my house all at once, knowing that few of them knew each other. But I needn't have worried. When they arrived I introduced everyone and before long we were talking, laughing, and gabbing like old friends about our jobs, children, and lifestyles.

Sunny commented, "The women I meet in southern Georgia are generally described as precious. You people aren't just precious, you're downright interesting!"

Tina piped up, "We should do this every month! Let's call it the Southeastern Wisconsin Interesting Ladies League! S.W.I.L.L."

I laughed. "SWILL! SWILL? We're going to form a club and call it SWILL?"

"Why not?" Sharon asked. "We can gather together and just unload all the swill that creeps into our lives periodically and get support from each other."

And so we began at the end of 1989. We decided to meet at my house each month since I had the largest family room and the fewest family members to uproot on Friday nights.

We kept it simple. SWILL had no dues, no minutes, no committees, no rules, no dress code, no bylaws, no agenda, and no purpose. We simply got together and shared whatever was on our minds. The only suggestion I gave at each meeting was that only one woman talks at a time. That way everyone could hear what everyone else had to say.

I never worried about cleaning the house before a SWILL meeting because nobody was there to do a white glove inspection. And I didn't worry about fancy refreshments. If one of us was having a chocolate or salty foods craving we'd bring a bag of candy or pretzels to toss on the coffee table to share. We resolved from the beginning never to get bogged down, as some clubs do, with a "fancy food" complex.

Over the years at least 100 women wove their way in and out of the SWILL meetings. Anyone could bring an interesting friend to SWILL and if that friend liked us she could come forever. Sometimes we had twelve or twenty women present, and other months, because of hectic schedules, only five or six.

But it didn't matter how many. What mattered was that as we got to know each other, we began to care more and more about each other. We became a family of friends, sisters to the core.

SWILL welcomed everyone regardless of age, race, religion or occupation. Everyone from Carrie, a young married woman in her late twenties with four small children, struggling with the possibility of her marriage ending, to Eunice, who had been married for forty-two years and taken enough college-level classes in her retirement to be one of the most interesting people in the group.

When one of our group, Linda, died of heart failure at age thirty-nine after only meeting with us a short time, we mourned together and discussed ways to solve the medical insurance problems that often face single, overstressed parents like Linda who must work three jobs to make ends meet.

When Jody's teenage son, Daniel, died in a car accident, we held each other and cried with Jody at the funeral.

When Mary shared with us that her ex-husband had decided to live on the street to avoid child support, we encouraged her to go back to court to get some disability funding, which would include child support for her. She did and the SWILL members were her biggest cheerleaders.

When Gail, whose children were starting college, went back to school to study nursing, we spent hours talking her into staying in school when she wanted to quit. One of our members, a counselor, helped her through some test anxiety problems one night. When Gail graduated from nursing school we all took a bow.

When Barb's son came home from the army and moved back into her "empty nest" home, and then a few months later her daughter moved back home with her new baby, we listened to the ups and downs of Barb's five-adults-in-one-house, three-generation family. We gave her lots of advice, including the fact that it was okay for her to go back to work full-time.

Diane, whose happy marriage rubbed off on all of us, pointed out that even a happy marriage isn't perfect all the time but that a wonderful sense of humor can get you through most of the "swill" that marriage can dish out.

Sunny became much more independent, found a good job in the school system, and eventually transferred to the Chicago area to start her own support network.

What did SWILL do for me, the one who was simply trying to find a few friends for Sunny? I'm the one who benefited the most. Those women who were married, single, separated, divorced, or widowed came from all walks of life to open their hearts and their lives at every SWILL meeting. They listened to me, laughed with me, and helped me through the rough times of being a single parent. When I had three children in college at once and a fatherless twelve-year-old at home, they helped me even more through the struggles by offering financial advice as well as emotional help.

When my youngest left for college 1,800 miles away from home, I talked about my fears, failures and fantasies. I learned from my SWILL sisters that it's okay to love your empty nest after thirty years of full-time parenting.

In 2004 I moved from Milwaukee to Florida and the SWILL Gang meetings ended. But one thing's for sure. What I learned from the SWILL Gang during those years will last me a lifetime. I learned that when you open your home and your heart to other women and nourish your friendships on a regular basis, good things happen. These days, it's working here in Florida with a whole different group of women friends.

~Patricia Lorenz

The Thriving Five

Grief knits two hearts in closer bonds than happiness ever can;
and common sufferings are far stronger links than common joys.
~Alphonse De Lamartine

It was 1999 when my world was shattered by a phone call. My son had died in an auto accident. I went through his funeral with the usual numbness and started down the long road of grief and mourning.

At the time, I was becoming familiar with using my husband's computer. In a desperate state one day I typed in a search for "mothers who are grieving the loss of a child." That was when I found a lady who had started a group for mothers who had lost children. They wrote to each other daily and helped each other through. Finally, I had found a place where someone would listen whenever I needed to spill my sorrow. They could tell me what was working for them, what wasn't working, and what to avoid. None of us felt absolutely certain of what we were doing, but we knew we could figure it out together. Talking about our sorrow each day, as we took tiny steps forward, was the most healing therapy I could have found. I was able to share stories about my wonderful son and also learn about their precious children. (And my husband bought me my own computer so he could have his back!)

Thirteen years later, five of us are still together! Some of the women came and went, feeling they no longer needed the help that was offered. Some even found that talking about it daily brought them more sadness; if it didn't work for them, we let them know that it was okay to pursue another avenue. It is true that some people can easily pour out their hearts in words, and some just find that too difficult.

The five of us who have stayed together are the closest of friends. In fact, we call each other sisters. Over the years, we have honored our children on their birthdays by making donations to hospitals, daycares, libraries, schools, or whatever charity a mom chooses. We still feel the strong connection to our deceased children, almost as if the umbilical chord had never been severed. Most of us have had little "signs" that we believe are from our children, letting us know they are always with us and want us to go on and live happy lives. We have shared pictures of new grandbabies, graduations, weddings, and the successes of our other children over the years. We know so much about each other and have watched children and grandchildren grow up through the pictures that we've shared.

Each year the five of us try to get together at one of our homes. Our last reunion was in Cleveland, Ohio, at Joellen's house. A reunion always starts with hugs, and lots of them! The mom who hosts usually has little trinkets of love for us in gift bags. We never spend gobs of money, but it's very special to have a candle to light on anniversary days, or a butterfly trinket that reminds us that our children live on.

When we met in Debbie's hometown in Kentucky, we purchased stuffed animals to take to the firehouse in town. They were given to children to comfort them after fires or other disturbing incidents. In Ohio, we purchased books for the middle school library. We've made quilts over the years for children's hospitals and the Ronald McDonald House in my hometown of Nashville. In Alabama, Suzy also donated quilts to a place that services children who have suffered a loss. We helped Ruth, in Massachusetts, provide a good Christmas for a family that needed help. A daycare facility in Virginia received art supplies, and a family with a child born on Debbie's son's birthday received a wagonload of baby gifts! These are just a few of our donations made in memory of our wonderful children.

A reunion where we talk about our children usually involves

some crying together. But not all our time is spent with tears in our eyes. Sometimes we shop till we drop at the nearest mall. Laughing together is just as important to us, and we know it fills our children with happiness and delight!

These women that I call my "sisters at heart" are a very important part of my healing journey, and I am so thankful that I met them thirteen years ago. Today, we talk less about our sorrow and loss, and more about how our lives are enriched by our children and grandchildren, and about the things we have learned from our loss that have made us more compassionate and caring people. We all believe that by writing and sharing our children over the years on our computers, and by our reunions when we can arrange them, we have broken down the barriers between the physical and the spiritual and keep our children ever close to us! We have an omnipresent feeling that our kids know we are together supporting each other. We believe that where there is a circle of love, our children are near.

~Beverly F. Walker

14

My Circle of Friends

There is no surer foundation for a beautiful friendship
than a mutual taste in literature.
~P.G. Wodehouse

er skin is the color of milk chocolate. Mine is the color of café au lait... without the café. She is short in stature, trim of figure, and fond of exercising. I am a bit taller, a lot wider, and allergic to jumping jacks. She is reflective and introspective; I shoot from the hip (and as a result, often blast myself in the foot). We're as different from each other as we can get. And yet we're best friends.

However, despite being a daring duo, Darice and I were each stuck in workaholic ruts. Neither one of us had a life outside work, and the stress was slaying us. Determined to spend part of our lives doing enjoyable, non-work things, we formed a book club. And although it started with the two of us, we were merely the beginning of something incredible.

We envisioned a high-falutin' group. Once a month or so, we imagined getting together and discussing a piece of literature over dinner. We had lofty aspirations, we anticipated civilized conversations, and we looked forward to expanding our minds. In reality, what we ended up with was, uh... different.

Darice invited two of her friends to join us. For our first gathering, we met for dinner at a restaurant near a bookstore. I was a bit nervous. Would they be witty and fun or deadly dull? Would the four of us gel? Most importantly (from my perspective) since they were already close friends, would they widen the circle for me?

I needn't have worried. That evening, Donna and Pat made room for me at the table at McCormick & Schmick's. They tossed barbed remarks in my direction as well as Darice's. When they saw that I could dish it out just as well as I took it, I was in. I was one of them.

Later that evening, we scoured the shelves at the bookstore, each of us eventually plopping down a pile for the other three's perusal. We spent a long time picking up books, reading the blurb inside the jacket, discarding some, and putting others into the "serious contender" stack.

Over the next six months, we read several books, including *Their Eyes Were Watching God* and *The Help*. Never relying on the discussion guides at the end of the books, we preferred to forge our own way. There was nothing snooty about our talks. We were loud. We were bawdy. And we were passionate. The words we highlighted and noted with Post-its struck chords with our own lives. Sometimes a couple of us, having been extra busy that month, would have to scream out, "Don't spoil the ending!" as the story was discussed, because we weren't quite finished with the book, but we all understood. There were times when work and family would sap all our time and energy, causing us to have to set the book aside.

Soon we invited two others: Diane and Karen.

It was apparent from the initial meeting that we were too rowdy to meet in public, so we moved. Most of the time we met at Darice's—a large, old, graceful home—and everyone brought a dish. Over appetizers and dinner, the talk flowed just as freely as the wine. One month Pat hosted our get-together. Because Pat is fiercely private with her personal life, I felt honored. Another month, Karen kicked her husband out for the evening, and we met at her house.

But when fall came, the hills of our state's wine country called to us like a siren's song. Why not take advantage of the cool autumn days (we were all menopausal, after all) and spend a Saturday touring the wineries?

For the locals who saw us meandering around town, they probably wondered what tied us together. People might have speculated, but a cohesive group we obviously were.

Pat has such a formidable face and active eyebrows, she could slice you up with just a glance. She also is a sharp dresser. Donna is so bubbly and her eager brown eyes always peek out over her reading glasses. Karen's gray hair is unfailingly pulled up in a bun, but some curling tendrils always escape. And Diane rounds out the group. Her bright blue eyes are often crinkled in laughter. That Saturday we tasted wine, and bought some. At each vineyard, we'd sniff and swish and sample, saying either, "Ugh. That's too sweet. Darice and Sioux, you'll love it," or "Yuck. That's dusty and dry. Pass that over to Donna and Pat." We wandered the streets and stopped in the shops. We ate a leisurely lunch and, reluctantly, headed back home in the late afternoon.

Now we call ourselves a "social club" instead of a book group. Some months, we bring a few books we've already read, and each of us borrows a book. This month, we're planning to go to the Black Repertory Group. And I've invited Jackie to join us. She's quiet, but is capable of getting spitting mad when she's passionate about an issue. Unfortunately, she feels like she doesn't fit in with her work colleagues. Just as the circle widened for me, we can enlarge our group to embrace Jackie.

It was books that brought us together. And part of me begs to compare our group to a bookshelf. The books that are lined up on the shelves are rich with texture and images, and they're varied. Darice compares us to wines—some of us are sweeter, some have more of a "bite," but we're all delicious. But it was Donna who made us all whoop with delight. She says we're like a sampler box of chocolates. Some of us are nutty, some of us are as soft and giving as the cream-filled candies, but we're all delectable.

~Sioux Roslawski

15

All That Jiggles May Be Old

Growing old is mandatory; growing up is optional.
~Chili Davis

Twice a week I take myself to what I secretly call my BHGLLD (hint—rhymes with jiggled) class. It has a different trade name, but I think of it as my Blue Haired Gringa Ladies Latin Dancing class. I can call it that because I happen to resemble the "BHGL" part of that remark, though I think the blond in my hair still edges out the white. Barely. But not enough to avoid using the purple shampoo that makes me fit right in with the rest of my classmates. Actually, I may bring the average age down a bit.

Unexpectedly, attending this class has me harking back to high school, and not just in a boy-do-I-feel-youthful-and-energetic-again way. There is a lot of hip shaking, shoulder shimmying, and pelvic thrusting, reminiscent of the action in front of the bleachers on Friday nights, let alone in the hallways between classes. Reminiscent, but in this iteration weirdly entertaining, as back then it was just nauseating. There are also the unspoken but hierarchical fashion norms, as some ladies proudly wearing (and working!) their belly dancer scarves with the shaky coins on them, and/or their BHGLLD official trade-name Spandex.

I'm probably creating more of a visual than you had anticipated. Sorry.

There are the flashy overachievers who consistently plant themselves inches behind the instructor so they can focus on their own strutting images in the front mirror.

Remember the hot shot in the front of the class who would shout out an answer before the teacher even finished asking a question? Mmm hmmm. She grew up to be the one to start prancing through a routine before the instructor has a chance to demonstrate the moves.

The introverts tend to gather in the back corners of the room, making no eye contact with anyone, and hardly able to see, let alone follow the instructor. Drably and loosely draped, they barely move in synch with the zealots, but smile, sweat, and come back again and again.

As in high school, the cliques in this community are impenetrable. Their members arrive early, within seconds of each other, stake out their territory and guard it more fiercely than rival gangs. Any new and therefore unsuspecting intruder is gradually and systematically salsa-ed out of the elite zone as class progresses, until flattened directly against the side mirror. The orchestration of this maneuver by all the clique members is really quite impressive.

For a few weeks I noticed the cliques were all wearing the same blinding neon color. Rumor had it that they were deciding among themselves each day which color they would wear to the next class. When the suggestion was made that everyone could participate if they would assign a color to a certain day of the week, such as Monday being yellow day, one of the ringleaders decided it wouldn't be "special" anymore, so they decided to quit doing it at all.

There are a few unique, or "token" attendees, such as a couple of men and a pair of über-youngsters who appear to be barely out of high school. These two are the artistic types, willowy and excessively expressive, gyrating in their eyeliner and musical theater T-shirts. The male of the pair has only come a few times, but he looks like a keeper.

BHGLLD class has become one of many new routines in my life since I quit working my eight to five job and joined my husband in trying to make a success of our small business. I have found many such positive routines, but the one negative is the significant decrease in social stimulation. The major change in my schedule does not jibe with my buddies who are still working weekdays, so I have been open to finding new acquaintances who share my current interests and timetable. So far, as you can probably tell, somewhat like high school, BHGLLD class has had few if any likely candidates.

One day I came in after the warm-up song had started, as usual, and tried to slip myself into a "neutral zone" opening as surreptitiously as possible. It had been a few weeks since I had attended, having planned, then survived, my daughter's wedding and gone on vacation thereafter. I glanced back to the introvert corner and apologized to a gray-clad, mousy-looking lady with glasses, asking if she could still see the instructor. She surprised me by actually looking me right in the eye and responding, saying with a smile that it didn't make any difference to her dancing whether she could see or not. Since then, whenever I come in, she has jokingly elbowed me aside or otherwise teased me about "these people who come in late and think they can stand wherever they want."

On a subsequent morning I noticed that she was happily chatting with another lady whom I did not recognize, but who absolutely fit right in the introvert corner as well. But wait, I guess not, because they were happily chatting. I maneuvered my way into a small opening, and between songs my new acquaintance jokingly and loudly pointed out to *her* new acquaintance how I had "barged in" and blocked their view.

The three of us are now not only on a first-name basis, but we cover each other's backs. They position themselves to keep a space for me when I am inevitably late. One of them has a short-term bladder, so we other two "guard" her spot when she leaves to use the bathroom during class. I know the name of one's grandson, and which plants are the other's favorites in her garden. So far we haven't made plans together outside of class, but it feels as if it's definitely headed in that direction. Even so, we aren't a clique. At least not yet.

~Robin Calkins Gwozdz

The Pregnant Gals

Strangers are just friends waiting to happen.
~Rod McKuen

I babysat when I was a teenager to make money to spend at the mall. But it was more of the "feed the kids, plop them in front of cartoons, and set the clocks ahead one hour to put them to bed early so I could chat all night on the phone with my girl-friends" kind of babysitting. Not the kind of babysitting that requires Early Childhood Education units, CPR training, and age appropriate play projects that today's parents look for when choosing a babysitter.

Fast forward to age thirty-nine and pregnant. I didn't know anything about pregnancy, let alone raising a child. My whole life, I'd been a career woman. I used my education, time, and expertise on work, not children. I could whip up a project in no time flat. Projections, spreadsheets, reports, marketing, retail, and customer retention came quickly and easily to me. Going through pregnancy and raising a child did not.

Where on earth could I get a crash course on pregnancy and child rearing? What I needed was CliffsNotes, if you will, on every-thing I needed to know, and the stuff I didn't really want to know, but probably should. Of course, I went to the Internet.

I searched for pregnant women in my area who might like to get together. Nothing. I thought briefly of going to the local parks to look for pregnant women to ask if they wanted to hang out. Creepy.

I thought how nice it would be to have a site, much like a professional matchmaking site, which would put fun groups of like-minded women together. A little more searching and I found the perfect one!

I typed in my zip code and found... nothing! So, I started my own group. I called it the Pregnant Gals. I touted it as a group for pregnant women to get together to share education and information, talk, laugh, cry (hormones, you know) and drink coffee (decaf, of course). Within the first week, I had twelve members!

In the beginning, we got together every week and shared our experiences. We took our ever-expanding bellies for long walks on the beach, drank decaf for hours at the local coffee bar, and tried the new hot restaurants downtown. Boy were we a sight! People commented often. We got everything from, "How sweet. Reminds me of when I was pregnant," to "Honey, I'm sure glad I'm too old to be in your club!"

We swapped stories about baby names, anxiety, weight gain, nursery colors, in-laws, and birth plans. Having such deep topics to discuss bonded us together faster and deeper than I've ever bonded with any other women.

As we approached our due dates, some girls began to drop out of the Pregnant Gals club to deliver their babies. Amazingly, we all delivered within six weeks of each other.

A couple of the Gals moved away, some we never heard from again, but six of us still remain extremely close. We see each other at least once a week, sometimes more. Our husbands get along with each other, so we expanded our group to the guys as well. We babysit and grocery shop for each other. We have lots of play dates with our little ones. We go wine tasting, and even manage a group date night once a week. We now call ourselves the Not-So-Pregnant Gals.

I love my new life. Lunch dates have turned to play dates. Morning meetings have been replaced with morning feedings. I no longer whip up projects; I whip up eggs and oatmeal. I love that I now know how to do all of these things, and I love that I was able to learn all these things from such wonderful women.

~Crescent LoMonaco

The Bridgman Bible Babes

We have been friends together
In sunshine and in shade.
~Caroline Sheridan Norton

My baby dared to defy me. What did my dear child do? The same thing his older brother dared to do two years prior. He went to kindergarten.

I used to be a teacher, working full-time, staying after hours, working weekends. Then when I had my children I began the not-so-smooth transition into being a stay-at-home mom. I mastered the diaper and tantrum stage, often commiserating with other moms at local playgroups, which was important to my sanity.

I began to miss the playgroup days, not just the time with my kids, but the time I spent with other moms going through the same stages in life as me. But many of those moms had gone back to work or made other commitments, our paths no longer crossing on a regular basis. It was time to find a new group to join. I needed to belong again.

About the same time I was looking for something more consistent to do, a friend from church told me about a group of moms that were starting a Bible study group. While I knew who several of the women were from the community, I did not truly know many of them. Meeting on Tuesday afternoons at each other's homes, we'd begin with conversation, at first about our children, as had been my experience during playgroups. Then we'd spend time going over questions and sharing answers to the questions of whatever Biblical-based book we studied. I enjoyed the camaraderie, and I began to look forward to our time together. After the six to eight weeks it would take to finish a book, we'd gather to share a potluck meal.

By the time we met about our second book, it started to become apparent that we weren't just a Bible study group. In fact one member of the group referred to us as the BBBs: Bridgman Bible Babes. Who says women in their thirties and forties can't still be babes? Some husbands jokingly called us a cult because of our tight bond. We even signed a sheet that essentially said, "What happens in the group, stays in the group."

Our second book was *The Five Love Languages: The Secret to Love that Lasts* by Dr. Gary Chapman. In the book, Dr. Chapman defines five ways people give and receive love: through words of affirmation, quality time, physical touch, acts of service, and receiving gifts. It was during this study that we started to really know each other, not just as "Connor and Luke's Mom" or "Grace's Mom." We started to know each other as women. While the love languages caused many of us to want to learn how our spouses gave and received love to better communicate with them, we also learned more about ourselves. We started to share our fears and our insecurities. Our prayer concerns became more significant. And while we had all giggled at the confidentiality sheet we had signed, we now felt confident that it was binding, as if we'd signed with a drop of our own blood. We weren't sisters, but we were fierce friends, and nothing was off limits as to what we would help each other through.

Several years have passed now since our first Bible study group. People have come and gone depending on their schedules. I have recently had to drop out due to a new venture into the work world. I miss these women I call friends. But the foundation remains strong. They have my back, and I have theirs. We've seen friends through failed marriages, mourning with them through the "ugly" cries. We've made meals and held tight to friends whose husbands became seriously ill. We've prayed for children struggling in school and hoped for the wisdom to guide them well. We've rejoiced in new jobs and new relationships and new babies. And we have laughed. Laughed hard. Laughed so hard we've wet our pants. Yes, when you have these kinds of friends, nothing is hidden.

What started off as something to do, something to fill the time and allow for the mingling of like-minded moms, has created a foundation of friendship that I didn't know could exist in my late thirties. Perhaps we were all yearning to belong, for somewhere to be free to share our darkest secrets. Yes, we are moms. Yes, we may also be wives. But we are women, too, and women need other women, in good times and in bad. So bring it, life. The Bridgman Bible Babes are ready to weather any storm together.

~Marcy Blesy

18

The Card Club Ladies

It takes a long time to grow an old friend.
~John Leonard

"I'm meeting my besties for lunch," I recently commented to an acquaintance.

"What's a bestie?" he inquired.

"My best friends," I replied.

"Best friends? Don't people have only one best friend?"

"I have six."

"Do they know that?" His eyebrows arched.

"Absolutely, they know," I retorted. "We embrace it. We are each other's BFFs."

We refer to our group as "The Card Club Ladies," mostly because we used to meet once a month, with our spouses, to play a game of cards. Over the years our friendship morphed into a wondrous thing. There are seven of us and we are tighter than the apron strings we tied each spring during graduation season.

You see, in our rural area, high school graduation celebrations resemble the festivities of a wedding. Families print and mail invitations to relatives, friends, and in some cases, someone you met last Friday in the grocery store. Karen, the eldest of the twenty-seven card club kids, was the first to cross the stage with diploma in hand.

Her six extra mothers converged on the home of her biological parents the day before her celebration. Together we chopped vegetables, shredded meat, diced potatoes, and cubed fruit. We tucked the prepared food in cold storage and retreated home for a good night's sleep. The next day, six smiling women greeted guests in matching "Card Club Catering" aprons. We invaded the kitchen with skills that rivaled the most seasoned catering company. We kept food bowls filled, plates and silver arranged for the swarms of people, and tables spotless for the continually changing groups. Janice and Joe, Karen's parents, were free to roam among their family and friends. They had the luxury of enjoying their visitors with no concerns about party details. We snickered our afternoon away as we divided the work. Party attendees began to ask, "How I can I join your card club? You have so much fun." We have hosted close to thirty high school celebrations over the years.

As the card club kids planned weddings, we switched to the art of hosting bridal showers. During the third one in as many months, my besties and I lamented about our own household goods. "My stuff is over thirty years old. It looks like trash. I wish I could steal some of these shiny, new things for my house." "No one will host a bridal shower for old married folks." "Let's do it ourselves," and we all agreed, we would do it for each other. We scrawled our names on paper and tossed them into a basket. In turn each plucked a friend's name, stuffed it down her shirt, and vowed to keep it secret. We typed registry lists and passed them to all by e-mail. Our shower for each other was a go.

"Let's have a 'Ladies Gone Wild' adventure," one of us suggested for our "bridal shower" gift-swap. We made arrangements for a motel room large enough for seven, and we converged in frenzied anticipation. Seven fifty-plus women became giggling girls as we shared stories, jokes, food, and two near-sleepless nights. We spent our days descending on every thrift store in town, enjoying meals that our husbands wouldn't eat, and sharing a glass of wine at the end of each day.

"Let's just have a night with nothing but junk food," rang out from my group of excited friends, and we scampered in seven different directions in a local grocery store. In a few short minutes we met at the checkout counter. A young woman rang up our bags of indulgences: granola, yogurt, vegetables and dip, fruit and dip, one package of cookies, and a six-pack of wine coolers. "Go knock yourselves out," she smirked as we carried out the bags with our "forbidden fruit." That evening we ate our treasures, guilt-free, and hooted about our "junk food" meal. Finally it was time for our gift exchange.

"How shall we decide who opens their gift first?" inquired one of our more organized gals, Joan. "We could do something boring, like birthdays, or we could have some fun," retorted Vicki, her contagious laughter spilled over to us all. I don't remember who suggested it, but we snorted at the decision: we opened our gifts according to our bra size. For some of them, it was no contest, and they ripped the paper off their gift. It came down to Joan and I, small versus smaller, so we stood shoulder to shoulder, chests out with arched backs. "It's rigged," I complained and grinned as I opened mine last.

All too soon, our time together was over. We entwined our little fingers and we pinky swore this would be an annual event. That happenstance gathering became a tradition. We kept the tradition and meet each summer. We visit vintage shops, eat, catch up from the events of the last year, and share shower gifts.

My besties, Joan, Cindy, Vicki, Kathy, Ruth, Janice, and I have forged a friendship that I treasure. We raised our children together. We kept close company by our yearly camping trips, ladies' luncheons, and Sunday gatherings with as many as two dozen offspring in attendance. Time passed and our bond grew deeper. We shared our faith, and discovered the glue that cemented our friendship. As members of our card club family battled cancer, divorce, death of parents and siblings, we knew help and support was only a phone call away.

2006 was a year I barely endured, doing my best to make it through each day. My daughter, Kathy, recently diagnosed with schizophrenia, recovered with us in our home; Trela, our eldest son's wife, diagnosed with a rare form of cancer six weeks after her second child was born, fought for her life; and Dean, our second child, had a son, Garrett, born with a defective heart. Garrett endured countless surgeries and hospitalizations, and my heart shattered when he left us at the age of five months and twenty-seven days in his daddy's arms. I felt my life unravel. Getting out of bed was almost too much some days. My "besties" gathered around me and helped me hang on for one more day. Sometimes it was an early morning visit, or a phone call to let me cry, but most importantly, they prayed. They lifted me up in prayer, continually asking for health for my family, and for me to have strength and wisdom as I fought the battle in my tormented soul. Meals cooked and shared; arms that helped squeeze the pain into a manageable force; tears that cleansed; and laughter that refreshed all helped stitch together the torn pieces of my heart.

And so I feel secure. I know when I need a shoulder to lean on, arms to hold me as I cry, a buddy to share a belly laugh, and most importantly a friend who will pray with me, I only need to call one of my six besties and I will be upheld. And for that I feel extremely blessed: I have six best friends.

~Mona Rottinghaus

19

The Monday Night Ladies

It is a good thing to be rich, and it is a good thing to be strong,
but it is a better thing to be loved of many friends.
~Euripides

My husband is an accountant and he works long hours during tax season between the months of January and mid-April. One Monday afternoon my girlfriend knew my husband would be working late and suggested we go out for coffee that night at 7:00. We spent several hours in a local restaurant, chatting and laughing and having delightful, much needed time together. It was a great release of tension for me, because I still had three children at home and no husband to help me. We continued to do this every Monday evening on a regular basis. After the first time, several other friends joined in and we would laugh, tell stories, and drink so much coffee we thought we would float away.

There are now six of us who meet at a local place called Chubby's. This has become a weekly ritual.

One night, one of the girls came in starving and decided to order a meal. That was the "AHA" moment for all of us. "Let's start meeting at 6:30 and eat dinner," we chimed in unison. Twenty-seven years and counting, we are still meeting like clockwork every Monday night and we still have more fun than anyone else in the place. We look forward to our ladies' night out and hate it when someone has to miss.

There is no topic left untouched in our many conversations. I can tell you what type of undergarments are preferred by each of my friends and vice versa. We like to solve all the problems of the world and always have a solution to nearly everything, or so we think. Politics, religion... all the way down to what type of toenail polish we favor. Any subject is up for grabs.

Truth be known, we are very refined, cultured, and ladylike older women until we walk through that magical door of Chubby's, where we are transformed for the next two hours into six unfiltered, carefree, loud, and exuberant women.

When we walk into our favorite establishment the waitresses fight over who gets to wait on us, because it's like a party going on the entire evening. They tell us we can be quite entertaining to them and break up their evening. It was the waitstaff who dubbed us "The Monday Night Ladies."

We tend to get very close to some of the younger waitresses and are interested in how their lives are going. We are genuinely interested in them, one in particular. There were numerous times she would ask our advice on certain things, and we were more than happy to share our opinions with her. She was a senior in high school from a highly dysfunctional family and trying to do her best to graduate while still working full-time. She was living alone in a cramped apartment with some old furniture that people had donated to her. The Monday Night Ladies decided to surprise her and give her a dream-come-true Christmas. Without her knowledge, we secretly adopted her. We bought her some new clothes, got her some gift certificates to her favorite places, bought her a little television and stuffed some cash inside a homemade card with a personal poem. She was so touched by our generosity, she told us it was the best Christmas she ever had in her short seventeen years.

The Monday Night Ladies, we are one fun bunch and we love

our time together. Stop in sometime and join us—there's always room for one more.

~Carol Commons-Brosowske

Chapter 3

Just Us Girls

She Knows

An Imperfectly Wonderful Friendship

A friend can tell you things you don't want to tell yourself.
~Frances Ward Weller

"Zoe, you need serious professional help, and I cannot continue to be a source of support for you until you get it. I need space from you." As I sat at my kitchen table my heart sank. I could barely read the words of Jessica's e-mail through my tears. The best friendship I'd ever had was crumbling right before my eyes. How had we let our friendship get to this point?

I met Jessica during my freshman year of college. She was two years older than me and had the same drive and passion for running that I did. I broke the ice by making her a care package for a big race she had coming up. From that day forward we did nearly everything together. We would make secret handshakes in the pool, whack giant marshmallows with badminton rackets, roast the remaining marshmallows over an open stove, blow bubbles and throw water balloons at each other, get way too competitive playing *Mastermind*, and watch chick flicks at her apartment. It was our nerdy, intense, quirky personalities combined with our inability to fit in with the "popular" crowd that made us absolutely inseparable. By my sophomore year she had definitely earned the title of "best friend."

Our beautiful friendship was the super-glue holding together the broken pieces of my soul. A lifelong disordered eater, I struggled immensely with eating in college. After knowing Jessica for two years, I finally felt comfortable enough to share with her what I was going through. She would comfort and console me. "You're a superstar," she'd tell me. She'd send me songs to brighten my day. She'd take me to church. She would touch my arm in support when I cried. She was always there for me. She would always take away my pain and leave me feeling like a champion. Our friendship was magical. Flawless. Perfect. The best thing to ever happen to me.

But behind the perfect illusion I had imagined it to be, our friendship was just as broken as I was. I couldn't see what an enormous burden I was putting on Jessica. Talking endlessly about my struggles was beginning to be more than she could bear. She wanted to help me but didn't know how. This went on for a year and a half until one day I took it too far. We were sitting outside at a picnic table on an unusually warm December afternoon. "I'm thinking about cutting myself," I confided to her. She stared at me with terrified eyes, a sharp contrast from the soothing demeanor she'd always shown me. She quickly began making excuses to leave. As I watched her walk to her car, tears began to form in my eyes. Her uncharacteristic response made me realize that something was terribly wrong.

The next morning I sat down with a warm cup of coffee, still feeling awfully shaken about my encounter with Jessica. I casually began checking my e-mail and noticed that she had sent me a lengthy message. I read the first line and curled up on the floor crying hysterically. "Zoe, you need serious professional help, and I cannot continue to be a source of support for you until you get it," the e-mail began. "I need space from you." How could I possibly distance myself from the girl that meant everything in the world to me? There were countless additional lines detailing why she needed time apart, but my eyes glazed over and the words started spinning all over the page. I felt like I couldn't breathe. I called her twenty-five times. No response. I sent her e-mails begging her to speak to me. Nothing. After a day of uncontrollable sobbing, I finally realized that I had become completely dependent on Jessica and that our friendship was no longer healthy. I sent her a final e-mail telling her that I needed space of my own.

The month I spent apart from Jessica was eye-opening for me. I realized that I was in dire need of professional help, and without Jessica there to help me I felt lost and alone. Forcing me to get professional help was the best thing she could have done for me. Thanks to Jessica's tough love I came back to school a completely different person, ready to face life courageously.

Jessica and I very slowly began to rekindle our friendship, which we affectionately referred to as a "work in progress." For months we walked on eggshells, afraid that saying anything wrong would send our friendship into an irreparable downward spiral.

And then it finally happened. "I beat you, Jessica!" I exclaimed as I jumped up and pumped my fist in the air. "Victory is mine!" We were playing *Mastermind* on the same picnic table where our friendship had taken a massive nosedive the previous December. I had just beaten my genius best friend by one point. I looked at her with a smug expression and we both started cracking up. From that moment on I knew that our friendship was back to being normal. No, make that back to being completely awesome. Like a rubber band, the tension snapped and we finally both let our guard down.

Our friendship is different now. We have more obligations and see each other less. But our friendship contains an element that it never had before: depth. The breakdown in our friendship helped us get our issues out on the table so we could move past them. It challenged our commitment to being friends. But being the strong, determined women that we are, we put our shattered friendship back together piece by piece. Our friendship will inevitably have many more bumps, twists, turns and roadblocks along the way. We'll stumble and we'll fall. We'll have tension and need some comic relief, and we'll likely resort to taking badminton rackets and whacking oversized marshmallows at each other. But because of Jessica, I refuse to dwell on the negatives in my life. It's probably for the best; now I can put all of my energy into whipping her butt in *Mastermind*. Bring it, Jessica!

~Zoe Knightly

Tesi

A friend accepts us as we are yet helps us to be what we should.
~Author Unknown

I could tell the pretty stranger wanted to come in as I peeked out at her from behind my half open front door.

She introduced herself politely. "I brought you some books."

I accepted her gift and looked over my shoulder, doing a quick survey of my living room. It wasn't "company clean" but it would have to do.

"Excuse the mess," I said as I stepped to the side, inviting her into my home.

So this was Tesi Pugh. She was certainly not what I had imagined. She was cute and really put together. The exact opposite of how I appeared at that moment. I suddenly felt self-conscious as I looked down at my ratty terrycloth sweats and remembered the messy bun on top of my head. She didn't seem to notice my disheveled appearance.

I had shared a single phone conversation with her at the insistence of a mutual friend and now here she was. I hadn't expected that we would actually meet.

"How are you doing?"

"Good," I lied. "How are you?"

Tesi selflessly shared her story, one that was so very similar to my own. When she finished we hugged. I waved goodbye to her from my front porch as she drove away.

I went into the house and collapsed on the sofa, exhausted.

Tesi's story, just like my own, was one of great loss. She'd lost her seventeen-year-old son, Alex, only nine months before my own daughter, Kyley, died in a car accident.

I half-heartedly placed the books, designed to help me through my grief, on my nightstand. I had no real plans to read them. It had been very sweet of her to reach out to me but I wasn't interested in making a new friend.

I had no intention of solidifying my membership in the "Grieving Moms Club" by hanging out with other members.

Months passed and as the one-year anniversary of my daughter's death neared, I threw myself into a local community outreach program. I arrived at my first volunteer assignment and found myself working alongside the pretty lady with the books, Tesi.

I knew I would be seeing her again so I went home that night, found the books, and started reading. I didn't want to have to lie to her if she asked me about them.

Tesi invited me to lunch one day. I accepted with some reluctance. What would we talk about? Would we talk about our loss and the accompanying pain that seemed so intense at times it threatened to swallow me whole? I didn't talk about that with anyone. Nobody understood what I felt. People were uncomfortable with my grief and so I maintained a good distance from family and friends. I couldn't really blame them. I was pretty uncomfortable with it myself.

I met Tesi for lunch. Three and a half hours and four glasses of sweet tea later, we emerged from the restaurant smiling and with plans to meet the following week for a fun-filled day of shopping.

"I'm going to call and cancel. I'm having a bad day," I told my husband.

"Don't do that. Just go. It will be good for you to get out of the house." I reluctantly gave in and headed for Tesi's.

She did most of the talking on the thirty-minute drive to San Antonio and that was just fine with me.

We arrived at a cute little shop, just the kind of place I would have loved before my world had been turned upside down. As I sat in the car, staring at the quaint storefront, I became overwhelmed with emotion. I sat in the car and grieved my loss. Not only the loss of my daughter, but the loss of the life I'd imagined for myself, the loss of that feeling of joy I had once found in the little things, like shopping trips with new acquaintances. I burst into tears with Tesi sitting next to me.

I waited for her to tell me not to cry. She didn't. I waited for her to start listing all the reasons I still had to be happy. She didn't. I waited for the pep talk designed to lift my spirits. It didn't come. Instead, she grabbed my hand and sat with me in silence, in understanding.

I didn't realize it at the time, but this woman was becoming my friend.

I began spending more and more time with Tesi. We found we had many common interests: decorating... writing... family. It was nice to be able to share those things again with someone.

We spent many therapeutic hours visiting about our lost children. We spent many hours visiting about our faith. Tesi eagerly shared about God's mercies during her struggles. When the time came that my grief turned to anger and I no longer wanted to talk about God, or our loss, Tesi quietly stepped back, whispering, "I'll be here when you do." And she was.

We shared times of light heartedness and plenty of "laugh 'til it hurts" moments, too. But the sacredness of the friendship being forged between us came from our mutual life experience and the bond we shared in our understanding of how precious this life really is.

Tesi was there with me the day a near stranger wrapped her arm around me and offered to pray for a sign that I might find comfort despite the upcoming anniversary of my daughter's death. Tesi was there with me when I received the e-mail from Chicken Soup for the Soul informing me that the story I had written about my encounter with the prayer warrior had been chosen for publication in one of their upcoming books. We laughed, we cried, we laughed some more.

Tesi celebrated with me when I felt good enough to host a gathering for friends in my home. After the invitations were sent out I remember saying to myself, "What was I thinking? I'm not ready for this." Tesi arrived before the other guests, her famous enchilada dip in hand, and went about the task of ensuring everything ran smoothly, allowing me to sit and visit with old friends.

When a local television station asked to come to my home to interview me about my story in *Chicken Soup for the Soul: Devotional Stories for Tough Times,* I couldn't help but feel more than a little overwhelmed at the thought of talking about something so personal on TV. I looked around my house, which was nowhere near camera ready. Tesi arrived, removed her jacket, and began cleaning, offering encouragement as we worked together.

It's been four years since Tesi showed up on my doorstep. I was prepared to go it alone on this journey; I thought at the time I would have preferred it that way.

As I emerge into the light at the end of the tunnel, I do so holding the hand of the woman who has walked beside me through the darkness. She is my God gift. She is my best friend.

~Melissa Wootan

Chicken Soup
for the Soul

Rekindling the Inner Spirit

In everyone's life, at some time, our inner fire goes out. It is then burst into flame by an encounter with another human being. We should all be thankful for those people who rekindle the inner spirit.

~Albert Schweitzer

I've had plenty of close friends throughout my life, but I always felt like I was missing that one big friendship that so many other women seem to have. As an only child, I had always longed for a sister. As an adult, all I wanted was a true best friend to fill that void.

When I was thirty-two, I was living my dream as a stay-at-home mom when the world came crashing down around me. On a Tuesday afternoon in May of 2009 I was diagnosed with stage two invasive breast cancer. My days of play dates, trips to the zoo, and lazy mornings at home with my twenty-one-month-old son turned into doctor's appointments, terrifying body scans and a whole lot of uncertainty.

In the months that followed I learned quite a bit about the people in my life, both friends and family members, some for better and some for worse. Over the course of eight months I had a unilateral mastectomy with reconstruction, six cycles of intensive chemotherapy and twenty-eight rounds of radiation. While the pain and side effects were almost unbearable, the fear and anxiety that developed was even worse. My husband and parents were an amazing support system but they couldn't understand what I was going through both physically and emotionally, nor could I expect them to. Plus, I wanted to be strong for them so they could in turn be strong for my son. I never missed having a sister more than I did during that time.

Eventually I found myself wishing for a "cancer friend" so that I could relate to someone who knew what I was going through. I would sit at chemo and look around the room, trying to find someone to befriend. I met some wonderful people, but everyone was always much older than me so I never connected with anyone.

I found what I needed in the most unlikely of places. When I finished chemo, I decided to enroll my son in preschool. It was the middle of the school year when he started, so many of the parents already seemed to know each other. I was still wearing my headscarf and knew it was obvious I was in the middle of cancer treatment, so I basically kept to myself. After a few weeks one of the moms from class approached me in the parking lot and asked me if I was in treatment. She told me that she was a recent lymphoma survivor and we made plans to meet for coffee the next day. That day I drove home from preschool giddy, suddenly feeling the weight of the world lifted off my shoulders. A simple five-minute conversation in a parking lot and I wasn't alone anymore. No longer was I the "freak" I felt I was.

Leah and I hit it off right away, and of course it didn't hurt that our sons were exactly the same age. My husband joked in the beginning that I was too eager but I think the feeling was mutual. I started to find myself again through this new friendship and it was a relief. Since then, Leah and I have become the closest of friends.

One day not too long ago, two different people e-mailed me separately, each asking me to reach out to someone they knew who was thirty and had been diagnosed with breast cancer. Sure enough, even though they didn't know each other in any way, it turned out they were both talking about the same woman. I knew that day we were meant to be friends. Vicky has been a welcome addition to the friendship that Leah and I have built over the past few years. And in a short time the three of us have truly become sisters. I feel incredibly lucky that I now have friends who understand the new me. It is an unexpected gift in the wake of such adversity.

Leah, Vicky, and I sometimes compare our situation to having been to war. We went to battle for our lives and we share a bond that people who haven't been there could never understand. We will never be the same for the things we experienced, but I'll admit we did get something wonderful out of it. Not only do I have the best friend and sister I hoped for so long ago—I have two. And although we can't predict the future, we have each other. Which, after all we've been through, is not too shabby. And the three of us are planning to be friends for another fifty years.

~Lauren Magliaro

Sunshine on a Rainy Day

Nothing but heaven itself is better than
a friend who is really a friend.
~Plautus

Have you ever marveled at the sun when it continues to shine through a cloudburst? That is the visual of my treasured friendship with Gen.

We were all packed for our yearly vacation with extended family the summer after our son's death. We had lost Davis in a traffic fatality the previous June. He loved going to the hot springs, golfing, and connecting with his cousins. The pain of his absence on this trip numbed my senses.

As the sun was setting on our vacation home in British Columbia and we were clearing the dishes from our barbeque, in walked a troupe of young people toting guitars and assorted musical instruments. One young girl was smiling shyly as she walked by with her African drum. Music has always been a big part of our family life. My sister and I grew up singing harmonies and my mom was a pianist. One of my sons is a guitarist. Everyone is gifted with some sort of musicality. The jam session began in earnest on our patio on this hot summer evening. It took me to a place of joy, something dear when you are grieving. Wanting to capture the memories, I began to take photos. My eyes were riveted on Mikelle, the lovely petite teen with the African drum. She and Davis would have been the same age. When my son died at eighteen years old, his future was lost to us. As I watched her, I knew how much Davis would have loved meeting this girl. I felt a respite from my sorrow that evening as we all sang together.

The following summer, I sat on our patio reading the newspaper, clutching my cup of joe and basking in the mid-morning sunlight. A headline snapped me to attention. There had been a terrible car accident down the coastline highway. A teenage boy had fallen asleep behind the wheel, resulting in the death of two of his passengers and serious injury to himself and another. My heart ached for all of the families, knowing how far-reaching the agony would be. I prayed for each of the families as I looked over their photos in the newspaper. My eyes kept going back to a photo of a pretty, blond girl, one whose life was taken in the accident. Soon after, I realized this girl was Mikelle, the one who had played her African drum at our summer place.

Wanting to share with her parents how meaningful the evening with Mikelle had been, I located their address and sent them a letter, along with the photos I'd taken of their daughter. With no expectations of a reply, I was surprised when Mikelle's mom, Gen, contacted me. From the first time we met, we felt an ease in sharing our grief. We carried an identical burden and fully understood the pain. We also took comfort in each other's perspectives. Although complete strangers, we felt deeply for each other's loss and trusted each other with our vulnerabilities. When the weather cooperated, we walked and talked for hours through our parklands. We discovered that we had many interests in common, which prompted diverse conversations and field trips. Being with Gen gave me courage to want to live fully again.

When a friendship is forged from tragic circumstances, an unmatched bond of heart and spirit takes place. I do not believe in coincidences but rather that everything happens for plan and purpose. Both Gen and I believe we were divinely appointed to meet. Despite the pain of loss and brokenness, a beautiful friendship has come from the ashes in our lives. Both of our teenagers are in heaven.

I often think back on the jam session that happened on our patio, and how I lamented that Davis didn't have enough time here to meet someone like Mikelle. Now a comfort washes over me when I picture them together, on the other side, while Gen and I continue to walk together, propping each other up on this side. Something very special has come from the ache we will carry for a lifetime. This gift of friendship keeps us moving forward. It is lifegiving, like sunshine on a rainy day.

~Sally Walls

24

Best Friends

Somewhere on this planet is your best friend.
Find that person.
~Omar Kiam

My best friend knows me well,
And reads me like a book.
She knows when there is something wrong
By taking just one look.

She also reads between the lines,
When I've got things to share.
She listens without judging me
And lets me know she cares.

She tells me what I need to hear,
I know it's for my good.
Otherwise, I'd never change
Or do the things I should.

She laughs when I am happy,
And cries when I am hurt.
She stands firm and takes my side
When others dish out dirt.

Our friendship is forever,
It's priceless and won't end.
I'm absolutely sure of this
'Cause I'm also her best friend.

~Lydia Gomez Reyes

25

Brassiere Basics

Friends are like bras: close to your heart and there for support.
~Donna Roberts

I'm a big girl. You know—curvy. Feminine. Buxom. Which, of course, leads to the inevitable need for a bra. I say need, here, in the most fundamental sense. I don't wear one to ensure a "smoother profile" or "better posture"—two of the many lies promulgated by bra manufacturers. No. My motivation for struggling into one each and every day is more a sense of self-preservation. You see, after breastfeeding three babies, they've become a tripping hazard. I can't say for sure, but my guess is that I'd be violating an OSHA mandate if I didn't keep "the girls" safely contained—for my own safety, and the safety of others.

Why am I exposing myself (figuratively and a bit literally) writing about such things? It's all my bestie's fault. She is one of those people who is funny, cute, and always looks pulled together and neat. During a break in a conference we attended together, she commented about how much she loved my dress, and asked me to take off my jacket so she could see the back. Thrilled to have impressed my fashionista friend, I started to slip my arm out of the sleeve, and then froze. I hemmed. I hawed. I made excuses, and blushed furiously. Finally, I had no choice but to admit the truth—I couldn't take my jacket off because the halter neckline of the dress would expose the back of my bra. Usually, this would not be a problem between buddies. However, my bra on that particular day looked like something out of a redneck fix-it shop. You can see, then, why I was hesitant to show it off.

The implement itself wasn't all that unusual. It was your typical Walmart bra—white, with a three-hook closure in the back, and made for nursing. The problem was, I hadn't nursed a baby in two years. Since the time it was purchased I had gained some girth, and had added a handy extender to give me some extra breathing room. The extender was black. And six hooks wide. And had been repaired in hot-pink thread. I might as well have used duct tape and baling twine. The final result couldn't have been much worse.

My friend, being the intuitive gal that she is, began to throw questions my way about the offending item of clothing. In short order she had guessed that I was ashamed to show it because it was a nursing bra, despite the fact that I was no longer a nursing mother. Thankfully, she accepted that as the reason why I was hesitant to flash some skin and show off the back of my dress, so I was spared the embarrassment of having to actually reveal my neon stitches and mismatched extender. I did, however, have to sit through a mild chiding about the importance of finding the right bra. Arguing was out of the question—partly because I knew I deserved the lecture, and partly because I was afraid she'd want to point something out and discover just how shockingly bad my undergarment really was.

At any rate, she was right. Since then, I've tried to be more mindful of my choice in brassieres. I no longer own a single nursing bra, and am down to just one extender, which happens to be the same color and width as the bra it is affixed to. Moreover, just last week I actually discarded a bra after the underwire broke, rather than simply pulling both wires out and continuing to wear it as-is, which is (I'm ashamed to say) something I've done in the past (hey, at least it's economical).

All in all, I'm glad to report that I've taken some major steps in the right direction, and am well on my way toward having an arsenal of support garments that's both attractive and strong enough to tote the load. And, not a moment too soon. After all, I'm raising three daughters who (if genetics are any indicator) are likely to be similarly well endowed. I'm determined not to let them down when it comes to brassiere basics. I'm sure the answers are out there — some mysterious combination of fact, science, lore, and Spandex — hidden deep within the pages of the Victoria's Secret catalogs, blueprints in the basement of the Vatican, and the annual OSHA safety guidelines. And if all else fails, I hope my daughters have a friend as good as mine, who knows exactly when to stage a brassiere intervention.

~Andrea K. Farrier

26

Finding New Valentines

Friendship is born at that moment when one person says to another:
"What! You too? I thought I was the only one."
~C.S. Lewis

"Ahhh, February 14th, the day you will learn to hate." My friend, Debbie, guided me through a tough separation and divorce, and then led the way through my first year of being single again.

"Should we make plans together?" I asked her.

"Do you really want to go out to dinner on a night when every couple in the world is renewing their love?"

"No, but I don't really want to sit home alone and feel sorry for myself either."

My brain churned. I had my own home now that offered a formal dining area with six matching chairs. I remembered Grandma's hand-me-down china, never-used cloth napkins, and stemware packed away in boxes. If Debbie hated the day so much, did others? I knew a lot of single females.

I selected five vivacious women, collected their addresses, and created elegant invitations.

Planning a menu suited to lighter tastes, I determined this would be no meat and potatoes night. Different colored cloths and lace draped the table, topped with a playful centerpiece of feather boas and candles.

My mother, recalling her first Valentine's Day as a widow, supported my excitement by purchasing a single long-stemmed red rose for each of my friends to take home from the evening. I tied them with ribbons and placed one at each setting of the table.

The ladies dressed up as requested, and came through my front door with smiles, saying, "I've looked forward to this all week," and, "Oh, how beautiful!" at the festive décor.

I introduced them by offering a small explanation of how I knew each, and then left them to mingle with one another. Once dinner was ready, the women were seated; dinner was served in courses.

The meal started with small appetizer plates, clear broth, and a salad of mixed greens. The easy-to-prepare main course of Turkey en Croute appeared impressive, the sides of roasted asparagus and candied carrots well received.

A lovely dessert wine had chilled all afternoon and accompanied a serving tray of fresh chocolate-dipped strawberries, and petit fours sprinkled with red and pink sugar for our finish.

With coffee, we played a slumber-party-type game with abandon, laughing and joking as we shared our experiences of first kisses, worst dates, and our hopes for the future.

Our evening ended with affirmations of one another and blessings. And everyone agreed—we had just experienced the best Valentine's Day ever.

~Cynthia Mendenhall

27

More than a Good Deal

Every action of our lives touches on some chord that will vibrate in eternity.
~Edwin Hubbel Chapin

Six men and one woman stood ready to pounce on me inside the dealership showroom. I was alone in unfamiliar territory; I'd never purchased a new car before.

A middle-aged man briskly approached me with his hand out. "Hello there," he said. "See anything you'd like to take out for a test drive?"

I smiled politely and extracted my hand from his. "Nice to meet you, but I'm already dealing with that woman over there." I pointed.

He raised his eyebrows, shrugged, but said nothing. I walked toward the woman and quickly read her nametag. "Lisa!" I said, a little louder than necessary. "I'm ready to buy that car now."

She smiled and nodded, then led the way to a back office. Once inside, she gestured for me to sit down and closed the door.

"It's kind of tough for a single woman to walk into a shark tank like our showroom, isn't it?" she asked. She took a seat across the desk from me.

I nodded. "Thanks for not laughing or pointing to my trembling knees."

Lisa's smile broadened. "No problem. Glad I could save you from the feeding frenzy."

She waited while I took a deep breath and exhaled slowly. "I really am in the market for a car," I began. "I've just never negotiated a deal myself, and I'm a bit nervous about the whole thing."

Again, she waited silently.

"So do you think you can help me find what I'm looking for?"

"What color?" she asked.

I laughed. "Not the make, the model, or the mileage first?"

"Oh, that stuff's the easy part," replied Lisa. "But in my experience, a woman is more inclined to want to match the car color to her personality before worrying about how many cylinders the engine has."

"Red," I answered. "But not the fire engine bright garish red. More like the hot metallic cranberry color on those Accords out there."

"That's the spirit!" said Lisa. She got out her pencil and started making notes. "Once we get a general list made, I'll use the computer to see what I can find at other dealerships and make a swap if we don't have exactly what you're looking for on our own lot."

I appreciated the way she thought, and the way I felt no pressure whatsoever.

My list was soon complete, and Lisa grabbed the detachable dealership license plates from the main office, along with the keys to several different models. We went out the showroom door, laughing like old friends.

"Let's do lunch!" she suggested as soon as I maneuvered the first car out of the parking lot.

"Lunch?" I queried.

"It's after one, and I'm famished."

"Okay..." I hesitated.

"Don't worry, I won't ply you with drinks, and you'll have to buy your own meal. Cars haven't been selling all that well this month."

I fell in love with the way the very first vehicle I drove handled, so after a delightful time at lunch, we returned to the dealership to crunch the numbers.

Lisa quickly located a car close to what I wanted at a dealership 300 miles away. "No extra charge for delivery," she happily told me.

"Why isn't it exactly what I want?" I asked cautiously.

"It's got pinstripes and a wing on the back. Very classy," she added.

"Pinstripes don't make the car run any better, and the wing is worthless."

"No, actually the wing adds about $500 to the cost of the car," Lisa replied with a straight face.

"It's worthless because it doesn't enhance the mileage or anything," I explained.

She did another quick computer search, but came up empty.

"How much will you take off the price of the car if I agree to take it with the pinstripes and the wing still on it?" I asked, not even trying to mask the twinkle in my eyes.

"Excuse me a minute," she said, closing the door behind her when she left.

When she returned, Lisa was all smiles. "I told my boss he'd either have to take the wing and the pinstripes off, or give you a discount for leaving them on. I explained to him that you were a tough negotiator and he told me he didn't want to pay the labor to have them removed so he'd throw them in at no charge."

I immediately jumped to my feet and hugged her. "It's a deal!"

"It's a first!" she replied, laughing. "People aren't usually so exuberant when they sign a new car contract."

"And I'll bet they don't usually invite you to a summer picnic, either," I replied. "But I've got a bunch of friends getting together this weekend for a weenie roast on the beach, and I'd love to introduce you to them."

Lisa and I became steadfast friends. "You know," she once told me, "I was about to start looking for other employment when you bought your car from me."

As it turns out, it's a good thing Lisa kept that job. One day a short while later, the man of her dreams walked into the dealership. He walked out with a new car and a date with Lisa. They got engaged a few months later, and were married in Hawaii. I was invited to the wedding as a "very special guest."

"I might not ever have met him if I hadn't kept selling cars," Lisa told me after the ceremony. "So in a way, I'm living happily ever after because of you."

I rather doubt the total validity of her statement, but my life too is far richer for having met her. Our friendship, like the car I bought, is still going strong.

~Jan Bono

28

A Cup of Comfort

Friends are those rare people who ask how you are
and then wait for the answer.
~Author Unknown

In my early college years, I worked at a little Starbucks coffee shop in my community. I loved the feeling of pulling my hair up into a high bun and putting my focus and care into creating each cup of joy. When the nights were slow, I would make myself tea and review my notes behind the bar. It was comforting to look out over the steamer and see one or two students enjoying their lattes and focusing passionately on their homework. When we closed up for the night, I would take a hot chocolate home with me and sit at my desk into the late hours, feeling comforted and encouraged to focus on my writing.

On lonely nights, I would indulge in steamers—steamed milk with flavored syrup—a beverage I learned about from a customer. One night, the shop was empty, and I was just getting ready to close when that same customer came rushing in.

"Are you still open?" Her eyes were red as if she had been crying and her long hair was caught in her sweater as if she had just pulled it on.

I couldn't say no.

"We just closed down the espresso machine, but I could still steam milk if you want a hot chocolate or steamer," I offered.

The girl didn't hesitate. "I need two raspberry steamers please."

"No problem," I said. "They are on us today."

I felt compelled to steam the milk as quickly as I could. She could tell.

"My best friend had a bad day," she explained.

When the girl left the store, I remember feeling numb. I couldn't think of one person in my life who would go through that much trouble to bring comfort to me. I can't remember if I took home a raspberry steamer that night because I was in the mood for a hot beverage or because I wanted to feel included.

It was hard to leave the comfort that I had found in Starbucks. The baristas whom I had grown close to were all following different career routes as they finished their college years. I remember watching them move onto new experiences and deciding that it might be time for me to move on too.

I was hired at a restaurant in the same community as my Starbucks a few months after applying. I loved serving from the start. I felt a sense of pride when I picked up a tray of drinks and would stride down my aisle smiling and assigning them to the right tables.

When Cathleen showed up for her shift at the restaurant, I was excited to see her. We had worked together at Starbucks and were familiar with each other. I was more than happy to share some appetizers with her after work.

I don't remember when small talk over appetizers turned into late night bonding sessions over chick flicks and a bottle of wine, but by the time summer rolled around, Cathleen and I had become inseparable. We got along well with each other's friends and shared a lot of the same quirks, such as our love of wearing new dresses and a terrible sense of direction.

Cathleen helped me through a lot of hard times that summer. I had experienced a bad break-up and found out that a childhood friend was really ill. Just when I thought I was pulling through my grandpa got cancer and dementia. It was Cathleen who kept me going. She never tried to play psychologist with me or to make me forget about it by dragging me out of the house. We kept hanging out in our free time as usual. On the hard nights, Cathleen would share noodles and wine with me as we caught up on the television series that had hooked me.

I had been having a particularly rough week that summer, and I remember looking forward to plans with Cathleen. We decided that it would be nice to sit out on a patio and let our skin bronze as we caught up with all the gossip that had been going on at work and the previous weekend's party. We decided that it would be fitting to bond over Starbucks coffees since we had originally met there.

When we had chosen the perfect table in the sun, Cathleen offered to buy the drinks. I was indecisive on what to order and told her that I would be happy with whatever she chose. It wasn't long before my best friend returned, two raspberry steamers in hand.

~Crysta Windsor

29

A Friend in Need

A friend is the one who comes in when the whole world has gone out.
~Grace Pulpit

Our friendship began in high school, more than thirty years ago. I was a shy and awkward scholar and Barb, well, she was the gregarious, fun loving, popular one. I can't recall how we connected but once we did, we became closer than sisters.

Barb and I lived in an apartment together after high school while we were both trying to find our way in life. We had crazy escapades, long conversations, and more than once spent the entire night talking, laughing, and eating tuna fish sandwiches. Sleep didn't matter much back then.

Throughout the years we have both shared all of life's journeys. We've been through weddings, babies, divorces, illnesses, surgeries, venting sessions, weight gains, and weight losses. We have eaten together, prayed together, laughed and cried together, attempted dance and aerobic classes, and have even had knock-down, drag-out fights. Yet we are friends and that will never change. I know that I can call Barb whenever, to share in my happiness or my pain. Ten years ago, unfortunately, I called Barb to help me with my pain.

My husband Ted, my daughter Elizabeth, and I had left for a Disney World vacation. We were sharing the week with my sister, brother-in-law, and niece, looking forward to a wonderful time exploring all of the theme parks and relaxing in the Florida sunshine.

Our vacation ended very early on our first morning with the jarring ring of the telephone. My dad had unexpectedly passed away while he, too, was enjoying a vacation with my mom. He died in their hotel room in Virginia as they made their journey back home from Florida to Ohio. The shock was overwhelming. My young daughter and niece were nearly inconsolable. Thankfully, Ted and my brother-in-law Jim took the girls to breakfast while my sister and I packed up all of our belongings that had just been unpacked the night before... and I called Barb.

My dear friend instantly went into care mode with, "What can I do? What do you need? How can I help?" I had no answers but simply appreciated the questions. As we packed up and began our solemn road trip back to Ohio, Barb checked in frequently. Barb knew that my dad and I were very close. She insisted that she talk with Ted so that he could tell her if I was truly doing as okay as I professed... which I really wasn't.

Not but a few minutes after we pulled into our driveway at home, Barb came roaring in (if you know Barb—she does tend to "roar" in!) with a plate of sandwiches and miscellaneous food items, knowing that we probably had little to eat at the house. More than the food, the tight hugs and shared tears were incredibly welcomed.

The decision was made to assemble at our house following Dad's memorial service. I gathered myself together to assure that there was a spread of food prepared, but I could hardly get it all ready while at the service. Again, Barb took charge to alleviate my stress. She offered, or actually demanded, to make a quick appearance at the service, head back to our house, and make sure that the food and drinks were set up. When we did arrive home after that long day, with my entire large family, we came home to everything set beautifully on the tables with additional dishes prepared by Barb. Barb, in her own knowing way, recognized that this was a private family celebration of life, as my mom had requested. She gracefully greeted all of us then quietly slipped out.

Personally, Barb has been, remains, and always will be my family. She would have been more than welcome to stay. I am just thankful that she has stayed through all of these years... with many more to come.

~Lil Blosfield

30

Chicken Soup
for the Soul

Mary and Me

In my friend, I find a second self.
~Isabel Norton

Mary and I hadn't known each other very long when our children were in a car accident together—struck by a drunk driver while walking home from a study date. My son Neil had been dating Mary's daughter Trista for just eight or nine months when the crash occurred, killing Trista and leaving Neil with a serious traumatic brain injury. We moved in different circles. Mary was a lifelong resident of our town, graduating from the same high school as her two children would attend. I was more of a newcomer. I had moved my family to this beautiful coastal community from a central part of the state some ten years earlier. My friends were like me—transplants from somewhere else.

Having kids who were dating each other brought us closer together. We took turns dropping our kids off at soccer games and picking them up from school plays. We snapped pictures of them dressed for their semi-formal, Trista in her shimmering blue gown, Neil in top hat and tux. Though their relationship was new, Neil and Trista's devotion to each other was compelling. Though Neil was headed off to college in the fall, he had decided to remain a couple with Trista, not look for other girlfriends. Trista told Mary she thought

Neil was "the one." With our kids' relationship progressing, I found myself wondering if Mary would someday be Neil's mother-in-law.

But it was not to be. Instead of walking our children down a wedding aisle, we walked down courtroom corridors together as the drunk driver was charged, tried and sentenced. Instead of reading toasts to family and friends, we read our victim impact statements to a judge. Mary spoke of memories of Trista, of shopping together and holding hands. She talked of all the things Trista would never experience: college, a wedding, children. I told the judge about physical therapy and antidepressants and academic modifications Neil needed because of his brain injury.

Though our children suffered very different fates, our experience was uniquely bonding. The night of the accident, Neil and Trista were taken to two different hospitals. Trista was on life support. Neil was confused. He thought he was in a gym. He didn't know what year it was. Mary and I spoke on the phone, updating each other on our children's conditions. Eventually, Trista was pronounced dead. While Neil was taken to the operating room to have his broken leg repaired, Trista was having her organs harvested for donation. While Neil was being intubated for his operation, Trista was extubated after hers.

Mary and I still move in different circles. We see each other around town from time to time; we catch up on our separate lives. Our friendship isn't one of coffee klatches and double dates or long walks together. Our friendship was born on the dreams of our children. It has survived the death of one and the alteration forever of the other. From Mary, I have understood pain and loss, but also learned of resilience and the infinite power of love. Our friendship endures still, strengthened by tears, solidified by our unique and tragic commonality, evolved to a place of acceptance and grace.

~Carolyn Roy-Bornstein

Chapter 4

Just Us Girls

Down the Block

Good Neighbor Helen

Friends are relatives you make for yourself.
~Eustache Deschamps

I always assumed that a best friend living next door came with those thirty-year mortgages—like Lucy had Ethel Mertz and Mary had Rhoda. My hopes were soundly dashed the moment I met Helen, the neighbor who lived next to our very first house. Looking at Helen I realized that there was going to be no rerun of Lucy and Ethel or Mary and Rhoda happening in my life. Helen was in her early nineties, gray haired, sharp eyed, and extremely willing to share her opinions. About everything.

"You burned the bacon this morning, didn't you?" was one greeting on a hot summer morning when I opened the back door and found her standing on the patio. "I could smell it clear over in my kitchen. You can't cook bacon quickly; you've got to let it fry nice and slow. You hurry too much. That's your problem."

Then there was the day my husband was installing a new side door. Helen watched him as he worked, waiting until he had invested several hours and a whole lot of frustration into the job before coming over to tell him what he was doing wrong. "I could see right off the bat that you were trying to put that door in backwards," she announced, "but you've got to learn these things on your own. I didn't want to interfere."

As the weeks turned into months and then years, we got used to Helen. I'm not sure if we mellowed or she did, but the longer we lived next door to her, the less she irritated us. That became even truer after our sons were born. Helen took a delight in first Joe and then Hank that surpassed their own grandmothers' interest. She baked cookies for them, gave them cards with dollars tucked inside, and encouraged them to play on her front porch whenever they wanted to. Suddenly the advice she handed out so freely was much appreciated by me, a nervous first-time mother. Helen had raised two children of her own and she shared her knowledge with me just as she shared everything else. "Don't worry so much," she advised me. "They'll survive and so will you."

Helen stayed in her house until she was in her late nineties, continuing to cook and clean and take care of herself almost until the end of her life. "Don't move until I'm gone," she requested one day.

"I'll try," I said, but it was a promise I couldn't keep. We moved to a bigger house a few months before Helen went into a nursing home.

We've had many neighbors since Helen. I've had neighbors I've enjoyed drinking coffee with, neighbors who like to take walks with me, and neighbors who are almost as zany as Ethel and Rhoda.

But I've never had a neighbor who was a better girlfriend than Helen.

~Nell Musolf

Friends in Dark Times

A friend knows the song in my heart and sings it to me
when my memory fails.
~Donna Roberts

The call came at two in the morning. I hadn't been sleeping well anyway. Something in my mother's heart, something buried deep, had known trouble was coming.

It was my twenty-year-old son's friend. "I need to tell you about Logan." Her voice was steady but I could sense ripples of fear. "He's stuck in a cave. He's been there for a while. You need to come."

My husband Lonny and I stood in the kitchen. He wrapped his arms around me and we rocked back and forth as we prayed. Our boy Logan had left earlier in the afternoon to go camping with friends. They were an hour away at a state park well known for its underground caves. My family had enjoyed spelunking through them since my son was small.

But tonight was different.

Tonight my son was trapped, head down, arms pinned, in a steep, narrow crevice in the cold, dark ground.

"I'll get to the park," my husband said. "You stay here with the other kids." Our four other sons slept soundly in their beds.

And in a moment he was gone. It was just me. The ticking clock. A pounding heart. And fear.

I knew at once what I needed to do. I needed to call my friends.

"Logan is stuck in a cave in Maquoketa," I whispered into the phone. "There are emergency crews. But they can't get him out. I'm sorry to wake you. I need you to pray."

I spoke the words. Over and over. A half dozen times or more. There was something about hearing those voices. Something about knowing my friends would be up, alone in quiet places, sitting in the dark, offering sweet whispers of prayer.

The minutes dragged slowly. I went outside for some air. The bricks were cold on my feet, and for a moment, I wanted to run. I wanted to run from the desperation of it all. But I went inside, started the teapot, more for something to do than for tea. If I didn't do something I'd surely go mad.

"God help me. I can't stand this. I don't know how to push through these minutes. I need your grace," I whispered at the kettle began to howl.

And that's when I heard the knock. It was a gentle rap at the back door.

I knew at once who it was.

My girlfriends had come.

Sarah and Tammy came right in and held me tight. We sat together, praying, reading Scripture, talking, until a stripe of dawn broke the nighttime gray. When my veneer of calm gave way to panic, Sarah held my hand. When doubt and grave thoughts slipped around me like a cloak, Tammy would speak truth.

At about seven in the morning, my husband called. "It's tough, Shawnelle," he said. "There are crews working. But oxygen is a problem and the rescue workers can only stay in the depths of the cave for ten minutes at a time."

I wanted to close my ears.

"They've dangled an oxygen mask down to him. But right now, he can't put it on."

Lonny shared more and while he talked I packed a few things. My dad had come in the night, and he and I were going to the park. I needed to be as close as possible to my boy. And even as I paced and packed and choked out words, my girlfriends made arrangements. When I got off the phone, Sarah spoke in clear, calm words.

"Tammy's going with you two to the park. I'm going to stay here and take care of your other boys."

And with that, we were off.

When we arrived at the park, the first thing I saw was a group of emergency vehicles. Eight or more. Then, coming down the hill that led to the cave entrance, came Lonny. His jaw was set hard and his eyes showed his worry. Together we traversed the hill, and with each step I wondered if I were standing above my trapped boy.

"We have to stay in this area, " Lonny said. "There are picnic tables and a shelter. The entrance isn't too far away, but we have to stay back and let the responders do their work." Lonny held one of my hands, and Tammy held the other.

And then, up the hill, came my passel of friends. The ones I'd called in the night. The ones who had spent the last few hours with hands folded in prayer.

"We had to come," Teresa said. "We want to be here for Logan. But we need to be here for you, too."

I didn't know when I'd been more grateful for the open arms of my friends.

Minutes somehow gave way to hours and the morning sun stretched high in the sky. My mom and sisters had arrived, and they joined the tight circle of my friends. We talked about Logan. We spoke of sweet memories of his growing-up years. We prayed. And once, when I couldn't stand it anymore, a friend followed me as I got up and ran deep into the woods.

I'd fallen to my knees, desperate for my son.

And as I sobbed and begged and finally made peace with God, she held me tight and then helped me to my feet. Together she and I walked back to the shelter.

Later in the afternoon I began to hear whispers of the potential for rain. "The cave is a wash gulley," I heard a rescue worker say. "We'll have to close off the entrance to the cave."

I knew that my son still couldn't move. I knew that he couldn't raise his head. He'd been there for almost twenty hours. I tried to push the panic away, but it moved around me like a damp, heavy fog.

And that's when my friends began to sing.

It was one voice at first. Then another—"Amazing Grace." I closed my eyes and listened to the sweet voices of my friends. Somehow their singing pushed away the fog. Somehow their voices allowed me to breathe.

It was late in the afternoon when we sat at those old, wooden tables and a rescue worker came near. He walked with authority. Tammy reached for my hand and held on tight.

Silence filled the shelter.

"We're going to begin the process of getting your boy out of the cave," he said. "He's no longer lodged in. Your boy has come free."

I would have fallen then, had my friends not held me up.

There was great rejoicing in the dear hearts of those who gathered under that shelter.

I don't believe I would have made it without my girlfriends that day. I'd asked for grace, and God brought my friends.

I learned something precious, too, as we gathered that afternoon with tears running rivers. If a friend stands by you in the darkness, you can bet she'll be there when you're standing in the sun.

~Shawnelle Eliasen

You Goof

No friendship is an accident.
~O. Henry, Heart of the West

We met the day I drove my family two hours north to look at their house. We were planning on moving the next summer and this house had just shown up "For Sale by Owner." It was a few days before Christmas, and Marion and her family were about to decorate their tree. With enthusiasm like the Energizer Bunny, Marion buzzed around setting all our kids up with a game. She was great with my shy children, and her two girls were friendly and kind.

The old Vermont Cape was awesome, but Marion was even more awesome. We stayed and visited as if we were old friends and my kids even helped decorate the tree. Even though the house was beautiful, it wasn't right for us. But that's not why I was disappointed. I was sad that Marion and her family were moving away to another state. I was so comfortable with her that I just came right out and said, "Hey, why do you have to move anyway?"

In her Marion way she smacked me on my arm (my first smack from Marion!) and said, "Oh, you goof."

By the time we found a house and moved, Marion's family had long since left. So imagine my surprise when I saw Marion and her children swimming at the local pond that summer. She told me that they were moving again, this time back to Vermont, but still hours away. And even though we barely knew each other, we chatted like old friends.

Over the next couple of years, Marion would show up here and there as her family came back to visit. I ran into her at a few parties and she always gave me that same quirky smile, and the now famous smack on the arm. One time we met at a mutual friend's house for an all-women's clothing swap. The dining room table was piled high with our clothes to trade, and we tried on all kinds of treasures. Everyone ooohed and ahhhhed when I showed off a skin-tight black suede skirt. "It's so you!" they said. "You look great!" I wasn't so sure. "It's kinda tight," I said, but my words were quickly covered up with, "No it's not! It's perfect! It's you!" I searched the crowded room until I met Marion's eyes. With the slightest, tiniest movement she shook her head and gave me The Look. I could almost hear her saying, "It's not you, it's not perfect, you look like a sausage in that thing. Take it off right now." Later she tossed me a skirt that was perfect. When I tried it on and showed her she smacked me on the arm and said, "You goof, listen to me from now on."

When her family decided to move back to the area, I was thrilled; Marion and I could finally have a real friendship. Never did I realize how strong this friendship would be. My twelve-year-old daughter had gotten very sick and the recovery was extremely difficult. On her own, Marion thought of something that she could do to help. With a pixie-like twinkle in her eye, she showed up at our house one Saturday with a gallon of paint and a handful of wallpaper scrapers. Painting has never been my thing, and I had not even noticed that my daughter's walls were covered with wallpaper more suited for a nursing home than a preteen. But Marion noticed, and she knew that for my daughter's recovery, a purple room was going to make a difference. And it did.

It took many Saturdays to peel off the layers of wallpaper; the bottom one must have been there since the 1800s, when the house was built! Through the weeks, Marion and I peeled and painted and laughed, our children played together, and the color returned to my daughter's cheeks. As her room took on new life, so did she, reemerging healthy and beautiful.

Even through our laughter and joking, Marion knew how much I had been hurting during my daughter's illness. She listened to me when I needed to talk, and held me when I needed to cry. But she's not one to let sadness rule. She always had a funny story to tell, usually about her own childhood—talk about a wacky family!

Even now when I try to thank her, and tell her how much it means to me that she was there during such a difficult period, she just gives me her quirky smile, smacks me on the arm and says, "Oh, you goof."

~Lava Mueller

34

A Friend Across the Street

> *If you have two friends in your lifetime, you're lucky.*
> *If you have one good friend, you're more than lucky.*
> ~S.E. Hinton

I met Colleen Tuthill about six years ago, when we moved from Bozeman, Montana to Whitehall. We bought a place with thirty acres. The Tuthills lived across the road from us. They had two boys, close in age to our older two.

I'm a pretty shy person and tend to keep to myself, and with three boys and a writing career, I don't have a lot of down time. So it took most of the summer before I had the courage to actually cross the road and introduce myself.

The first social thing we did was go to their house for supper. We liked each other immediately. We had similar families and backgrounds. And we had a lot of parallels in our lives. We were both stay-at-home moms, we both had houses full of males. We both married men ten years older than us, we both enjoyed being at home, and we both liked to walk.

Over a few months time, we started going for daily walks, spending an hour together getting to know each other. And the more we talked, the more I liked her. I found someone I could confide in, someone I could share secrets with. Sometimes you just need a woman in your life who understands.

As the last six years have unfolded, four of our combined five boys now have driver's licenses, one has graduated, one is a junior, one is a sophomore, and one is a freshman. My youngest is in third grade. Her boys call me Mom. Mine call her the same.

We rely on each other to get our kids places and to do chores. But most important? We know we can call the other one at any time.

There are days when I'm sad for no reason or I've had a bad mothering day or I've had a fight with my husband. I know I can call Colleen, talk for thirty minutes and have a whole new outlook on my day. And the same goes for her.

We started going to Butte together once a week—it's a community about twenty-five miles from us. We do our grocery shopping and other errands together, and we usually splurge for lunch. We've gone Christmas shopping together, and we have our favorite restaurants, depending on what town we're in. In Butte, it's the Greek place. In Bozeman, it's Cajun.

Our birthdays are close together—mine is December 1, hers is December 3. We try to have some kind of celebration around that time—we treat ourselves to lunch or something fun.

A couple of years ago, Colleen introduced me to her homemade "tea." It was actually Irish cream, but she drank it out of a tea mug. It has become our private joke. And when we have the need, we can whip up a bottle for sharing and drink our tea during the afternoon. The same goes for margaritas. Some summer days, when all the boys are occupied, we'll get together for icy, slushy margaritas, and just enjoy.

We have a fire pit in our east pasture, and we normally host cookouts during the year. Typically, we have one on Memorial Day weekend, Fourth of July, and Labor Day weekend—if the boys don't have any rodeos. The Tuthills have a standing invitation to those.

The best part of my best friend is that she doesn't judge me. I can be my petty, neurotic self around her, and she gets me. We don't agree about everything, but we're okay with not agreeing.

One great thing I've rediscovered with Colleen is that I'm an interesting and fun person. I had forgotten about my life before I was "Mom." My youngest still needs me to be a full-time presence in his life, and I cherish that. But my older two boys are carving out their own lives now and I find that I have more available time to cultivate my life again. Colleen helps me remember that I can be witty and charming. I can tell bad jokes. And I can try new things.

We're good for each other. Together, we're brave enough to take on projects that alone we wouldn't dare. And we give each other the kick in the butt that is sometimes needed. But above all, we listen to each other. And we empathize with one another. And we laugh!

The best compliment that I've had in a long time came from Colleen. She was making a list of ten nice things she could do for herself. And one of her ten was "Call Jodi." How great is that?

~Jodi Icenoggle

35

Girlfriends, Near and Far

Friendship is a sheltering tree.
~Samuel Taylor Coleridge

The moving van, packed full, chugged away from my dream home in the Arizona desert. I settled back into the front seat of my car, snapped my seat belt tight, and took one last look at the sunrise that painted orange and yellow hues across the sky. I inched my foot closer to the gas pedal, then reluctantly put the car in gear and pulled out of the driveway. The stately saguaro cactus that lined our property stood at attention with outstretched arms that seemed to be begging me not to leave.

My husband Ray drove the van while our daughter Lindsey and I followed behind. I glanced at Lindsey, who was sitting with her nose just inches away from the window. Her small frame wiggled with excitement over this new adventure. She pointed out every sight that appeared on our route. After a few hundred miles she asked, "How much longer, Mommy? Are we there yet?" I leaned over, brushed her cheek with the tip of my fingers and stifled the sadness in my voice. "It'll be a few hours, sweetheart. I'll let you know when we're getting close."

I turned my attention to the road before me. Thoughts about the people I'd miss tormented me. How could I leave behind extended family, familiar streets and places I'd known all my life? But it was moving away from girlfriends I'd known since high school that weighed heaviest on my heart. These girls were my support team—the ones I called in the middle of the day when the baby had chickenpox or I was exhausted from being up all night and wanted to run away. They were the ones who would go to the store, buy calamine lotion, bring it to the house and then sit with me for hours listening to me cry through a flood of tears. Memory after memory played back in slow motion.

The farther I drove toward unknown territory, the sadder I felt. When I glanced in the rearview mirror, I saw a picture peeking from behind the pile of clothes jammed in the back seat. It was a farewell gift with an inscription about girlfriends. What was I going to do without them? My gaze turned to Lindsey, who was sleeping. I silently prayed that one day she might have a special place in her heart for good friends.

The loaded van creaked heavily as it entered the circular drive of our new home. I inched the car to a stop behind it. I took a deep breath, willed my lips into a smile and stepped out of the car. Lindsey woke and sprinted toward the house. "Daddy, Daddy, look at the big trees. Can we build a tree house?" Stopping to get my bearings, I let my breath go, surveyed my surroundings and said, "Oh my gosh, this place is beautiful."

A fortress of fifty-foot cottonwood trees graced the driveway. In the distance I saw snowcapped mountains with pine trees that reached toward the blue sky, peppered with billowing white clouds. Grassy fields bordered both sides of our property with horses calmly munching on alfalfa. Their ears twitched back and forth as if they could hear us intruding on their serenity.

Within a few days, our new life started to take shape. With items unpacked and furniture arranged, I sat down to assess my progress. Startled by a knock on the door, I nearly tripped in my hurry to answer it. An older woman stood in front of me with a basket in her hands. She introduced herself as a neighbor who lived behind us. "Wanted to welcome you to the neighborhood. Thought you might need a few staples until you can get to the store," she said. The corners of her mouth seemed to reach the edges of her eyes. I felt the hair tingle on my arms. We chatted, I thanked her, and back in the house, I fell into a chair and cried.

I enrolled Lindsey in her new school while Ray resumed his duties on the road with the highway patrol. One by one, neighbors came to visit, always with something to share: food, flowers, suggestions, and smiles. Before I knew it, I was volunteering at the school, joining the PTA, and starting classes at the local college. Ladies at the school introduced me to an organization called Beta Sigma Phi. We did charity work and planned fabulous socials with our husbands. The people at the little church we joined opened their arms to us. Bible studies enriched and soothed my heart. Riding my horse became a new experience. Instead of the cactus blooms I used to see, I took in the aroma of sweet pine and the sounds of a babbling brook.

We moved one last time—another transfer for Ray. This time, I embraced the move with enthusiasm. Once again, people met us with open arms in our new neighborhood. We embraced them and they embraced us. Now I had a bigger list of girlfriends to stay in touch with. Past memories can never be stolen from our hearts. New memories don't replace the old.

Most importantly, I realized that people are people no matter where you live. If you open your heart to a stranger, you are strangers no more. Girls can become girlfriends anywhere. A move is just another location, a small interruption in life. I didn't lose the "old" girlfriends. I made new ones. With today's technology I'll never be out of touch with the girls I left behind.

Today, Lindsey is grown and on her own journey. Ray is retired and filling a larger portion of my life. But... I still have those girlfriends that come to my aid whenever I call on them. They don't bring calamine lotion. Instead they bring their hugs, smiles, encouragement and their ears. Oh... and tissues!

~Alice Klies

36

Chicken Soup for the Soul

A Friendly Rescue

Begin challenging your own assumptions. Your assumptions are your windows on the world. Scrub them off every once in awhile, or the light won't come in.
~Alan Alda

"I do not want to move to Maryland," our daughter Jill said firmly, her blond hair swirling as she shook her head.

"I don't either," her sister Kay agreed. "We like it here in Texas. I have a job, Jill's in college and has a job. We'll get an apartment and live together."

So, as empty nesters, my husband Fred and I moved to Takoma Park, Maryland, just a few minutes from Washington, D.C. A real estate agent found us a small house in a reasonably good neighborhood, close to Fred's office and within our budget. It was a one-and-a-half story brick Cape Cod built for soldiers returning from World War II.

That house impressed nobody except me. I loved it. To me it represented a blank canvas that I could improve to my heart's content without worrying whether what I did was the most "with it" in terms of decorating. I also reasoned that all the physical labor involved would be good therapy for a lonesome mother.

I scraped layers of paint off door casings and painted the walls and trim a light cream color. Fred and I pulled up the carpets and refinished the beautiful red oak floors. The clean smell of latex paint and sharp odor of polyurethane permeated my pores and worked as medicine against the doldrums. A small room upstairs, lined in old knotty pine paneling, endured multiple applications of sandpaper and changed from dark brown to gold.

I worked outside the house also, helping Fred dig up overgrown junipers, tearing up the ugly fence between us and the neighbors, mowing grass, and sanding and painting porch railings.

Carroll and Julie Davis, an elderly couple, lived in the house on the corner lot and were our next-door neighbors. Outgoing Carroll walked back and forth between our houses and watched my frenetic activity. I knew he kept his tiny wife informed of my progress but even the few times I caught her outside and tried to make conversation, her replies to my questions were monosyllabic and she scurried inside quickly. This was a disappointment. I missed my girls and needed a friend.

"My wife doesn't 'neighbor' much," Carroll explained. "It's not you. She just never has warmed up to any neighbors." Until one day when I needed to be rescued.

After I finished sanding the knotty pine walls in the upstairs bedroom, I brought up a bucket of warm water and old towels to wash the window. The window was the kind you rotated a handle to open and shut. I washed the inside, then opened the window and stepped out on the kitchen roof to wash the outside. I scrubbed with my usual enthusiasm and didn't notice the window gradually close. Finished, I stood back to admire the clean glass and realized only a sliver of space was left between the window casing and the window. Desperately I tried to squeeze my hand through that slender opening and reach the handle. No luck. I did not want to force the window.

Finally I shrugged and gave up. I was stuck on the kitchen roof. Nuts. How idiotic could I be? The street we lived on was one short block with three houses, not counting Carroll and Julie's house on the corner. Undeveloped parkland filled the other side of the street. The traffic consisted of the three of us householders and an occasional lost soul.

Standing on my kitchen roof I scanned the neighborhood. This was a lovely afternoon. Where were the neighbor kids riding their bikes? They often came over from the park to ask for a shovel or a rake to build up the jumping mounds on their bike trail. No young voices shouted to one another today or knocked on our door. The neighbor to the left was at work, ditto the neighbors on the other side of him. Carroll and Julie were likely home, but our kitchen was on the wrong side of our house for me to call to them.

I sat down and pondered my situation. Even if someone came along, they couldn't walk in the house and open the window. The doors were locked. That was my husband's doing.

"When you're engrossed in an indoor project, anyone could just open the door and come in," he would say. "Keep the doors locked."

I needed a ladder.

I sat, disconsolately thinking how stupid I was and wishing a book would magically appear, when I heard the distinct sound of a dribbling basketball. I stood up and peered down the street. Sure enough, it was a preteen boy. Was this ordinary looking kid my key to freedom?

"Hey, boy," I yelled. The kid looked around, puzzled at this voice coming from nowhere. "Up here. On the roof." He looked up, saw me, and grinned. It's not every day you see an old lady on a roof.

"Whatcha doing up there?" he asked.

"I'm stuck. I was washing the window and it shut. Could you go to the corner house and ask one of those people to come?"

He gazed at me for a while, grinned again and disappeared. Soon he was back, with Julie in tow.

"Is Carroll home, Julie?" I asked. "I need a ladder."

"Carroll's not home but I think I can carry the ladder."

My young basketball player gave me another huge smile, picked up his ball, and went merrily on his way, no doubt thinking of the great story he could tell at dinner. Julie soon came, dragging a ladder behind her. She set it up and I climbed down.

My rescuer smiled a shy smile. "I suppose your doors are locked and the key's in the house."

"You supposed right."

"I baked cookies this morning and could put the coffee pot on," she volunteered hesitantly.

"That sounds wonderful, Julie."

The two of us celebrated my rescue with coffee, cookies, and laughter, and for the eight years we lived in that little Cape Cod house, we kept our coffee pots hot and our conversations lively. I delighted in her friendship.

~Georgia L. Alderink

37

The Dead Body

Mistakes are part of the dues one pays for a full life.
~Sophia Loren

I never thought I would make a new friend by finding a body on the porch. But one day I happened to look outside our spare bedroom window, which faces directly onto our next-door neighbors' back door and porch area. I was surprised to see an older woman I did not recognize and had never even seen around our street. She was sitting peacefully with a small plastic Tupperware box on her lap containing what looked like candy.

Her body was slightly slumped, head tilted back with a small bathroom towel wrapped around her hair. I thought she was asleep.

So I went about my day and later returned to the window again. I noticed the woman had not moved at all. As I looked more closely at her face, I thought her skin looked abnormally pale. At this point I thought she was dead but was not one hundred percent certain. There was no movement of her chest or stomach, or any sign of breathing from what I could see.

My first thought was that maybe I should go to my neighbors' door and let them know. I wondered how long she had been there; my guess would be a matter of hours. I waited a short time, and just as I was about to leave, the back door of my neighbors' house opened and my next-door neighbor stepped out onto the porch. She walked straight past the body, almost as if she did not even see it. My neighbor went straight down the stairs carrying a laundry basket in her hands. She was down the stairs and out of sight for at least ten minutes.

Then the neighbor came back up the stairs, mopping each step from the bottom to the very top. At this point I thought that surely my neighbor would notice that this woman was dead. It was very strange. To me, it was obvious that there was a dead woman on my neighbors' porch, but she proceeded to clean around the chair where the body was without batting an eyelash. I was really starting to wonder what was going on, so I decided to take a photo of the woman.

I mentioned to my husband that I was going to go around to our neighbors' door to see if they realized there might be a deceased person on their porch. Of course, I understood that this was a very sensitive issue. I was only going to mention that there might be a woman on their porch... and maybe they should check to see if she was okay.

My overactive imagination couldn't be contained. I started to wonder, "What if the woman on the chair was murdered? Maybe they sat her outside on the porch because of the smell, or maybe she had been hit on the head and the bathroom towel's purpose was to cover the obvious wound!" I was being crazy, I thought. Or was I?

So my husband stayed at the window while I went next door to speak to my neighbor. He was waiting to see if anything happened to the body while I was next door. Off I went, nervously, with my cell phone in my pocket.

I rang the doorbell of my neighbors' house and waited patiently behind the iron gate. Through the glass door, I could see my neighbor approaching with a huge friendly looking smile on her face. She opened the door and asked, "Would you like to come in?" I felt a bit apprehensive but accepted her invitation.

Once inside, I blurted it out. "I'm really concerned about the woman on the porch." I had barely finished my sentence when she burst out laughing. Her husband looked at me over the top of his glasses and smiled. She took me out onto the porch and her husband followed.

They went straight to the body, picked her up, and started flopping her around. I was shocked. It turned out she was a dummy!

My neighbor explained, "Our house was recently burgled, and somebody gave us this dummy to give the impression there are people in the house whenever we're away. We just left it on the chair for now because we were going to give it a good clean before using it."

A little embarrassed, I laughed. "From our window, it certainly looks real, all dressed in tracksuit bottoms, sweatshirt, and a pair of running shoes." My neighbors certainly saw the funny side. I don't know who was the biggest dummy here but I sure felt like one, and of course every time we see each other now we can't help but laugh. It's probably something I will never live down. As neighbors we never really had the opportunity to be introduced or know each other at any great length. The dummy on the porch was a great icebreaker for us. Sometimes the craziest situations lead to making a wonderful new friend.

~Karen E. Lewis

Strength in Numbers

> *In prosperity our friends know us; in adversity we know our friends.*
> ~John Churton Collins

I t was dark and cold at four o'clock that October morning. The dim orange streetlights illuminated my husband as he stood at the end of our driveway. Headlights entered the cul-de-sac, then turned broadside to our house. Jason heaved his sea bag into the trunk and climbed into the passenger seat. His gaze turned towards the house and the window where he knew I was standing, and then the door shut. The engine revved, and those red taillights slipped around the curve and beyond my sight. He was gone.

I was two months pregnant and my husband was being deployed. His ship was leaving in a matter of hours on a trans-Pacific tour that would take God-knows-how-long. The Navy claimed it would be four months. Other wives laughed at that. "The Navy tells time about as well as my five-year-old," one woman said, rolling her eyes.

I wasn't laughing. For the first time in my life, I would have to handle everything on my own. My husband was going to be on the other side of world, in harm's way. He might very well miss the birth of our child. My parents were a thousand miles away in California. I had a house to myself—well, myself and the two cats. I was all grown up and scared witless.

I also had my pride. I didn't want anyone to know how vulnerable I felt. I didn't have a driver's license, but I didn't let that slow me down. I had the post office, grocery store, and a bus stop all within half a mile of my house.

"I can do this," I said out loud, staring out into the dark morning. I had to do it. I had no choice. I had to prove to everyone—and to myself—that I could survive on my own.

I didn't go back to bed. I dozed in a chair and then paced the house, and at six in the morning I kept a very unusual appointment. I walked across the cul-de-sac to my girlfriend Stephanie's house.

Stephanie and another neighbor, Joy, had approached me in my front yard a few weeks before. Stephanie was president of the military spouse group and Joy was parliamentarian, and they encouraged me to join the group before the deployment. I was very shy; I had lived there for eight months and hadn't made any friends yet. There was nothing shy about these two women.

"Come on! We can introduce you to everyone," Stephanie said. They proceeded to do just that.

That particular morning, Stephanie had the duty of standing on the pier and being interviewed by local news crews as the last sailors boarded the ship. She asked me stay in her home while her kids slept, and to help the oldest get ready for school.

I turned on the television and sat back to try and calm my nervous stomach. Flipping between news channels, I saw Stephanie again and again, standing there on the pier with her wind-tousled hair. The heavy gray ship loomed behind her. My husband was in there. Was he thinking of me right now? When would I see him again? I pressed my hands against the nub of my belly and felt the tears well up in my eyes. No, I had to stop thinking like that. I didn't want her kids to see me upset.

Stephanie's son awoke and I helped him get dressed and ready, all the while eyeing the television in the background. Eight o'clock arrived, almost time for the school bus. We walked just outside the front door. Across the cul-de-sac, our other friend Joy emerged with her son.

The two boys met on the sidewalk and headed towards the bus stop. Joy waved me over to meet in the street.

"I'm going to do some shopping in town tomorrow. Want to come?"

I balked. "Are you sure it's not any trouble? I mean, I can walk to the grocery store easily enough...."

She gave me a look. "You don't need to be doing that. It's going to rain. It's always raining here. You walk and get all wet and you get sick, what good's that going to do for you and the baby? Come on now. I'll even pick you up in your driveway."

"I'm only two houses away! I can walk that far."

"Well, you don't need to. That's what I'm saying. I'll be ready at 8:30."

I headed back inside, abashed but grateful. Stephanie returned from the media blitz a short time later.

"It was cold out there!" she said, shuddering as she took off her coat. I turned the television to a kid's show for her toddler.

"It looked it," I said. "Listen, I'm going to head on home..."

"When's your next doctor's appointment?" she interrupted.

"Um, about two weeks, I think."

"Call me later and let me know. I didn't write it down on my schedule."

"Stephanie, you don't have to take me just because you did last month. I can walk to the bus stop and go from there."

She gave me the same look Joy had given me earlier. "In the rain?"

"I'm not going to melt! Honest!"

"Well, I can't promise I can take you, but I want to try. I have to find a babysitter."

I was getting exasperated by that point. "Listen. I don't want to be a bother, okay? That's the last thing I want. I was trying to get that through to Joy earlier, too."

Stephanie let out a heavy sigh. "You're not a bother. You have to remember, we've all done this before. We know what deployments are like and how it is to be pregnant or all alone with little ones when the men are gone. It's hard. It's hard just on a duty day, let alone a deployment. You don't have to go through it alone. You have girlfriends to help." Her voice creaked with emotions she had withheld during her series of interviews.

They knew. They all saw through my fragile facade and understood the vulnerability within. I thought that being grown-up and dealing with this deployment meant mucking through on my own. Chin up, no tears. They knew I wasn't going to ask for help.

So, they just made the choice for me. And I knew the mature response, the only thing I could say in return.

"Thank you," I said. "I'll give you a call later, but please remember if it's a hassle for you I can find a way to get there on my own."

"I know you can," she said, smiling. "But hopefully that won't be necessary."

I went back to my house. I shut the door and locked it. One of my cats lifted his head and yawned. I slipped off my shoes, sucking in a breath as I saw them all by themselves on the mat. Jason's shoes were gone. He was gone. Everything was my responsibility now—household, cats, bills, lawn, me, baby.

I could do it all on my own. I knew that I could. But Joy and Stephanie had made me realize that with my friends to help me along, I didn't have to.

~Beth Cato

Good Neighbours

Great opportunities to help others seldom come,
but small ones surround us every day.
~Sally Koch

I agree with the proverb that says "it takes a village to raise a child." The trick is finding that village when you live in the metropolis of Toronto in 2013. Sure, there are communities within the city, but not the type of small, cohesive group that is required for this purpose. Several years into the mayhem of motherhood, I concluded that you really must create your own village, wherever you are, in order to do this job properly.

I have managed to do this by forming some special relationships with neighbours on my street. Paula is one of these neighbours, and I have been grateful for her presence since my children were small. In the summer, Paula was always the first to admire the chalk artwork on my driveway. When the kids drew roads, she walked on them. When they drew stores, she pretended to buy things, and when they wrote cryptic messages in pre-school handwriting, she tried valiantly to read them. She always made time to talk to the kids, and seemed to know just what to ask to prompt an animated conversation—she had a knack. She gave all of them their first jobs too—walking her dog, Max, giving them clear instructions, a true sense of responsibility, the requisite plastic bag, and probably too much money.

As they grew, my children appreciated Paula's surrogate

grandmotherly attitude towards them, and were always happy to lend a hand if she needed help with something.

One snowy winter evening, as we were finishing dinner, Paula phoned. She was feeling under the weather and wondered if our son Jason would mind coming over to shovel her back deck—just a little—so Max could go outside to do his business.

Jason had recently moved past the point of thinking shovelling was fun, but had adopted a stoic, typically Canadian attitude towards the task. Knowing that Max is a diminutive white dog, easily lost in a snow bank (and admittedly, a bit of a princess), Jason knew Max would be reluctant to obey Paula and go out if there was more than a centimetre of snow on the deck.

Jason said he'd be right over. Heading out the door, shovel in hand, he called, "I'll be back in a few!"

About a half an hour later, a figure closely resembling the yeti arrived on our doorstep. Apparently, the snow was still falling thickly; Jason was covered with it.

"How was it out there?" I asked, taking his jacket and wet mitts as he stepped carefully onto the mat in the hall.

"Icy—not too cold," he replied. "I wiped out and fell down Paula's back stairs when I was shovelling. I guess she heard the thump—she poked her head out the door, looking all concerned."

I looked him up and down. "You all right? Any major damage?"

"Just a little cut on my hand from the edge of the shovel." He held up his hand to show me. "Paula felt really bad so she ran in for a Band-Aid. It was kind of embarrassing; she insisted on putting this on for me."

I smiled. "Once a mom, always a mom. Looks like you'll survive. Had you finished the job by that point or should I pop over?"

"No, it was pretty clear—Max can get out, no problem," he responded. After I thanked him for helping out, he headed upstairs to change.

In the past, Paula had hired one or both of my boys to do the full driveway-clearing job. I was happy that she felt comfortable enough to call for a little casual help every now and then. Give the kids a chance to do something nice for someone they know and trust — a chance to learn how to be good neighbours.

A few minutes later Jason arrived in the laundry room and tossed an armful of wet clothing onto the floor.

"Paula tried to pay me, you know," he said. "It wasn't a big deal or anything — the job, I mean — but I think she felt bad that I fell down the stairs. I just slipped; it was my own fault, and I'm totally fine."

"How'd you handle it?" I asked him, stuffing his things into the dryer.

"I told her it was okay, she didn't need to pay me, and it was just a quick job. I was happy to do it for free. She sort of insisted, though. It was one of those awkward times, you know, where you say, 'No, it's okay, thanks' and the other guy says, 'No, really, I insist.' And you go around in circles for a while... I finally caved."

"What, she wore you down?"

"Yeah, but I got her," Jason replied, with a twinkle in his eye.

"What do you mean?" I asked, tiny parental alarm bells starting to jingle in the distance. "How exactly did you 'get her'?"

"She finally just asked me to name a fair price for the job. I told her my fee was one Band-Aid."

He held up his injured hand, wiggled his fingers, and with a self-satisfied grin, loped up the stairs. I stood in the foyer, rather at a loss for words. When had my self-absorbed little kid turned into a thoughtful, helpful, and maybe just a little devious adolescent?

Paula enjoyed being outmaneuvered by Jason that evening. She said as much, when she came by the next day to drop off some warm homemade cookies for him. I thanked her for the baking, and then I thanked her for helping us show the kids how it's done — how to be a good neighbour. We may not have a whole village, exactly, but I think a few wonderful friends may just do the trick.

~Julie Winn

Chapter 5

Just Us Girls

It Works

A Rare Book

A book must be an ice-axe to break the seas frozen inside our soul.
~Franz Kafka

I'm shy. I've always been shy. When I was in school I was practically invisible because I hid behind books. If I was reading a book, I didn't have to try to talk to anyone.

People thought I was cold or unfriendly but I wasn't. There was nothing I wanted more than a friend but I never felt good enough to have one. I thought I wasn't pretty enough or smart enough. I didn't think I was interesting or funny and my family was poor and I had to wear clothes that were handed down from my cousins and everything seemed to be either too big or too small. I was ashamed of the way I looked.

I grew up and got a job and although I worked with some nice people, they weren't friends, they were coworkers. They were pleasant, but as soon as the store closed for the day, they went home to their families and I went home to my books.

I joined clubs I didn't really want to belong to and went to lectures at the library that bored me to death. I looked into joining singles' groups, hiking clubs, yoga classes and I even took classes at the community college. I took two language classes, Italian and Japanese, but I didn't make a friend.

I must have read twenty books on how to make friends and be popular but nothing seemed to work. I even copied a list out of a book about how to start a conversation and keep it going. I carried the list in my purse so if I met someone and I got tongue-tied, I could look at it. One suggestion was to ask people who they would choose if they were stranded on a deserted island with three people. I never had the courage to ask anyone that question but I had a good answer if anyone asked me, I'd say I wanted to be stranded with a doctor, a chef, and a boat builder. No one ever asked.

I decided it wasn't anyone's fault but my own that I was alone. I just wasn't meant to have a best friend and I'd have to live with it.

One day I'd just gotten out of my car and was walking into the mall when a strange woman hollered at me.

"You have a sock on your back!" she said.

She reached out and pulled a white sock off the back of my black sweater.

"Static cling," she said as she handed the sock to me. "It's happened to me before, you never know what might be sticking to your clothes when you take them out of the dryer."

"Thank you," I said and shoved the sock into my purse. "I would have been embarrassed if I had walked around all day with a sock clinging to my sweater."

"No problem," she smiled. "I'm headed to the bookstore. They are going out of business and everything is seventy percent off."

"I'm going there, too," I said.

"Let's go together," she said. "I love poetry. I'm hoping to find some books by Emily Dickinson or Robert Frost."

"The woods are lovely, dark and deep..." I quoted Frost.

"But I have promises to keep..." she answered.

"And miles to go before I sleep..." we said together and laughed.

Linda and I went into the bookstore. We both left with bags of books and Linda suggested we have lunch at the food court. I didn't have to worry about thinking of something to say because Linda was a talker and had lots of funny stories to tell. She made me laugh and I forgot I was shy. I didn't even have to ask her the question about being stranded on a deserted island.

Linda and I began discovering things about each other. We both loved poetry and all kinds of books. We liked a lot of the same things and completely disagreed on other things, but it didn't matter that we didn't always agree.

I told her how lonely I had been and how hard it had been to talk to people. She said she was sorry I'd been lonely but that some very famous people also had trouble making friends and I wasn't alone.

She gave me a beautiful plaque that read, "A good friend is like a rare book of which only one copy is made."

I cried when I read it.

She became my first real friend, because we both loved books and because we made each other laugh. Finally, at the age of thirty-four, I had a best friend.

It was strange. I'd spent years trying to find a good friend and then it was something as simple and as silly as static cling that brought my best friend into my life.

Last Christmas Linda gave me a book of poetry.

I gave her the sock that brought us together.

And we both laughed.

~April Knight

Picker Sisters

What is a friend? A single soul dwelling in two bodies.
~Aristotle

We started out as nurses at the same hospital, although never the same unit. The night shift has a way of unifying NICU and gerontology nurses just by virtue of being fellow night stalkers. Later, we found ourselves on the same bowling league, although not on the same team. Mutual pregnancies and raising children solidified our bond. Over our thirty years of friendship we have seen and lived it all while dealing with chronic diseases—mine, multiple sclerosis, and hers, systemic lupus erythematosus. We supported each other through wheelchairs, crutches, and hospitalizations with teasing and laughter. But it was our mutual love of picking—finding funky, eclectic, unusual, artsy fartsy beauty in objects that most cannot envision as anything other than mundane—that made us related.

We are picker sisters. And we dubbed ourselves this long before the History Channel embraced the notion.

Usually, Marion's style is decidedly different than mine. When she taught me the fine art of jewelry making with Swarovski crystals, her style was big and bold, mine much more understated. Yet we appreciate each other's "eye," or lack thereof, with a keen sense of humor.

After the kids had grown, our families seldom had the opportunity to spend time together. Yet, barring exacerbations of our illnesses or other calamities, Marion and I made an effort to meet over coffee once a month and then visit one or two haunts to pick over the goods.

"Oh, look at this!" I said one day at a local thrift shop, while holding up an old wooden perpetual calendar.

"You have one," she replied wryly.

"It would look good on my new porch," I said, ignoring her.

"This would look good on my new porch," she said picking up a gaudy wicker basket filled with faded dusty plastic flowers.

"You don't have a new porch," I said.

"Exactly my point," Marion said. "Now back away from the calendar."

Instead, the calendar went into my cart.

Marion found a limited edition Barbie in impeccable shape. She slipped it into her cart, hoping I didn't see. But I did see it and so began my tale of finding the perfect limited edition Ballerina Barbie for a ten spot, worth triple digits. I gave it to my two-year-old granddaughter, who promptly dunked it in a bowl of salsa at a Mexican restaurant.

Marion grunted. She had heard the Barbie story many, many times.

I found a storage box in the shape of a book. "Oh look! *War and Peace*! It will go great on my bookshelf."

"You have three of those," Marion reminded me.

"But I don't have *War and Peace*," I said, while placing it in a cart.

"What do you do — hide money in those?"

"Its function will be determined," I said defensively. "It has yet to speak to me."

Down another aisle, Marion picked up an antique rose patterned jacket with brass buttons. "This baby is saying, 'rescue me, Mommy.'" And it went into her cart.

And then I saw it, hanging on a distant wall. Marion looked up and spied it too. "On your mark, get set..." she began. But I had already taken off with my cart, at record speed, despite my gimpy legs.

I beat her to the wall and carefully retrieved the black, white, and red purse. I gently ran my hand over the leather pattern. The sexy figure on the bag looked back at me with big eyes and a familiar pout. It was a gently used, vintage handbag that I had researched many times online, but just couldn't justify the money spent. This, on the other hand, was priced just fine.

"Let me have it," Marion begged.

"Finders keepers, losers weepers," I replied.

"I'll give you my Betty Boop bedroom slippers if you give her to me now."

"Your feet are bigger than mine," I said, placing the leather softly next to my cheek. "The lady belongs to me."

A third shopper cleared her throat. It was apparent that we were being watched.

"Don't mind us," I said, with a smile. "We have no life."

Our observer tilted her head. "Quite the contrary," she said. "I had a friendship like yours once. It was sad when she moved away. What you two have is quite the life."

I looked at my longtime friend—this sister from another mother—and we simultaneously broke into infectious grins.

Indeed. We have had a wonderful life.

~Diana M. Amadeo

42

Bonding Over Books

Every reader finds himself. The writer's work is merely a kind of optical instrument that makes it possible for the reader to discern what, without this book, he would perhaps never have seen in himself.

~Marcel Proust

The elderly gentleman stood in front of the checkout desk at the small branch library where I'd just taken a job as manager. "Do you know of a book I might like?"

I chatted with him a few minutes and learned of several things he was interested in. Then I found a couple of books that I thought might work and sent him happily on his way. The scene repeated itself a couple of hours later, only this time the inquirer was a stay-at-home mom. Again, I found some reading material that seemed to make her happy.

All in all, a successful first morning on the job.

The afternoon was a little more challenging. A teenager with numerous facial piercings came through the door in a huff. "I have to write a book report for school," she told me, "and I want to read something really non-traditional." Luckily, I'd familiarized myself with the contents of our young adult shelves and was able to steer her toward a book that seemed to satisfy her.

"Hooray!" I said to myself as I locked up for the night. I love people. I love books. Putting the two together was the main reason I'd taken this job.

But something unforeseen began to happen when my library patrons returned the books they'd borrowed. They wanted to talk about them. To tell me what they'd liked and disliked. To discuss intricacies of plot and character. At length and in depth. Problem was, I didn't have time for all that.

Or did I?

Why not invite a group of book enthusiasts to meet after hours at the library and talk about what they'd read? It would be a good way for me to get to know my patrons. A chance for everybody to share their love of the written word. And for all of us to make new friends at the same time. Thus was born the idea for the Book Bunch.

Seven library patrons and I met for the first time on a warm spring evening. I served take-out pizza and soft drinks. The oldest person at the meeting was an eighty-five-year-old retired nurse. The youngest was a sixteen-year-old high school student. (Yep, the girl with facial piercings, who easily devoured three or four books per week.)

After introducing ourselves and scarfing down every single morsel of pizza, we each took a few minutes to discuss a book we'd read and enjoyed over the past month. Then came the big question: Is this how we wanted to format our future meetings or did we prefer that everyone read and discuss the same book?

"How about both?" Barbara, the nurse, suggested.

That's what we decided on. I found enough money in the budget to purchase several sets of used paperback books that I thought would stimulate discussion.

Every other month, we all discussed the same book. On alternate months, each member gave a ten-minute book report. Every meeting started with a simple potluck supper, served on paper plates.

You know what? Those seven people became some of the best friends I ever had. And good friends to each other, too. Melissa, the high school student, began giving Barbara a ride to and from the Book Bunch meetings when she became too feeble to drive herself.

Albert and Rob became fishing buddies. Suellen organized meals both for our meetings and to take to any member who was under the weather.

Three years after I began working as library manager, I accepted a job in a different town. Leaving the Book Bunch was one of the hardest things I've ever done. But we've kept in touch via phone and e-mail, and I'm happy to report that the group is still going strong.

I'm also happy to report that even though I no longer work at a library, I've joined a book discussion group at the library in the town where I now live. Not surprisingly, the members of that group have turned out to be wonderful new friends.

I guess there's just something about a love of reading that brings people together.

~Jennie Ivey

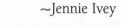

Tooty and Me

*A good friend is a connection to life—a tie to the past, a road to the future,
the key to sanity in a totally insane world.*

~Lois Wyse

er name is Pat. I call her Tooty. We met when I was a first-year teacher at a small, private school. Early in the year, I felt overwhelmed and was beginning to think I had made the worst decision of my life. Tooty, a veteran English teacher, convinced me that I could handle the pressure and be successful at my job.

We realized quickly that we had a lot in common. We had gotten married in the same year, and we both loved traveling, reading and going out to eat. Our shared sense of humor was similar, often childish, sometimes bordering on sick.

We spent all of our free time at school together. We ate lunch together, sat beside one another in faculty meetings and assemblies, and graded papers together. Tooty and I were as bad as the students we made fun of, completely inseparable and unable to walk to the restroom without the other.

Eventually, our friendship began to bloom outside of school. We went to restaurants, visited each other's homes and celebrated special occasions. And in June of that year, Tooty called me with an exciting invite.

"Do you want to go to Myrtle Beach for a week?" she asked.

"I'd love to. But you know I can't afford it right now."

She did know. Our miniscule salaries were another commonality.

"You only need money for food," she continued. "My friends Kay and Bucky own a timeshare, and they have an extra room. We'd have to share it but they're not charging us."

Hours later, I agreed to go. Tooty drove and we spent the week talking, eating, drinking and laughing. One night, we decided to go out by ourselves. Our condo mates wanted a relaxing evening at home.

"Do you have your key?" Tooty asked, as we hopped in the elevator.

"Yes. I have it. You ask me that every time we leave. It's in my wallet."

A few hours and several cocktails later we were outside the condo door again. I fumbled through my purse for the key, but I couldn't find it. I dumped all the contents of my purse onto the ground and started searching.

"You don't have it, do you? I thought you said it was in your wallet."

"It is in my wallet," I answered. "But my wallet is in my beach bag. And my beach bag is in the condo."

We had no choice but to wake up our friends. At two o'clock in the morning, they were less than pleased when they heard our fists pounding on the door. But they couldn't control their laughter when they opened the door and saw us.

There we were sitting cross-legged on the ground, with Krispy Kreme hats perched on top of our heads, glazed sugar crystals on our mouths, and our purses upside down on the sidewalk.

We thanked our friends and crawled (literally) in the door and into our beds. We woke the next morning bloodshot and achy. Then, like real soldiers, we trudged back to the beach.

In the heat of the South Carolina sun, Tooty and I talked about the night before, our jobs and our friendship. I told her that I was really glad we had met, and that I appreciated having her in my life. I babbled on for a while about career goals, family plans and traveling dreams.

"This has been so much fun, Tooty. We should take a cross-country road trip together when I retire," I said.

"Melissa!" Tooty laughed. "I'll be almost ninety when you retire!"

I hadn't thought about that. Sure, I knew she was older. But I had never really thought about it. After all, Tooty doesn't look (or act) her age, and she certainly doesn't dwell on it. If anything, I'm the one who acts older. I worry constantly, complain about aches and pains, and refuse to go out on a "school" night. And I'm the one with the failing memory. I needed Tooty to help me remember my key.

Tooty and I are teaching at different schools this year. We talk on the phone regularly, and we meet occasionally for Tuesday night tacos. But it's not like it used to be. I consider her one of my closest friends, and I miss seeing her on a daily basis. Chronologically, we are separated by twenty-three years, but spiritually we're the same age.

And though our relationship is great, it is not without the occasional argument. Every now and then (when I do something stupid), Tooty likes to tell me, "I could be your mother you know. I'm old enough."

"You could be. But you're not," I remind her.

I've got one mother. I do not need another one. But I do need my friend. I need Tooty.

~Melissa Face

44

Chicken Soup for the Soul

Our Friendship Is a Treasure

Each friend represents a world in us, a world possibly not born
until they arrive.
~Anäis Nin

Our friendship is a treasure
beautifully wrapped
in shared adventures.
It has its own language
packed with meanings
known only to you and to me.
It is filled with
cherished memories,
candied confidences,
and revealed dreams,
all tied up with
ribbons of laughter,
understanding,
and deep connection.
Our time together
turns an ordinary day
into a celebration.

What an elegant gift
we offer each other
in the simple word
Friend.

~Ferida Wolff

45

Over a Cup of Tea

The most beautiful discovery true friends make is that
they can grow separately without growing apart.
~Elisabeth Foley

When my girlfriend moved with her family to a sprawling acreage outside the big city of Calgary, Alberta, I thought things might change between us. She had her dream house, a large family, and a thriving home-based business. To me her life seemed picture perfect.

One day I went to visit and took the tour. I admired the layout, fine furniture, and original art on the walls. Her kitchen window overlooked hills newly planted with fir trees, a children's swing set, and a nearby bright red barn. Then I noticed a broken teacup on the sill. It seemed out of place.

I asked her why she kept the cup, which couldn't hold tea if it tried.

"Because you gave it to me," she said with her trademark smile.

I took a closer look at the cup, and the memory of it came flooding back. It was off-white fine china with a pastel floral design. Along the rim ran the words, "You'll always be my friend. You know too much." I laughed and put down the cup. I gave her a big hug, while her four girls and one boy watched quietly.

I'd given her the cup back in the day when we were roommates sharing a large duplex with four other single women. The house was always full of people and the ongoing dramas of young people looking for love. My girlfriend and I sat up plenty of nights drinking tea and divulging secrets. She was detailed and disciplined — she worked in a bank and had been engaged forever. I was a struggling student attending journalism school and not quite sure which end was up when it came to love and marriage. She got her facts straight and made plans. I pondered possibilities and made it up as I went along. Despite our differences, we needed and appreciated each other.

Plus, after two and a half years as tell-all roommates, we knew too much to not be friends for life!

At her fairytale wedding, I was her bridesmaid in spiffy downtown Calgary. Six years and as many moves later, her daughter was my flower girl in small-town Banff. We stayed in touch, called often and never forgot a birthday or anniversary.

At first, I thought the new house and hard-earned success might change things between us. But her loyalty ran deep. I knew my secrets were super-safe with her. And the details! She never forgot a detail. For her, my stories were never long enough. She wanted to know everything. She always remembered to pray for me and send an annual invite to a marriage retreat she and her hubby were attending. I always declined, preferring to work things out on my own. She kept inviting... but I knew she was a champion of my happiness. Despite the cracks, she saw the beauty of my life.

So, when I saw the cracked cup on her otherwise perfect sill, I paused.

The teacup symbolized our friendship. And there it was — in the open, where everyone could see. My friend made no effort to put it in a private corner, or on a shelf away from curious eyes. Anyone who asked about it, she would tell. My very loyal friend, who usually held her secrets close to her heart, was proud of what we meant to each other.

She'd put it in a place of honor, as a reminder of our friendship. As she did the dishes and watched her children play, she remembered me. As she talked over future plans with her husband, she remembered me. No matter what, I realized I'd always be an important part of her life. She loved me. Forever.

Houses come and go. One day the cup may go too. But our friendship is one of life's treasures I plan to take all the way to heaven, where all the cracks will be mended, all the tears we've shed together dried up, and all the secrets something to laugh about together—over a cup of tea.

~Dayna E. Mazzuca

46

My Front Row Friend

How old would you be if you didn't know how old you were?
~Satchel Paige

ervous anticipation fluttered through my stomach as I ripped open the envelope. Yes! I clutched the letter triumphantly. I'm finally going to be published!

That night as I cleared the dinner table, a rush of excitement hit me. I tossed the dishcloth toward the sink and raced to the computer. "I've gotta tell Grace!" I hollered back to my husband still standing by the sink.

I typed "Guess what!" on the e-mail subject line. Then I paused, remembering when I first met Grace. It was an unexpected friendship that all began with an e-mail.

Grace and I attended the same church for several years, but our paths never crossed. Why would they? I was a young mom; she was a grandmother. I sat in the balcony in case my fussy baby required a quick escape; she sat in the front row. My wardrobe included a handy burp cloth draped over my shoulder. She wore lovely scarves from Talbots. I couldn't imagine what Grace and I might have in common—until the church newsletter.

As a full-time mom, the church newsletter satisfied my creative cravings. Each afternoon I tucked my babies in for naps and tiptoed to my office. Then I cranked up the baby monitor and escaped for a few hours, writing articles and designing page layouts. When the need for a new proofreader arose, the church secretary suggested I contact Grace.

I soon learned that Grace was a fabulous proofreader. But her knack for spotting a typo wasn't the only quality I liked about her. When it came to encouraging others, Grace had a gift—and impeccable timing.

I remember one particular morning, when I was struggling to start an article after a sleepless night with a cranky baby. I plopped into my chair and stared at the computer. My mind felt as blank as the screen. I knew I shouldn't let my lack of sleep and raging hormones dictate my mood, but I didn't care. How did I ever think I could write? Looking for an excuse to procrastinate, I opened an e-mail from Grace:

Hi Sheri! I just finished reading the final copy of the newsletter. Another great job! Thank you for all the time and thought you put into it. You are one special gal!

I smiled. Maybe Grace scrutinized the newsletter with a critical eye, but she always looked for the best in me.

In time, our e-mail topics expanded beyond the newsletter. We chatted about marriage, realizing we both chose ambitious, professionally-driven men. We talked about motherhood. Grace offered a different perspective from friends my own age. She empathized with my struggles, but reminded me to enjoy every passing stage. We discussed our faith, our families—even our love of shopping. Then one day we realized we shared something else.

"Imagine that," Grace said, "born on the same day, only three decades apart. We should meet for lunch!"

Over the years, our birthday lunches became a tradition. We kept them simple, just getting together and exchanging cards. Except one year when I couldn't resist a little surprise.

I stepped inside Applebee's, scanning the busy lunch crowd. Grace waved from a table near the windows. As usual, she looked like a stylish grandmother in a ruffled cardigan and sparkly beaded necklace. I scooted into the booth, discretely placing a gift bag beside me.

"Happy birthday!" Grace reached into her leather handbag and gave me a pink envelope.

"Happy birthday," I said, passing her gift over the table.

Grace raised an eyebrow and gave me a lighthearted "shame on you" look.

"It's no big deal." I fidgeted with my napkin. "I just saw it and thought of you."

Grace drew back the tissue paper and uncovered a small stuffed teddy bear in a red cheerleading outfit.

"You're always so encouraging to me," I said, hoping my unexpected gift didn't embarrass her. "You're a great cheerleader."

Grace's blue eyes glistened as she propped the bear on the table. "Well, these days I'm not sure I've got the energy to be a cheerleader." She dabbed her eyes and laughed. "I can't believe I'm seventy!"

"Me either." I plunked my water glass on the table. "You certainly don't act like you're seventy. Aren't you supposed to dress like an old lady and drive a white Buick?" I teased. "I wish I had your wardrobe, and you drive a red Corvette for heaven's sake!"

Grace knew I was teasing, but in some aspects I was serious. For years I had watched her, and I was impressed. It wasn't the clothes she wore or the car she drove. It was her attitude. Even at seventy, Grace never stopped learning, never stopped growing and never stopped giving. She didn't care for the spotlight, but was content connecting with people one-on-one in her own soft-spoken way. During a phase of life when she could easily focus on herself, she intentionally touched the lives of others.

That year I also began a new phase of life. After devoting ten years to full-time motherhood, my youngest started kindergarten. At first I felt lost. My days had revolved around three little girls for so long. Now what would I do?

I took my first small step out of my comfort zone and signed up for a writer's conference. Then I finally worked up the nerve to tell someone besides my mom and husband about my aspirations to write. I told Grace.

"So... how was the conference?" Grace leaned forward, resting her elbows on the restaurant table.

"I loved it," I said without hesitation.

Grace nodded as I rambled on.

"The speakers were excellent. They shared great tips for improving my writing, and I got to meet other women who also love to write and..." I stopped for a moment, hoping my enthusiastic chattering wasn't disturbing the stuffy-looking businessmen at a nearby table. I took a deep breath and softened my voice. "I just felt like I was right where I was supposed to be."

"That's wonderful!" Grace said.

"I know, but me? A writer?" I said. "I've got nothing to say."

Grace straightened in her chair. "Apparently God thinks you do."

So when I learned that I would be published, I couldn't wait to tell Grace. And when my article came out, I gave a copy to her. A few days later a group of ladies gathered around my dining room table.

"How exciting! What page is it on?" one lady asked, thumbing through the table of contents.

I thought for a moment, but Grace answered immediately.

"Page 241," she said with a wink.

When I first attended our church, I sat in the balcony. Sometimes I'd watch the people below, pondering who might make a good friend. My eyes gravitated toward other young moms.

But I've learned the best qualities of a friend have nothing to do with age. A friend is someone you can trust and confide in. Someone who believes in you. Someone who cares about you—and you care about them.

From the balcony, it can be difficult to see the people below. I used to think a grandmother sat in the front row. Now I can see she's a cheerleader—and she has all the qualities I need in a friend.

~Sheri Zeck

Super Friends

Ah, how good it feels! The hand of an old friend.
~Henry Wadsworth Longfellow

I pushed the supermarket cart around the store, barely paying attention to my shopping list or to the items on the shelves. Instead, I kept asking myself the same question over and over: What had happened to my circle of friends? Earlier that morning, I'd received another one of those unfortunate phone calls. So and so had said this or that. Someone else was caught snickering behind someone else's back. Yet another person had been found rolling her eyes about something or another.

My crowd was rapidly dwindling thanks to the dissension within the corps. I certainly could understand that; I was sick and tired of it myself. What I needed, I thought, were some new friends. I backed my cart toward the produce section to retrieve a forgotten head of lettuce, and there, in between the bins of potatoes and onions, she stood. I hadn't seen her in over twenty years, yet I recognized her instantly: the cut of her hair, the curve of her shoulders, her voice. Especially her voice. There was no mistaking it—I was looking at Milli.

I first met Milli at the age of six when I was a small, shy student in her Sunday school class. Our crowd of five girls stayed together well into our teens, with Milli at the center of our circle, socializing at our parties, attending our youth group events—even singlehandedly chaperoning us five adventurous teenagers for a three-day visit to Boston for a church-related event.

Throughout it all, Milli had been someone special to me. Her positive attitude encouraged me and gave me confidence. Though I didn't speak of it at the time, my childhood had been marred by family illness and its related unhappiness. Milli was an inspiration for me. She had endured hard times, too, but she overcame. A single mother at a time when single motherhood was rare, she managed to maintain a home in which her three children flourished, all while making giant strides in her own business as an artist, teacher, and gallery owner. She was the quintessential example of a take-charge woman. It seemed as though nothing could keep her down for long. I looked at her now and realized that without benefit of her example, I never would have become the woman I was today.

"Excuse me," I said as I approached her, "are you Milli?"

She scrunched her brows quizzically. "Yes."

It took a moment, but then the memories came back fast and furious. "Remember that trip to Boston?" she asked.

"Remember the time you took us girls to visit your art gallery?" I asked. "Remember the art lessons I took in your studio? Remember that backyard barbecue?" We laughed about the old times, but then I turned serious. "You know," I told her as tears welled, "those were the brightest moments of my childhood."

"I had no idea," she answered. She reached over and took my hand. "We have to talk more."

That afternoon we exchanged phone numbers and what had started out many years before as an association between a teacher and a child blossomed into a wonderful new friendship between two grown women. In the year that has passed since we reconnected, I have helped her prepare for an art exhibit and she has sat in the audience and cheered for me as I received a poetry award. We get together whenever, as Milli says, the spirit moves us, which is pretty often. We chat over the phone or over lunch or most recently, outdoors in her backyard where we created our own individual pieces of artwork side by side: hers in watercolors and mine in pastels. Each time is a joy-filled occasion with talk of old times and new times in that same positive style that Milli always had and helped to nurture in me. She continues to encourage and inspire me and perhaps, I like to think, sometimes I do the same for her.

That's what true friendship is all about: building each other up, recognizing the best in each other. In this crowd of two, there is no whispering behind anyone's back, no snickering or eye-rolling. In this crowd there is just friendship. True friendship. Or as Millie said yesterday as we sat and painted together, super friendship.

~Monica A. Andermann

The Inncrowd

Find a job you like and you add five days to every week.
~H. Jackson Brown

I work with an incredible group of women at two beautiful seaside bed and breakfast hotels called the Channel Road Inn and the Inn at Playa del Rey. Though we all started as strangers and mere coworkers, we have become great friends and help each other overcome challenging situations both at work and in our personal lives. I call us collectively "The Inncrowd."

Like any family, "The Inncrowd" has developed an internal dynamic, utilizing each individual's characteristics and strengths.

Liz is "The Leader." She's the General Manager of the Inn at Playa del Rey and has nerves of steel; the worse the situation is, the calmer Liz gets. Liz is a leader both at the Inn and within our community. In the past six months alone she's attended the Kentucky Derby, Michelle Obama's First Lady Luncheon, has hosted a "Toast for a Cure" fundraiser for breast cancer research and was recently installed on the Board of Directors for the Chamber of Commerce. Earlier this week I had lunch with Liz because I've been feeling stagnant and stuck in a rut. By the end of lunch I was so rejuvenated, I found myself vowing to find a volunteer opportunity that would stimulate me. When I need assurance the world holds wonderful possibilities, I turn to Liz.

Heather is "The Sensible One." She's the General Manger of the

Channel Road Inn. Heather reminds me it's okay to have boundaries and encourages me to stay centered even when faced with uncomfortable situations. I remember calling Heather one night because a guest was distraught her room was decorated with red accents. All the other guests loved their rooms; however, when I showed this guest to her room she stopped in the doorway and said, "I hate the color red and cannot possibly sleep in a room that has any red in it." The Inn was sold out so I had no other room to offer. I did what I could, removing the red chair and the red throw cushions, but the guest said she was still "highly uncomfortable." I called Heather and she suggested the obvious—give her a cookie and turn off the light! Whenever I find myself facing an unreasonable situation in my personal life, I think of Heather and try to channel her solid sense of self.

Nicole is "The Enforcer." Originally from Chicago, Nicole is the friendliest, most vivacious girl I know—but there's a "don't mess with me and don't mess with my friends" undercurrent. I remember one night, a repeat corporate guest came downstairs and asked why there were "naked people" in his bathtub. I thought he was joking but as our front desk phone rang, I heard Nicole say, "Why are you in his bathtub?" and then, "I'm coming upstairs." Turns out, some guests who'd booked a standard room snuck into the suite and were using the Jacuzzi bathtub when our corporate guest checked in. Thanks to Nicole, our guest now has a funny story he loves to tell and the unruly guests were quickly back in their standard room and had paid an additional $100 cleaning fee for the inconvenience. Nicole and I often go on "pizza-walk-and-talks" together. First we eat pizza, then we walk it off while sifting through the events of the day. I enjoy recapping with Nicole because she is so supportive. Even when I've clearly made a mistake, Nicole finds a way to twist the story so I end up feeling like the hero.

Dominique is "The Artist." She spent most of her life as a professional ballerina and carries herself with grace. Dominique is introspective and reflective. Her presentation in terms of personal style and the baked goods she creates is unsurpassed. She says both in her dancing and when she creates new recipes for the Inns she "searches for harmony, light and balance." Dominique adds a soft, graceful element to "The Inncrowd" and reminds me that it's okay, and actually quite beautiful, to be vulnerable. She takes risks both in her life (and in her recipes) and accepts the fact that most things she tries will work out, but some won't. When I stumble, I turn to Dominique to remind me that success and failure are simply two sides of the same coin and the only way to grow and create is to keep trying new things.

Rachel is "The Free Spirit." Not only does she not stay within the box—I don't think Rachel even realizes there is a box! She doesn't think twice about altering a recipe that's been made the same way for twenty years or about plating food in creative, unconventional ways. Rachel brings a breath of fresh air to the "The Inncrowd" and reminds me there are new ways to approach innkeeping—and life!

Carmen is "The Angel." When I first started working at the Inns, our owner Susan said, "You'll enjoy meeting our head housekeeper, Carmen. I'm not particularly religious—but I think she might actually be an angel." Carmen is the most loved and respected member of the "The Inncrowd." She is steady, sympathetic, unflappable and possesses a wise, otherworldly spirit. I remember the morning that a guest stood over me in the kitchen reading a list of complaints as I prepared breakfast. This was highly unusual because most of our guests are completely charmed by the Inns. At first the guest didn't notice Carmen—then she paused and glanced at Carmen, who was washing dishes. Carmen dried her hands and asked the guest if there was anything she could do to help. The woman suddenly began to tear up and said, "I'm sorry I'm being difficult. It's not the room or the food or anything else—I'm just stressed my daughter is getting married this weekend and I'm acting like a basket case." As the woman left the kitchen, Carmen gave me a small smile. I turn to Carmen for wisdom and assurance that whether it's a good day or a difficult day, it's possible to stay peaceful inside.

As the owner of the Inns, Susan is "The Innspiration." Like most of us, she came from humble beginnings but through incredibly hard work, she's become one of the most successful female entrepreneurs in Los Angeles. Susan empowers each and every member of "The

Inncrowd" by tasking us with duties that make us stretch and grow. She expects all of us to act like business owners as we negotiate rates, make sales calls, and handle guest service needs. Whenever I've mumbled the words "can't", "try" or "but", Susan looks at me blankly. Both in my professional and personal life, I turn to Susan for inspiration. When I stand beside her I feel anything is possible. Susan is fair. She is creative. She is generous. She is fearless and she is the heart and soul of the Inns.

Liz, Heather, Nicole, Dominique, Rachel, Carmen, Susan and I are not the only members of "The Inncrowd." There are those who have come and gone before us and there are those who will follow in our footsteps. For anyone lucky enough to join this sisterhood, they will have the privilege of knowing what it's like to work side-by-side with talented, smart, resourceful women and I guarantee you it's an experience they'll never forget!

~Rebecca Hill

Chapter
6

Just Us Girls

Taking the Plunge

Making Lemonade

Sometimes things fall apart so that better things can fall together.
~Marilyn Monroe

"Honey, you need to dry your eyes and mix things up. Host a 'Turn Lemons into Lemonade' party" and everything will change!" Char said. She went on to explain that each party guest was supposed to bring a friend the other guests didn't know, as well as a lemon treat to share.

Char was like a second mother to me, and she was the sole person I knew who had experienced the isolation of divorce. She, too, found herself divorced after a long marriage and was the only divorced member of her immediate family.

She knew I'd been spending too much time alone and lonely, and two years of grieving meant I needed a social facelift.

I was hesitant about having a party, yet logic told me it was a positive step toward getting out of the divorce doldrums and putting my marriage behind me. So I agreed to host the party.

Party day arrived, and I made pitchers of fresh lemonade and put them in the refrigerator to chill. The pretty miniature lemon cheesecakes I'd baked were sitting on their own white paper doily, just asking to be eaten.

Susan, who was my guest, placed dishes of candy lemon drops throughout the kitchen, dining, and living room areas. I was mildly unsettled about meeting so many new people at once in my own home where I couldn't leave if I wanted to make an early escape. I kept telling myself that half of the women coming to the party today were just friends I hadn't met yet... it seemed to ease my apprehension.

The first to arrive was Linda. I was delighted to see her dressed in a yellow shirt and Capri pants, with her friend, Margie, wearing a yellow and white dress. The party was getting off to a terrific start.

I introduced Linda and Margie to Susan. The doorbell rang as I was pouring the first glasses of lemonade. Lemon bars, lemon biscotti, and lemon poppy seed cake were filling the table; all were serving as perfect conversation starters.

"I hear there's a lemonade party going on here!" Bobbi belted out when I answered the door. We all burst into laughter. Bobbi was a people person with an infectious laugh that lit up a room. She introduced her friend Rae, whom she'd known for many years.

The ladies streamed in and before long it was standing room only in my tiny house. All the invitees came and each brought a friend, as requested. The party started out lively and the fun continued with a generous amount of chatting, laughing, eating, drinking and, in general, getting to know each other.

Char, the inspiration for the party, was the last to join the group. She made a grand entrance, acting as if she was the Queen of Spring, wearing a wide-brimmed yellow straw hat accented with orange Gerber daisies and lime green ribbons. It was very much out of character for Char to wear anything frilly; most everyone knew her as a sweats and tennis shoes kind of gal. The flamboyant hat lent an immediate frivolity to the party as Char and her friend Doris joined the other guests.

Like most parties, the food was the main attraction. Bobbi and Rae were cracking jokes; Mom and Arlene circled the refreshment table for the fourth time; Denise and Christine discussed how I'd decorated my kitchen with antique utensils.

As I watched the interaction among the ladies, I sensed that my life was taking a turn for the better.

They were exchanging recipes and telephone numbers, sharing

quips and anecdotes, and joking with each other like old pals. A warm feeling came over me and at that moment I knew most of these ladies were going to play an integral part in my ability to move on and grow into my new self.

I admired them all for stepping up and attending a party where they knew so few of the guests. It occurred to me that these connections with other women were basically how they managed to survive losses of every imaginable sort. Of course these ladies knew how to do some serious socializing and networking—it was the key to their survival.

"What do you think of my party idea?" Char asked, throwing one arm around me and adjusting her hat with the other.

"I'll admit I was a bit nervous about the party," I said. "But it's reassuring to know my friends will come through for me, and I've had a great time meeting new ladies who have 'been there, done that!' And today, just like magic, I've doubled my social circle. Thanks for helping me see my way out of a post-divorce funk."

"Hey, you just needed a nudge in the right direction!" She winked.

The party confirmed to me that it was time—time to come out of my shell, shed the past, and embrace new beginnings. My friends, longtime as well as new, started the process of guiding me out of the bitterness and into the sweetness. Why? Because that's what we ladies do for each other.

~Cynthia Briggs

Comrades in Moms

Friends are like walls. Sometimes you lean on them,
and sometimes it's good just knowing they are there.
~Author Unknown

The earth shifted under my feet when my son Ty telephoned. "Hi Mom, I just enlisted," he said.

In the following months I felt ignorant in my new role as a home-front mom. I also felt isolated and irrelevant. I didn't know other mothers with children in the military nor did I know where to find them.

Later, my world shook again when Ty called and said, "Hi Mom. I just got orders. I'm deploying to the Middle East."

My emotions seesawed. One moment I felt ready to explode from swirling, nervous energy. The next moment I felt like a weight on my chest made it hard for me to breathe.

The morning Ty boarded a plane on the other side of the country to deploy halfway around the world I drove to work under icy-blue skies. I gritted my teeth and held my emotions in check until a song on the radio undid me. When I arrived at work, I wiped my tears, called the Christian station, and asked for prayers for my son.

The DJ had sons in the service. "Have you heard about the Blue Star Mothers?" he asked.

"I haven't."

"It's a group of moms with sons and daughters in the military.

The local chapter meets upstairs in our office building. They're packing care boxes for the troops this Saturday."

I didn't have anyone to go with and when I arrived I didn't know anyone at the packing party. A gal with an in-charge attitude walked past me and pointed to a desk. "We need you over there."

Like a good soldier, I reported to my assigned station where I shared the desk with another mom. We hand-addressed stacks of postal shipping labels while being careful to write legibly and also pressing hard enough to make all five copies readable.

I glanced up from my work from time to time and flexed my cramped hand. The area resembled Santa's workshop, peopled with moms instead of elves. In several rooms women chatted while sorting donated items into blue plastic tubs. Others moved bins filled with granola bars, beef jerky, crackers, toothpaste, toothbrushes, white tube socks, and paperback books to a large room where long tables formed a packing assembly line.

In another room, laughter mingled with rip-rip-ripping sounds as women applied strapping tape to the bottom seams of priority mailboxes. Other moms carried the boxes to the assembly line, where they filled them to the brim, then brought them back to be strapped shut.

I would never have had an occasion or opportunity to meet these wildly diverse women elsewhere. Over time I found the differences that can divide people didn't matter to us. Instead, a common denominator—love for our children—united us.

I joined forces with these women with a renewed sense of purpose. I no longer felt as ignorant, isolated, or useless as a home-front mom.

Strangers became acquaintances and many became stalwart friends: Jan, Myra, Nina, Carolyn... and the list goes on. We've worked hard, played hard, and prayed hard together.

My new friends helped me through Ty's first deployment. When I hadn't heard from my son for longer than I wanted, Jan said, "No news is good news and bad news travels fast." Although I wanted to hear from Ty, I decided I'd rather have no news than bad news.

Because these moms and I developed strong friendships I could rejoice with Carolyn when her son came home from a deployment, although that day I felt weepy because my son was still overseas and would be for months.

Right before Ty returned from his first deployment I felt giddy at the prospect of giving him a hug. I e-mailed him: "Do you want me to meet you at your homecoming on post?"

He didn't. His reasons were valid but I still would have felt hurt if I hadn't spent time around my new friends. "He might need some breathing space," Myra said. "Give him a little time."

I gave him time to get his house in order. A few months later I gave him a hug. My relationship with my son is stronger because I took Myra's advice.

The next year I got another one of those calls that tips a mother's world on edge: "Hi Mom, I'm going back to the Middle East."

I felt more apprehensive than before Ty's first deployment.

Jan didn't hesitate when I mentioned my son's departure date from a distant airport. "That day, why don't you attend a welcome home at the airport here?" she said.

I'm glad I joined the crowd greeting a returning soldier, a stranger to me. Standing in a long cordon of flag bearers just outside the airport security area, I held the Blue Star Mothers' banner upright.

When a young soldier came through the security gate, he paused a moment and looked surprised that we all were there to celebrate his homecoming.

Along with other civilians, I smiled, cried, and cheered when I saw the wide grin on his face. Jan was right. Welcoming home some other mom's returning son prevented me from holding a pity party the day Ty deployed.

I tried to be brave, I really did, but six months later I whined to Jan about Ty being overseas. She didn't judge me. Instead she listened, then gave me a gift of grace, a sisterly hug, which I needed at that moment. She has two military sons and knew I was exhausted from holding my emotional breath for the duration of each deployment. That day I learned from my friend to give other home-front moms hugs when I see a scared look in their eyes. We recognize another's fear because we've seen it often enough in the mirror.

Jan also provided relentless encouragement—she calls it nagging—for me to get a passport.

"I don't want to even think about it," I said.

"Just consider it insurance," she said. "If Ty is injured and sent to a military hospital in Europe you don't want any delays getting there."

Neither of us voiced the obvious worst-case scenario.

"If you're faced with a situation when every minute counts getting to Ty's bedside," she said, "you'll be thankful you already have a passport. I'm not saying you'll need it. But if you do, you'll have it."

Thanks to Jan's persistence, I've tucked my new passport into a safe place with my other insurance papers.

My new friends invited me to be part of something bigger than myself. I birthed only one child, but we home-front moms share a heritage of adopting all our troops into our hearts.

Because of the examples set by my new friends I've written condolence notes to parents I've never met who have lost children I'll never know. I've sat beside Nina and other moms dressed in navy-blue suits as we filled rows of pews in candle-lit churches. We attend these memorial services to honor those who have died while serving our country and to pay our solemn respects to their families.

I've heard that troops forge strong bonds of friendship while battling through hell together, fighting side by side and protecting one another's backs.

So do their moms.

~Linda Jewell

51

Texas To-Do List

The nice thing about teamwork is that you always have others on your side.
~Margaret Carty

Promptly at 6:00 a.m., I stepped out of my car and into one of the hottest July days ever recorded in Houston, Texas. My thick cotton T-shirt was soon drenched in sweat as I waited in the local church parking lot. Experienced runners surrounded me, all wearing appropriate attire for intense heat and humidity. At the age of fifty-three, I was about to train for my first half-marathon with the assistance of an organized program. This was my plan for building friendships in an unknown city!

Houston was quite a change from Southern California, where I grew up, went to college, married, and raised two daughters. It's home to the world's richest rodeo, glorious barbecue, and bedazzled wardrobes. I had bravely faced my husband's job transfer, at a time when many couples were contemplating retirement. However, the last checkmark on my Texas "to-do" list was daunting: "Find friends." My future no longer consisted of PTA meetings, team mom activities and my children's' high school social functions. What would each day look like? Would two aging Labrador Retrievers be my sole companions?

The answer arrived one week after a moving van spilled musty cardboard boxes throughout our new suburban house. Annie, the real estate agent, phoned. "Dana, would you be interested in joining the local chapter of USA Fit here in town?" Honestly, I had no idea what she was talking about. What I did know was that Annie was a runner. I had even heard her mention marathons. I felt anxious already.

"What does it involve? I mean, is this about running? Because that's just not my thing." I was hoping she would hear the disinterest in my voice. Not Annie! She didn't give up easily.

"Come on! You'll love it! It's a group of both runners and walkers who meet for six months, training for the Houston Marathon and Half-Marathon. I think you would meet some nice friends. I'll be there!"

Excuses filled my head. "Annie, I am a walker, but who in their right mind walks a marathon? I've never heard of such a thing." It didn't matter. I was about to get schooled in the brilliant ways of USA Fit!

That day in the church lot, the beauty of Annie's plan came to light. We were divided into groups according to marathon or half-marathon, and pace. I decided to stand amongst the "purple people." That's code-speak for half-marathon walkers. I had a group. I had friends!

From the first day, four women with experience took me on as their personal project. Diane, Karen, Jill, and Betsy walked every step with me that initial Saturday. When we returned from the steaming three-mile course, my face was an unusual shade of red. Diane noticed immediately. She sat with me in the shade and covered the basics of proper clothing and hydration. I marveled at her kindness as I sipped a thick, green sports drink.

For the next six months, those four women never left my side. When fall arrived, we rejoiced in the beauty of the changing leaves and inhaled the scent of crackling fires as families rose and prepared breakfast. By now, our Saturday morning chats had become more personal. Kids, jobs, houses, dogs—no subject was off limits as we raced past the tranquil lakes surrounding our town. The sun rose, great blue herons soared, and deer wandered on the edge of the woods. I came to believe I could actually walk the half-marathon at the rapid pace required by the sponsors. My confidence grew not only from strict preparation, but also from a collective courage.

The USA Fit training schedule was taped to my kitchen wall. Every day for six months was recorded, with the required activity listed. I diligently crossed off each square until only the final week remained. With that realization, panic set in.

That was also when I understood just how supportive my purple friends were. On the Monday before the race, I saw Diane in the busy produce aisle of the grocery store. "I'm so happy to see you!" I gave her a massive hug and, without warning, the tears started. They came from a place deep inside, from insecurity and the realization that I might not be up to the challenge ahead.

Diane steered me toward the racks of bread. The air smelled delicious, and a soothing calm enveloped me. "You are going to be just fine. You're ready! I'll be waiting for you inside the convention center first thing that morning. I'll help you through the whole process." Another hug and I was on to cereal and canned goods.

Then came a piece of bad news. Karen was experiencing knee problems. On Wednesday, she made the tough decision. "I just can't walk the course. Look for me at mile seven. That's when you'll need a cheering section the most. I'll be there." I wasn't certain I could accomplish the enormous task ahead without the full team; each woman added a different component to the group's success. Karen was steadfast. "Do not let this take away any of your joy."

Race day was exciting. Spectators lined the streets with noise-makers, banners, and loudspeakers. I found my purple friends at the designated meeting place without any problem. A group photo was taken, and then we clung to each other as 24,000 racers made their way to the starting line. The four of us huddled in the early morning chill, pep talks were given all around, and then the gun sounded. Finally, I would face the challenge Annie had invited into my life.

Back in July, my target had simply been to finish the half-marathon. At some crazy point, I decided to complete the race in less than three hours. In order to meet that goal, Jill and I kept constant watch on the time. "Dana, I have a plan. We need to walk for five minutes, then jog for one. That should keep our finish time to three hours." We grinned at each other, knowing that this rather large detail should have been worked out in advance!

The last mile was nearly intolerable. Our pace had been much quicker than during training. Luckily, the final stretch was bursting with enthusiasm from the crowded sidewalks. I sped along to cheers from Elvis impersonators, sumo wrestlers and a youth group dressed as chickens. Diane yelled from far ahead, "It doesn't get any better than this!"

Six months of preparation finished with one step over a thin black line. An aquamarine spiral of balloons reached into the cloudless sky. Confetti blanketed the road. On the other side of the line, my friends waited, patient as always. Enthusiastic volunteers, who had been so generous with their time, placed heavily inscribed medals around our necks. I fingered the shiny, grosgrain ribbon with an overwhelming sense of accomplishment. At that moment, I realized I had become part of my new community. A town where strength is a team effort and a dear friend will dry your tears in the grocery store.

~Dana Sexton

52

Heaven Sent Friend

A faithful friend is a strong defense;
And he that hath found him hath found a treasure.
~Louisa May Alcott

"Laurie, I need a volunteer," my pastor husband Dale sheepishly said. As a pastor's wife in a small New England church, being asked by my husband to volunteer for something was not a new experience. Nursery—I'd done that. Sunday School teacher—why not? Baked goods for the annual Christmas bazaar, casseroles for potlucks—I could usually come up with something. I'd even reached out of my comfort zone to be a junior high youth leader. But something in his approach this time set off my warning sensors. My gut told me I wasn't going to like this.

"A volunteer to do what?" I suspiciously asked.

"Well, you know that new Prayer Partner program starting at the church?" I knew about it—I had quite intentionally not signed up for it. I was an introvert—not always the best trait in a pastor's wife, I'll admit. But an introvert I was, with a capital "I"—and a very shy introvert at that. I was a private person. And for me, Prayer was Private. Prayer was Personal. Prayer was something for which I most definitely did not want a Partner.

"What about it?" I asked.

"I have an odd number of people signed up. I need one more volunteer."

"How about you, Dale? Maybe you could use a prayer partner?"

"I've already committed to one. Besides, the extra person is a woman—you know the plan is to pair up men with men and women with women; it's just less complicated that way," he went on to explain. And then, as if he were reading my mind he added, "She's brand new to the church, I'd hate to make her feel unwelcome by saying we've run out of prayer partners."

So, he was not only asking me to take on a Prayer Partner, he was asking me to take on a total stranger as a Prayer Partner. After twenty years of marriage what part of the word introvert did he still not understand?

"Do you think you could please give it a try?" he begged.

I thought of flippantly answering that I would pray about it, but I wouldn't have meant it—and I knew there wasn't time. The program was set to begin, and all his other "go to" women in the church were already signed up. Totally against my better judgment I reluctantly agreed. He'd better appreciate this!

Phone numbers were exchanged, and of course with me being the pastor's wife and she being the newbie, I quickly realized it was my job to make the first call. I hesitantly dialed the number I'd been given—maybe she wouldn't be available when I was; that would solve everything. "Hello, Kate? This is Laurie Edwards. I'm signed up to be your prayer partner?" Not only was she available, she was as thrilled as could be. And she couldn't believe her luck—she'd actually gotten the pastor's wife as her partner! Wasn't this going to be wonderful? She had no idea....

Kate showed up at my doorstep on the agreed upon day and time, just bursting with enthusiasm. "Oh no," I thought. "She's the energetic, bubbly type. This is definitely not going to work." I invited her to sit down, offered her a cup of tea, and she reached into her canvas bag and pulled out two matching prayer journals—one with my name on it and one with her name on it. "I'm really in for it now," I thought.

We started to share with each other about our lives—we couldn't have been more different. Kate was a nurse from the West Coast. I was a pastor's wife from New England. Kate and her family were athletic and always on the go, while the Edwards preferred hanging out at home in our free time. Kate was always eager to try out something new and different. I knew what I liked and tended to stick with it. Kate was an extrovert; I wasn't. But week after week, we would meet, talk about our concerns, and pray for our families and for each other. At first it was about surface stuff—stuff you felt you could safely share with a stranger. But little by little our conversations became more personal and we found ourselves praying for real heart issues. And those little green journals started to fill up.

Sometimes Kate would show up with baked goods. Sometimes she would suggest we go out for a walk together. It was her idea to meet for prayer at a local café I'd never tried. She'd regale me with tales of her family's latest weekend plans—the new RV they were eager to try out. When my daughter started having chronic migraines, it was my friend Kate the nurse who finally convinced me to get her to a headache specialist. When I was struggling with worries about an overworked husband and my own premenopausal symptoms, Kate was ready with an encouraging word and prayer. When the youth group needed someone to provide snacks, Kate came to the rescue and got other parents to sign up as well. We'd pray together about our kids, our husbands, our inner and outer struggles. When Kate's husband's job just wasn't working out, we began to pray that he would find a new one.

Those weekly meetings, which I'd begun with so much hesitation, quickly became one of my lifelines. I was in for it, all right. In for a new and wonderful friendship. I didn't realize how lonely and isolated I had become. Then at coffee hour after church one Sunday morning, Kate leaned out of the kitchen serving window and announced that her husband had found a new job—another answer to prayer! Except the job was back on the West Coast. They would be leaving in a matter of days. My heart sank and the tears started to come. God couldn't have given me this wonderful new friend just to take her away!

Well, He did and He didn't. Before she left, Kate gave me a beautiful Willow Tree Angel of Prayer ornament that always brings her to mind when I take out our Christmas decorations. The year I got a Christmas card from the "Surf Clan" I knew just who it was from—her family had started an exciting new sport! And Kate gave me a plaque that sits on my wall and reminds me that "A Friend Is God's Way of Coming Alongside." I couldn't have put it better!

The next time the call came out for a Prayer Partner I didn't hesitate—someday I'll have to tell you about my new friend Jeanne!

~Laurie Carnright Edwards

53

The First in the Neighborhood

Decide that you want it more than you are afraid of it.
~Bill Cosby

I saw the woman again when I looked out the kitchen window. She appeared to be around my age, and she was with the same little girl I'd seen her with on several occasions. They walked to their mailbox, and the woman helped the girl as she reached up on her tiptoes, opened the door and stuck her small hand in the box to pull out the mail. The woman smiled and stroked her daughter's hair. I turned to look at my toddler son who played on the floor beside me as I washed the dishes.

He and I could both use a friend. I was born and raised in a small Midwestern town with friends and family surrounding me, and no need to reach out to meet anyone new. Jason's friends were ready-made when he was born—children of my friends and former coworkers. But my husband's job had recently relocated us a thousand miles away, and I had no idea how to begin to make the connections with other women that are so important when raising a child.

I had seen the woman across the street a number of times in the several months I had lived in this new home in a strange town. She looked like a person I could relate to, and she was my neighbor after all. If I could only get over the fear that gripped me when I thought about knocking on her door. I am an outgoing person and talk to people easily, but something about starting this first move towards making a friend in this new place paralyzed me.

One day after playing with my son all morning, I felt so strongly the need for us both to have someone near our own age to relate to. I picked Jason up and told him, "We're going on a little visit."

He looked confused—the past few months we spent all our days alone together until his father came home after work. I realized Jason had likely forgotten the time before our move, when family or friends dropped by with regularity. It was something I had not forgotten, and missed more than I could express.

Now that I had announced our intention to visit, there was no turning back. I locked our front door, walked across the street and knocked tentatively on the woman's door. I secretly hoped no one was home or no one answered, so that I could tell myself I had given it a try.

I was about to turn away, but the door swung open. Standing in the doorway was the woman I had seen at the mailbox. The little girl had her arms wrapped around her mother's leg, and she looked as scared as I felt.

"Hi, we're your new neighbors from across the street," I said, as I gestured at our house and Jason gave a little wave. "We've seen you outside—just thought we'd come over and say hello."

"Well, hello," the woman said. "I'm April and this is Katie. Come on in." I was grateful for April's genuine smile.

I set Jason down and Katie grabbed him by the hand as they ran off to play with her toys. I was left without the buffer that children give in such situations, and had no choice but to get to know April.

"Do you drink tea?" April asked as she led me towards her kitchen.

We settled in and began to compare notes. April had not been in the area long either, and had lived all her life in a city far away like me, so there was common ground. And of course we could talk about our children. I had forgotten how good it felt to compare notes on child rearing with other mothers. A couple of hours went by very quickly. Jason wasn't ready to go when I told him it was time, so I knew he needed these moments with someone his own age as much as I did.

Before we left, April and I exchanged phone numbers. The simple fact that I now had someone to call if I had a question about the neighborhood or a problem during the day gave me a peaceful feeling.

"I enjoyed meeting you both," April said as Katie smiled. "Let's get together again soon," she added.

"Next time it's our turn, right Jason?" I replied as Jason nodded. "I'm sure Jason wants to show you his toys, Katie, and I have lots of tea to choose from."

As we walked across the street Jason turned to wave at Katie several times. I smiled. The whole thing didn't hurt after all, not a bit.

~Nancy Hatten

54

What Mommy Learned at Playgroup

Remember, we all stumble, every one of us.
That's why it's a comfort to go hand in hand.
~Emily Kimbrough

The e-mail subject line simply read, "Got the call." I held my breath and opened it. "Well girls, my nightmare just came true," it said. "I have breast cancer."

I slumped down in my chair and shook my head in disbelief.

How could this be? My mind flooded with all the irrational reasons this couldn't be happening. She's only thirty-five. She's a mother of three. She's my friend.

I remember a time when I didn't understand the value of a good friend. As a new mom, I was happily consumed with motherhood. Sure I had friends, but they were more like acquaintances than true friends. That was fine with me. After all, once you're a wife and mother, your priorities change. I had my husband and my mom. I didn't need more friends. But sometimes God gives us what we need—even before we realize we need it.

When my first baby was a year old, I decided to quit my job and become a full-time mom. I loved being home with my daughter, but wished she could interact with other kids. I wanted her to learn how to share, make new friends, and have fun. I decided to start a moms' group.

I was excited about the possibilities, but nervous about the unknown. What if no other moms wanted to join? Worse yet, what if the moms that joined weren't a good fit with my personality? Soon I was convinced I'd either be the leader of a one-woman moms' group, or I'd be spending playgroups with a room full of cigar-smoking, tobacco-spitting moms.

One by one, other moms in our small community joined the group. Each week we gathered our little ones for playgroups, park days, or trips to the zoo. We pushed our babies in swings and shared our joys and frustrations of the day. We chased busy toddlers and laughed at how drastically our lives had changed since we became moms.

Over time, our friendships extended beyond weekly meetings. We found comfort in knowing others who faced the same challenges, and shared advice for our most maddening mommy moments. (Like how to convince a stubborn two-year-old to sit on a potty.) We visited sprinkler parks in the summer, picked pumpkins in the fall, and acted surprised when Santa crashed our Christmas parties each winter.

Even my husband appreciated the group. I'm not sure he fully understood how a few hours of eating munchies and playing games with the girls transformed his tired, grumpy wife into a pleasant woman, but he knew it worked. One night of laughter with friends always gave me the extra boost I needed to tackle life's troubles.

But kids grow up quickly and now many of us are caught up in the typical busyness of life with tween-agers. Our schedules are packed with football games, piano lessons, softball practices, band concerts, and dance recitals. But we still carve out time to keep in touch.

Staying in touch looks different every time we get together. Sometimes we might discuss a problem at our child's school. Another time we might debate a favorite *American Idol* contestant. Recently, we hosted a "pink party" for our friend who was diagnosed with breast cancer. As lunch drew to a close, one of the moms spotted a picture of my kids.

"I can't believe how much your girls have grown," she sighed.

"I know." I smiled, admiring my three little ladies. "When our group first began, Emily couldn't even walk. Now she's in junior high."

I sat quietly for a while and observed the camaraderie around the kitchen table. Every mom had dressed in pink in solidarity with our friend, sharing laughter and the occasional tear, sipping our pink lemonade and supporting our friend during the biggest fight of her life.

This is true friendship, I thought. When you're struggling, there's someone to strengthen you. And when you're rejoicing, there's someone to celebrate with you.

It's easy to see how our kids have grown, but over the years, we moms have grown as well. We've grown closer. We've grown wiser. We've grown stronger.

Being part of a moms' group taught my kids many great lessons in their early years of life. They learned how to share and how to make friends. They discovered that having a good friend is not only fun, but an important way to face life's challenges.

When I think back to those morning playgroups and summer days at the park, I realize my daughter wasn't the only one who needed a friend. My heart fills with gratitude because I learned those important lessons as well.

~Sheri Zeck

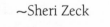

55

The Call

In all affairs it's a healthy thing now and then to hang a question mark on the things you have long taken for granted.
~Bertrand Russell

I'll never know why Linda pursued our improbable friendship with such determination and purpose, but I'm so happy she did. On the surface, we were two women unlikely to become best friends. Linda is talkative, animated, and buzzes from one topic to another like a pollinating bee. She is open and friendly and easy to know. Linda will stand in line at the grocery store and walk out ten minutes later with the phone numbers of three new friends. Conversely, I am a type-A personality who eschews buzzing in favor of to-do lists and set game plans; pleasant but private, I am not open with strangers.

On October 1, 1990, I started a new job. Linda had been employed with the company for several years. We were agreeable acquaintances at work, but not friends. She is a few years younger than I, and at the time I had already celebrated ten years of marriage and two children. Linda was a young divorcée with nothing but footloose-and-fancy-free weekends on her horizon. Considering the vast differences in our lifestyles, a friendship with her outside of the office was not on my list of things to pursue.

One Saturday morning the phone rang while I was busy housecleaning. I ignored it at first, but the caller was persistent so I finally picked up, totally clueless as to who chattered on the other end of the wire. Whoever it was, she certainly talked fast.

"Excuse, me," I said. "I'm sorry. Who is this?"

"It's Linda."

"Linda." I racked my brain, but came up empty.

"From work."

A Saturday morning call could mean only one thing, and that was trouble at the office. Had another coworker been in an accident? Did the building burn down? All the possible scenarios filled my mind.

"What's happened? What's wrong?" I dropped the dust rag on the table and sat down, bracing for bad news. "Is everyone okay?"

"Why wouldn't they be? Did something happen?" she asked.

"Uh, not that I know of," I said, baffled. "So... you're calling why?"

"I just thought I'd see how your Saturday is going."

"Do you need help with something?" I asked, still digging for a clue.

"Nope. I just called to say hi."

We stayed on the phone about fifteen minutes. Linda asked general get-to-know-you questions and chatted about random topics. In the end, I sat puzzling over why this single, active young woman took time from her busy Saturday to jaw with the old married lady from the office.

After that call Linda and I grew a bit friendlier, often eating our bag lunches together and rolling our eyes over office shenanigans. I looked forward to Monday mornings when she would tell me all about her weekend—the single girl in the city—and we laughed together over some of the dud dates she endured. Still more coworkers than friends, she persisted in calling me outside of work "just to chat."

One Friday night Linda suggested we hang out after work and share a pizza. My husband Joe offered to take care of the kids, so I agreed.

"Early night," I promised him. "Linda's a sweetheart, but we don't have anything in common."

Linda and I ordered a pizza and talked... and talked... and talked. I called home around 9:30 to apologize to Joe and tell him I'd be a little longer. When I looked at my watch again it was almost 2 a.m.

As surprised as I was by the time, I was even more surprised to realize I enjoyed myself, laughing and swapping life stories with this young woman who was so different from me in so many ways.

Linda planted the seeds of friendship with that first Saturday morning call and watered them with strong persistence every day thereafter. That they bloomed into a glorious sisterhood is one of life's miracles I will never understand but for which I am eternally grateful.

Our friendship has now spanned more than twenty years. We are still opposites in more ways than we are alike, but we're such good friends that our differences now are simply traits we've come to love in each other.

Linda met the love of her life and married, and our husbands became best friends. Over the years Linda and I have been pregnant at the same time, have watched our kids play and grow together. We've celebrated birthdays, graduations, and anniversaries, cheered each other on, offered consolation when sadness struck, and become true sisters of the heart. I can't imagine not having this wonderful woman in my life. She's been a constant source of support and friendship for more than two decades. She's the little sister I always wanted and now feel so blessed to claim.

The one thing I don't know, and will never understand, is why. Why did she try so hard to be friends with me when I didn't return the effort? What did she see in me, in our potential friendship? What made the idea of our connection so important that it was worth it for her to persevere, despite the fact we had so little in common?

Over the years I've asked her why she pursued our friendship with such purpose, but she doesn't have an answer. Ironically, she doesn't even remember that first Saturday phone call. But I do. I will never forget it.

That call changed my life.

~Lisa Ricard Claro

56

The Tax Girls

Soul mates are people who bring out the best in you. They are not perfect but are always perfect for you.

~Author Unknown

The voice inside my GPS said, "In fifty feet turn right." I followed the instructions and turned my car into the unfamiliar parking lot, driving slowly to read the signs on the stores in the small neighborhood shopping center. The tax school had to be here somewhere. Tucked back in the corner I spotted the familiar name. Parking the car nearby, I walked into school and took a seat.

My husband and I had moved to a new town only a few months earlier. I'd been unable to find a job so I enrolled in tax school hoping it would open up some new opportunities. Being an accountant, I loved doing taxes. I wasn't worried that the class would be too difficult. But I was apprehensive about fitting in with new people in a new place. I'd left the big city for a quiet small town. Life was different here.

"Hi. My name's Linda," I said, as I introduced myself to a woman who appeared to be about my age.

"Kay," she said. "Nice to meet you."

I looked around the room at five women and two men, all fidgeting in their seats waiting for class to start. The instructor, Larry, stood up and introduced himself before explaining the rules of the classroom. He asked us each to tell the others something about ourselves.

The other women all told similar stories about needing to find work in a weak economy. I felt camaraderie with them from the start even though their ages and priorities seemed very different from my own. The two men, both retired, were looking for something to fill their time and extra money to boost their pensions. The women seemed much more driven in their quest for employment, a quality I could relate to.

Three mornings a week, Larry calmly led us through the rules of the Internal Revenue Service, including filing status, dependents, and adjusted gross income. Nightly homework and weekly quizzes reinforced our lessons.

"Linda, what answer did you get on yesterday's practice problem?" Carrie asked one morning before class began. She closely examined papers spread across the desk in front of her.

I pretended to look through my briefcase. I didn't want to admit I hadn't done the homework.

"I got a refund of $180," one of the Susans said.

"You must have left out some of the income. They owe taxes," Debbie added. Over time we had learned that Debbie's homework was always complete and correct. The odds were great that it was this time too.

"Deb's probably right. They took a distribution from their retirement fund," I added, feeling pressure to contribute to the conversation.

Kay slid into the seat next to me and whispered in my ear, "I didn't do the homework. Did you?"

I shook my head no.

Larry rapped on his desk to get our attention. The other Susan flung open the front door.

"What did I miss?" she yelled out while she jogged to her seat.

The men sat quietly not saying a word. As the weeks wore on they stopped coming to school. We didn't miss them. The bantering amongst us was rapid and lively. Their absence gave us more room to spread out, compare notes, and speak our minds. Most days Larry sat back in his chair, arms crossed, and smiled, watching his students learn from one another.

"Next week the district manager will be here to conduct interviews," Larry announced one day. "I've told her how well you're doing."

A look of panic crossed Carrie's face. Debbie took a big hard gulp from her bottle of water. Susan brushed her long blond hair out of her face. Kay laughed. The other Susan threw open the door, took one look at our faces and said, "What did I miss?"

I watched the group's anxiety quickly melt away.

On the day slated for interviews we all showed up in well-pressed suits with colorful blouses. I put on make-up for the first time. Not dressed in our usual attire of shorts, sandals and T-shirts, we barely recognized each other.

The district manager called us to the back of the office one by one. Larry wasn't teaching a lesson that day so while we waited for our turn, we spoke freely as a group. We talked about books, our favorite television shows, and sports we enjoyed. The conversation never missed a beat as each of us rotated in and out for our interview.

We had to wait a week to learn if we'd been hired or not. When I got to class on the big day, in unison the group burst out, "Did you get hired?"

"No," I answered. "I haven't heard anything yet."

"We all heard. We're hired!" Susan number one shouted out.

My heart sank. I needed a job. And working alongside this wonderful group of women would make it extra special.

Kay put her arm around me. Carrie scrolled through her cell phone looking for the manager's number. Susan, Susan, and Debbie prodded Larry to do something, anything for me.

Carrie handed me a piece of paper with a phone number on it. I went outside to make the call. I got the manager's voicemail.

They all sat up straight when I came back through the door. I shrugged my shoulders.

I sat through class that day under a cloud. My friends did their best to try to reassure me. All gave me their good thoughts that everything would be fine by tomorrow.

When I got home the phone rang.

"I sent your hiring documents to your e-mail. You've been assigned to a high volume office," the manager told me.

I thanked her profusely, a weight lifted. The next day the women barraged me with questions. When I couldn't hide the smile on my face any longer, they knew I'd been hired too.

On graduation day Larry proudly handed each of us our diplomas. We'd all passed the course with flying colors. We agreed to meet the following week for lunch at a local restaurant to celebrate.

The lunch conversation volleyed back and forth across the table, a mix of questions, answers, and laughter. We revealed our ages and birth dates, told tales of children and grandchildren, husbands and boyfriends. The plates had long been cleared before anyone even thought to get up to leave.

While the waitress refilled my glass again, I remarked, "This was so much fun. Let's do this again."

A monthly lunch with the tax girls was born. I never miss it. Each time a different tax girl picks the spot and I put the address into my GPS. In addition to a delightful afternoon, I've learned my way around town. Even with several tax seasons behind us, we never lack things to talk about.

At tax school, I met five wonderful women, from different backgrounds with different points of view. My tax girls will forever hold a special place in my heart as friends I found when I needed them most.

~Linda C. Wright

57

Finding My Friend

*You can't stay in your corner of the Forest waiting for others to come to you.
You have to go to them sometimes.*

~A.A. Milne, Winnie-the-Pooh

I looked around the sanctuary. The pews were packed with mothers chatting. I picked at the seam of my jeans. Sighed deeply. Wondered why the loneliest place in the world could be smack in the middle of a crowd.

My husband and I had moved months before, and I needed a friend. A mom's group seemed a likely place to look. And I had. But so far all I'd found was a greater dose of lonely. I arrived early each time, checked my boys into their classroom, and headed to the fellowship hall. But it was impossible to penetrate the mom clusters. I ended up standing on the fringes, engrossed in a plate of fruit, staring at red grapes, and smiling too hard, as if being Lone Ranger Mama was the most desirable thing in the world.

Clearly it was not.

I'd never had trouble making friends before. And it wasn't that the women in the group were unkind. They were just established. Rooted deep. Most women had joined the group with an already-friend. There was a group that lived in the same neighborhood. Another group scrapbooked together, sharing time and hearts and double-sided tape. Another group went to the same church and another consisted of women whose husbands worked at the same plant.

I was alone. Looking for someone who was looking for someone, too.

There were a few moments for conversation before the guest speaker was introduced. I gathered my courage and turned to the mother next to me. "How are you this morning?"

She smiled big. "I'm good. Doing very well." She looked at my nametag. "And how are you, Shawnelle?"

"Fine, just fine," I said. "Do you..."

But she had turned and was, in a moment, deeply engaged with the friend on her left.

I tried to smile and then pawed through my bag. Better to be on an imaginary hunt than to sit alone, staring ahead.

A moment later the guest speaker took the podium. And the topic of the day? Friendships of Women. Great. I didn't want to stay. I thought about a quiet exit. Slipping to the back of the room. Passing though the heavy oak doors, gathering my children and going on home. I wrapped my hands around the handles of my bag. I didn't want to hear about friendships when I couldn't seem to find one.

But then the speaker began.

For the next hour I half-listened, moving in and out, hearing about why friendships are important and thinking about the ones I'd left behind. I missed sitting at my kitchen table, sharing from deep places while the children laughed and played. I missed the ringing phone and a sweet voice on the other end that sometimes was just a request: "Pray for me? My day is wild." I missed days at the park, pushing swings, when sentences came fragment-style because that's life and the season of it all.

It was all good. So very good.

"Let's take a moment," the speaker said, "and share about what you want in a friend. We'll move around the room. Just share, in a few words, what friendship means to you."

My pulse picked up tempo and I glanced at the back door. Share about friendship? Here? Now? The very thing I lamented over, each week?

No way.

I felt the sharp sting of tears and I blinked hard to push them away. But the question had rippled through the room and the spotlight was only three mothers away and knew I'd better string it together fast.

All I could do was speak from the heart.

When I felt all eyes shift to me, I stood and breathed deep. "Friendship to me is quiet. It's listening. It's sitting at a table, hands wrapped around a mug of something warm, listening to the heart of the woman across from you."

I took my place on the pew and only remembered to breathe again when the mother next to me stood. There. I'd said it. And I hadn't cried.

Now I could slip out and leave.

It only took a few moments to gather my boys. Toddler room. Nursery. Coats and hats and bags and bottles. In no time at all we were ready to go. I walked down the hall, one child in my arms, one child at my side. There was a solid flow of chatter from my toddler, the most conversation I'd had all morning.

I almost missed the voice. It was strong and sweet and coming from behind me. "Shawnelle?"

I turned to find a mother I hadn't noticed before. Her smile was bright and wide and her eyes were a gentle blue. I could tell from her approach that she was comfortable, confident, and kind.

"My name is Sarah. And I just wanted to find you because, well, I liked what you said."

"What I said?"

"About friendship. About listening. And sharing something warm. I like those things, too."

Sarah and I began to talk. She bent on one knee to speak to my son. She whispered to the babe in my arms. And in a short amount of time I learned that she and I shared hobby interests like reading and crafts, and she was nearly my neighbor, too.

I also learned that I'd found a friend.

I continued to attend the mom's group, with Sarah there, by my side. We learned to look for other moms who were new and unsettled, maybe looking for a friend. But we found those sweet, quiet times, too, and we shared many while our children played and laughed and stretched and grew. There were summer picnics and fireworks. Walks in the parks. Swims in the sun. There were fun times and tough times and laughter and tears.

And somehow the years whispered right past.

Sarah no longer lives in the neighborhood. She lives in another state. And our children have become teens, those mom group days are gone, and many things have changed.

But Sarah is still my friend.

And once a year she comes for a visit. We sit at my table. We sip from mugs and enjoy something warm to drink. Conversation flows fast and free. The common ties still bind us. Things pick up right where we left off and it's like no time has passed. And I feel the same way I did all those years ago, standing with my babes, in that hall....

I'm so grateful to have found my friend.

~Shawnelle Eliasen

Chapter
7

Just Us Girls

Second Looks

58

The Atheist and the Preacher's Wife

Two people of similar nature can never get along,
it takes two opposites to harmonize.
~Ram Mohan

When I was a kid, I had no trouble making new friends. "Just look for someone like you, and talk to them," I would instruct my younger sisters, showing them how to easily create a circle of friends.

But now that I was in my mid-twenties, newly married to a minister, and living in a town far away from my family and friends, meeting new people wasn't so easy.

My husband, Mike, was the pastor of a large church, in a town where people had grown up together and already had all the friends they needed.

I found a job waitressing at a family restaurant, hoping to find a friend, someone just like me, with similar values and interests. But most of the staff there were young and single — their lives consumed with school and parties.

A petite blond girl was instructed to show me the ropes at the restaurant. Melynda had moved to Canada from Ireland a year earlier, and with her thick Irish brogue I could barely understand her. "So, yer a preacher's wife?" she snickered. "Aye, if I ever darkened the doors of a church, it'd fall down on top of me!"

She had a temper, with a foul mouth that could make a sailor blush, and was about as polar opposite from me as you could get, or so I thought.

As I walked home after my shift, I realized she was walking right in front of me, and I saw her go into a little house just around the corner from mine.

The next day we met, while walking to work, and I reluctantly joined her, cringing at her crude stories. However, it turned out she was actually my age, married, and lived in that small house with her husband and numerous cats.

She made it immediately clear that she was an atheist, and wanted nothing to do with church people.

Frankly, she terrified me, and was about as far from my conservative upbringing as you could get. She told me stories about her wild teenage years when she would wear clear plastic dresses with nothing underneath.

And yet, we met to walk to work together, and home again every day.

One of the benefits of waitressing is always having pocketfuls of change. "Why don't we stop in a couple of shops on the way home?" she suggested one day. And that began our daily habit of thrift store shopping, where we'd buy dresses, sweaters and shoes.

Then Melynda introduced me to auction sales, where we bid together on beautiful antique furniture, as well as strange and crazy items to fill our homes.

We bonded over our interests in vintage things, art and gardening, but also over our mutual dislike of our waitressing job. We became a twosome at work and we were always paired to work together—whether it was waitressing, decorating the restaurant, or buying flowers for the restaurant patio.

Mike and I were hunting for our first house to buy, and she searched with me—she had a critical eye and a harsh tongue. I think our real estate agent was afraid of her too!

Soon, we were inseparable, spending every weekend together, and going places that the other girls in the restaurant wouldn't dream of going, like junk shops and art stores. The restaurant uniform required wearing a tie, so we began to make our own and sell them to the other staff.

We started a booth at the farmer's market, selling artsy things we'd make, or find and make over. I was the quiet, calm vendor, trying to keep Melynda's crazy temper in line so we didn't drive the customers away.

We talked about everything... everything except our religious beliefs. Yet, somehow it didn't matter. I was tolerant of her language and crude jokes, and she listened to my stories of the activities at church, and the interesting people I was meeting.

One day I invited Melynda and her husband Mark to a sports and dinner night we were having at church. Surprisingly, they came, and even more surprisingly, they participated with great enthusiasm. At the end of the night, she responded, "Boy, I really like your church. I would join right away if it wasn't for the religious part!"

We have both since moved away from that town, and live over a hundred miles away from each other. My life has changed, as I've become a mother and raised three children, while Melynda has built her dream home along a lake and filled it with pets. Neither of us works as a waitress anymore. But we've remained close girlfriends, and still share our love of collecting junk, being creative, and renovating our homes.

Each Christmas we mail each other gifts, and I eagerly look forward to the box I'll get from her, full of treasures she's found for me through the year—a vintage blanket, old Christmas ornaments, a teapot she's made. No matter what it is, I know I will love it, because even though she's still an atheist, and I'm still a preacher's wife, those aren't the things that matter in our friendship.

I'm glad we were both able to overlook the things that might have initially stopped us from enjoying a creative friendship. And since then, I've learned that when you're looking for a girlfriend, don't bother looking for someone just like you—because what you really need might be just the opposite!

~Lori Zenker

59

Chicken Soup for the Soul

Samers

Friendship isn't a big thing—it's a million little things.
~Author Unknown

indsay and I met on the worship team of our campus ministry group during our freshman year of college. She played the drums and I sang. Everyone in the band listened to her suggestions on what songs to play and I—well, I just talked to myself and made snorting noises into the microphone for entertainment while they made their plans. I thought she was conceited and she thought I was weird. We weren't off to a very good start.

In spite of my resentment, however, we actually had a lot in common. We wound up having so much in common, in fact, that at times it felt like she was following me.

Shortly after I moved from my all-freshman dorm into a different building, I learned that Lindsay had decided to do the same. Not only did she switch buildings, but she moved into the same building, on the same floor as me. Directly across the hall, in fact.

But that wasn't all. The week after I told the worship team I was considering applying to the campus newspaper, Lindsay came to practice with an ear-to-ear grin and asked the band to guess who the newest staff writer at the *Northern Student* was. I decided not to apply.

Not long after she got the job, Lindsay took a sudden interest in learning to play the guitar. Normally, this wouldn't be a problem, except that I had recently shared with her how I had been struggling to teach myself for several years. It irked me even more when her guitar skills surpassed my own and she started offering me tips. Whenever I could hear her practicing new chords across the hall, I closed the door and cranked my music.

Finally, the copycat did the unthinkable—she changed her major. And can you guess which major she switched to? Bingo. My major—Creative and Professional Writing. And to top it off, she also declared a minor in Spanish, just like me.

I don't like being closely followed. When I ran cross-country and track in high school, it drove me crazy when I could feel someone running right behind me. I would speed up to escape the clicking of their spiked shoes and the sound of their labored breathing.

I wanted to run away from Lindsay Larson.

Which is why it was so surprising when, on the first day of our second semester, I felt only relief when I walked into Spanish class to find her sitting there. I had been so nervous about the class that I actually studied vocabulary and verb tenses over Christmas break. When I saw her familiar face in the class, the worry vanished instantly.

It didn't take long for my bottled hostility to leave, either. Through hours of visiting each other's dorm rooms to quiz one another and giggle at strange-sounding Spanish words, we became not only neighbors, band mates, and fellow writing majors, but also friends. We were all-around "samers," as Lindsay called it. No longer did I feel she was threatening my most closely held passions, but that we were sharing in them. She wasn't chasing me anymore, but running beside me, a welcome companion.

We needed each other. She taught me how to cook and to dress more fashionably, and I taught her some of the more unconventional arts, like "dorky dancing." We proofread each other's papers and bounced story ideas off each other. We exchanged encouraging Bible verses, prayed together, and kept each other sane.

I especially needed her support during our sophomore year, when I became very interested in a senior named Ryan. My way of showing him I liked him involved a lot of teasing and obnoxious pranks, some of which I'd roped Lindsay into helping me with. I reasoned that, if we were meant to be together, Ryan might as well know my true personality from the get-go. But that was just the thing—I didn't know if we were meant to be together until, at some unidentifiable moment during that semester break, I knew I was going to marry him. Simple as that, I knew it.

There was a problem, however. When it came to girls, Ryan acted completely disinterested. He seemed much more intent on hunting and fishing and tromping through the woods—which completely surrounded our little northern Minnesota college town—than finding his future spouse. Still, I told Lindsay how I felt about Ryan.

Lindsay had also taken interest in a young man, Ben, whom she had met at a Christian music festival that year. Like me, Lindsay was cautious when it came to dating. She wanted to make sure that if she dated someone, there was potential for a future. When we prayed for my future with Ryan, we also prayed for God's direction in Lindsay's life regarding Ben.

And then one day it happened. The familiar clicking of Lindsay's high-heeled boots sounded behind me as she shared the news that she too knew who she was going to marry. Her voice shook with excitement as she described what happened. "When I was driving yesterday, I asked God if Ben was the one for me, and I saw a vision of Ben and me facing each other, smiling. I was wearing a wedding dress. I know it probably sounds like I'm trying to copy you, but I know I'm going to marry him."

I believed her just as she had believed me. We clung to that belief when Ryan ignored me in church and when Ben took weeks to respond to Lindsay's e-mails. We rejoiced over it when Ryan apologized for being aloof and when Ben started calling Lindsay.

Slowly, steadily, surely, the time did indeed approach for both of us. To the surprise of many, Ryan and I started dating that April, just before Ryan's graduation. He opened up about his feelings for me one evening as we walked along the lake our campus bordered. A year and four months later, we were married.

True to her pattern, Lindsay wasn't far behind. She began her journey with Ben on — get this — an evening snow-covered stroll the winter of her junior year. They were married the following December, just five short months after Ryan and me.

Ryan and I are currently living in Wyoming, and Lindsay and Ben reside in Florida. She already has two children and I have none, so I guess it's my turn to follow her! I just pray that, despite the many miles between us, we will continue to write many more stories together.

We are both writers, after all.

~Loni Swensen

The Assignment I Never Wanted

A true friend reaches for your hand and touches your heart.
~Attributed to Heather Pryor

A new family of eight joined our church. Their first Sunday at church, they sang, as a family, a beautiful hymn for the congregation. Their perfect pitch and blending of voices awed me, humbled me, and filled me with envy. Why, I wondered, couldn't my family do that?

Following church services, I mentioned it to my husband. "We can't sing," he said bluntly.

I knew he was right. Our family members weren't singers. And sometimes we didn't even get along very well either. We love each other. But sometimes we just get on each other's nerves.

I made up my mind then and there that I couldn't possibly like the mother of this talented, happy brood. Not only had she accompanied her family on the piano, she appeared to have it all together. She was young, blond, and flawlessly groomed. Obviously, she was perfect—very unlike my own flawed self.

Life has a way of throwing us curves, though. I found myself assigned to visit this lady to welcome her to the church. How could I do that with any kind of sincerity and warmth?

Reluctantly, I paid her a visit... and was immediately charmed. Her humor, her unstudied grace, her matter-of-fact approach to life put me instantly at ease.

Within minutes, we found that we shared much in common. We each had roots in Appalachia. We each had big families. We each knew how to pinch a penny. We were each avid garage salers.

More than a little ashamed, I confessed to her that I had decided that I couldn't like her. She laughed delightedly. "You thought my family was perfect?" she asked.

I nodded.

She laughed again. "We're as far from perfect as you can get."

"Tell me."

We proceeded to share stories of our imperfect selves, families, and lives. We discovered that both our husbands were independent-minded, didn't take orders well, and had started their own businesses. We shared stories of living on rice and beans and love and little else.

Today, this woman and I are best friends. Every Friday, we attend garage sales together and compete to see who can find the best bargain. On birthdays, we give each other gag gifts and delight in playing practical jokes on each other.

We have been friends for sixteen years now and grow to appreciate each other more with every year. How had I ever thought that I couldn't like her?

Hasty judgments and foolish pride had almost turned me away from a woman who would become an important and precious part of my life.

Friendships are frequently found when we aren't looking. I stumbled across this one and have been thankful ever since for the assignment I never wanted.

~Jane McBride Choate

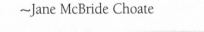

My Bully, My Friend

I destroy my enemies when I make them my friends.
~Abraham Lincoln

I stared long and hard at the friend request on my Facebook page. I hadn't thought about her in thirty years, not since high school. But her friend request quickly transported me back to eighth grade, which I called "The Year of the Bulldog." I recalled with sharp clarity more details about her than I cared to. I'd named her The Bulldog because that's what she reminded me of. Two long folds of skin ran down each side of her face, nicely complementing her pug nose and dull black eyes.

My eighth grade class was housed at the high school and labeled sub-freshmen, a derogatory term in itself. There was a group of older kids who made it their mission in life to terrorize sub-freshmen. In study hall, a group of them sat behind my friends and me. They regularly fired spitballs at us, said hurtful things, and enjoyed many laughs at our expense—a real hell on earth. The Bulldog was part of this group.

She also rode my school bus home in the afternoon. The bus ride home had once stood for freedom. I had loved the moment the bus doors closed and created a cozy world of chattering kids and laughter. Windows snapped down as soon as we were seated—the fresh air a taste of the freedom that would soon be ours once we spilled out onto our home turf. All that fun came to a halt during The Year of the Bulldog; the bus was no longer a safe haven.

She was alone on the bus, and not as scary solo — or so I thought. My bus driver appointed me Safety Patrol, but I didn't want to be Safety Patrol. It involved putting on a bright orange vest and getting off the bus to hold a red flag out across the road to stop oncoming traffic when a kid had to cross to the other side of the road. Isn't that what the big octagonal stop sign attached to the bus was for? Nevertheless, I couldn't say no. An adult asked me to perform a task and to refuse this "honor" felt rude or disrespectful.

On my first day as Safety Patrol I had to pass The Bulldog as I made my way down the aisle to perform my duty. She always sat on the end, hanging over the edge of her seat. When I walked past her, her elbow ripped into my side. Another time she reached out and pinched my arm to the snickers of her seatmates. I hated those bus rides home until the driver reserved the front seat for me. But even then, the long ride home never held the same allure it once had.

My friends and I got through that awful year and were soon freshmen on the way to The Rest of Our Lives. The bullies disbanded their pack and found other things to do, or rather another group of sub-freshmen to harass, and I filed the incident away.

That is, until this new friend request. The ill feelings came flooding back. Whoever believes that bullying is a common childhood occurrence and bears no negative consequences is dead wrong. I rarely turn down a Facebook friend request, especially if we share at least a mutual friend or two. But I did have to think about this one for a while before I accepted.

I did accept, and the funniest thing happened. We became friends — and not just of the Facebook variety. When I recently decided to start writing again, I posted some notes on my Facebook profile because I didn't yet have a blog. My new friend became one of my biggest cheerleaders. She particularly identified with a post about grandparenting and left some thoughtful feedback. When I wrote about donating peripheral blood stem cells (PBSC), she told me about a family member who'd been the recipient of a bone marrow transplant. Who knew I'd share so much with my former childhood adversary?

Recently the high school we both attended held a reunion for all graduates. I sought out my new friend immediately; such was the bond I now felt with her. We chatted easily during our short visit, sharing many laughs. As we hugged goodbye and promised to keep in touch, my gaze landed on the shiny school bus parked on the football field behind us. I smiled at the irony, and at the same moment my heart loosened up. Light flowed in as love flowed out. It felt good to forgive.

~Candyce Deal

Melissa Grace

Enemies are so stimulating.
~Katharine Hepburn

I hated Melissa Grace. I couldn't stand her. I knew I didn't really have much ground for not liking Melissa. I hadn't interacted with her much. She was a photographer, but without the artsy air that I thought was supposed to follow artists around. She wore blue jeans and T-shirts like every day was Friday and had brown eyes that I envied, but I wouldn't admit that to myself. She seemed to get along really well with men, which could only mean she was a flirt and a tease. How distasteful.

And, strangely, it seemed like she wasn't too fond of me, either. All the more reason for me not to like her.

Weeks and months passed, and we continued to perform the delicate, yet subtle, dance of avoiding each other. It was our mutually unspoken dark secret that no one else knew about. She didn't talk to me, I didn't talk to her, and we lived perfectly happy lives hating each other. I was fine with that. What a beautiful relationship.

One cool and clear night in October, my friend Kenna invited me over for a movie night. When I got to her place, she stepped out and told me that the movie night was at Melissa's place because she had a nicer television.

Excuse me?

Thirty minutes later, the popcorn had been popped, and I was just a few feet away from Melissa, as her guest. If I had had a steak knife, I would have been able to cut the tension in the air. It was a little awkward, passing popcorn while avoiding eye contact and trying to not let our fingers accidentally brush.

Surprisingly, it was one of my favorite movies. I was glad someone picked out a good film, saving me from focusing too much on the antagonistic atmosphere.

"This is one of my favorite movies," Melissa mentioned casually to her friend.

Pardon me, Melissa, I thought, but you aren't allowed to like this movie. Bad people can't love good movies. It's a rule.

Our small audience laughed, cried, and sighed at all the right times throughout the film. When the credits rolled, we all started talking. I realized this was the most time I had actually spent with Melissa, and horns had not yet sprouted from her head. In fact, she seemed pretty down-to-earth and friendly.

Kenna teased Melissa, prompting a quick and comical reply that sent the rest of the room into a fit of giggles.

Oh God. I laughed at one of her jokes. What was I becoming?

I think my laugh caught her off guard, because Melissa turned and looked at me with a surprised expression on her face. I could almost see her questioning whether I was laughing with her or at her. Staring into her beautiful brown eyes, I wondered what thoughts were running behind them. I knew so little of her, and I had never really considered her thoughts or feelings before. She had good taste in movies, and had a great sense of humor. What other traits had I overlooked?

The hours passed faster than I would have liked, and I learned about Melissa's quirky family in Kentucky, her love of Japanese cuisine, and her older sister who worked as a fitness instructor. Laughing at the ridiculous fears and antics of our childhood and sharing fears of the future, we gave of ourselves until the wee hours of the morning.

And we didn't stop. The next day, I wondered if the previous night had been a fluke. Perhaps we were unknowingly still at odds with each other. I was so very wrong, because we started talking at lunch as though we were back on her couch.

We talked. For days and weeks about everything and anything from moral messages in Van Gogh paintings to why we think reality television is a waste of time. Then we cried over our failings, prayed over our fears, and laughed at the silliness of everyday life. We snickered at the foolishness of thinking that we disliked each other.

It was as though that one giggle at a joke on that movie night banished my presuppositions and dislike for the woman I now dearly love. She is the opposite of me in all the right ways. It makes me wonder how many other potential friends I may have overlooked.

~Nan Rockey

That Haggerty Woman

*Stubbornness does have its helpful features.
You always know what you are going to be thinking tomorrow.*
~Glen Beaman

I never referred to her as Mrs. Haggerty or as Bertha Haggerty. To me she was always "That Haggerty Woman" because I didn't like her.

I didn't exactly know why I didn't like her except I didn't like the way she dressed like an old hippie in tie-dyed skirts and shirts. I didn't like that she drove a big noisy truck when everyone else in the neighborhood drove quiet, sensible cars. I didn't like the changes she was making to the house next door, the house where my best friend Joyce had lived before she moved away three months before.

One day, my eight-year-old son Peter was using his magnifying glass to look at leaves when he discovered if he held the glass close to the leaves the sun would set them on fire. Peter also set a nearby pile of leaves on fire, which started a small grass fire. The wind blew the flames straight into That Haggerty Woman's yard.

Luckily, I saw the fire and put it out with the water hose. There was no serious damage except for a small black patch of grass in my yard and a big black pile of burned ashes that had once been grass in the Haggertys' yard.

There was nothing I could do but march my son to her house. Both of us would have to apologize, and I would offer to pay for the damage.

There was no one on earth I hated apologizing to more than that woman.

I considered baking a cake or taking her some homemade jelly, but that would look like a bribe. No, I had to show up empty handed and repentant and grovel at her feet.

Peter and I looked at each other. I don't know who was more nervous and scared when I knocked on her door.

The door opened only wide enough to show one eye.

"I've come to apologize," I said quickly, "I'm afraid my son was playing and accidently set a fire and burned some of your grass. I'm sorry and I'll pay for the damage."

The door opened wider.

"You didn't get hurt, did you?" she asked Peter.

"No," Peter said, "I'm sorry about the fire."

She looked past us at the black patch in her yard.

"That's not so bad. The grass will grow back," she said. "Don't worry about paying me anything."

I was overwhelmed by her unexpected generous, forgiving nature.

"When I was twelve, I had a junior scientist chemistry set. I started a fire in my father's garage," she smiled, "He forgave me and in that same spirit, I forgive you. After all, we shouldn't discourage a young scientist, should we? No hard feelings, okay?"

I was feeling small and petty.

"I guess we haven't formally met. I'm Bertha," she said.

"I'm Holly." I took her hand.

"Would you like to come in for coffee?" she asked.

"Yes, thank you. Peter, run home and get the blueberry muffins I baked this morning and bring them back here," I said, and followed Bertha inside.

"You aren't a very friendly person, are you?" she asked bluntly.

What? I couldn't have heard her correctly. I'm very friendly! I have lots of friends. I help people all the time. I volunteer at my church. I help the Boy Scouts. I belong to clubs and charitable organizations!

I was friendly to everyone! Except, she was right. I hadn't been friendly to her at all. When my friend Joyce sold her house and moved far away the loss was sharp and deep. Childishly, I was determined not to like whoever bought the house, as if Joyce leaving was their fault.

"You're right," I confessed, "I'm afraid I've resented you moving into my friend's house and changing things as if you were erasing her ever living here. Joyce loved her rose garden and she spent years planting bushes and caring for them and you dug all of them up and got rid of them the first week you lived here."

"I'm allergic to roses. I have hay fever and asthma. I donated the rose bushes to the Valley View Retirement home. Your friend's roses are alive and well and being enjoyed by many people," she said.

"Oh," I said meekly, "I wish I'd known. I've misjudged you terribly. I'd like to start fresh. Welcome to the neighborhood. We have sixty-two very nice people and one old grouch, which apparently is me, but I'll change."

She laughed.

"Do you play cards?" she asked.

"No," I said. "Do you like to cook? Do you knit?"

"No," she said. "Do you like hiking, rock climbing, or canoeing?"

"No," I said.

The list went on as we searched for common ground.

We discovered that we had nothing in common, agreed on almost nothing, didn't share any interests, disagreed on religion and politics, but in spite of it all, we liked each other and made each other laugh.

That Haggerty Woman turned out to be a good neighbor and a good friend.

She's not Joyce, but that's okay. I like that Haggerty woman and I hope she never moves away.

~Holly English

Middle School Mentality

*Treat everyone with politeness, even those who are rude to you—
not because they are nice, but because you are.*
~Author Unknown

"If you put your yoga mat too close to mine, we won't have room for poses with outstretched arms," I said with a smile to the redhead in Spandex who was crowding my space.

"We can stagger our positions," she said with an icy stare as she plopped down with determination.

"This woman has no yoga manners," I said to myself. "I don't like her."

Later in the week, I was first to enter class, and like my yoga friends, I hurried to claim my favorite place in the room. As I prepared to lower my mat, the redhead appeared, unfurled her mat, and bumped me from my spot. I moved away, feeling a tightening in my stomach that didn't come from strengthening my core. After that, I was uptight around her. We avoided eye contact. My hostile attitude reminded me of my middle school mentality, many years ago, when I disliked a mean girl who bullied me.

"I can't stand this tension. I have to do something," I vowed.

One day, the scowling redhead arrived and unrolled her mat too close to mine. She sat and stared ahead, her mouth turned down.

"It's time," I told myself. "Do it now."

"Hi, I'm Miriam," I said.

She turned to me... and broke into a beautiful smile. Extending her hand she said, "I'm Rachel. Pleased to meet you."

We chatted like old friends, and adjusted our mats so there was room for Sun Salutations. The knot in my stomach disappeared. I liked her.

I wish I had approached Rachel earlier. She no longer competes for my space when she arrives. Instead, she greets me with a smile, reaches for my hand, and asks how I am doing. I return her warm responses, and wonder if perhaps she felt I was the one who was unfriendly and competitive.

With the tension behind us, Rachel and I are friends.

I realize yoga class is not the place to start off on the wrong foot... with a middle school mentality. Namaste.

~Miriam Hill

Unexpected Friendship

In a world full of people who couldn't care less,
be someone who couldn't care more.
~Author Unknown

When school started on that warm August day, I was ready for it, maybe even excited about it. It was senior year after all. I threw myself into everything I did for those first couple of weeks, including playing volleyball, which I loved.

I decided that year that I was going to fix myself. So I started my quest for perfection. I was desperate to be successful. I had to become beautiful, or at the very least, skinny. I stopped eating completely. I knew what anorexia was, but somehow I looked up to the girls who could do it. I was jealous of their willpower and drive. I knew I would never go that far. I had control.

After a while, my newfound diet started to take a noticeable toll on me. I was losing weight, which thrilled me, and I even grew to love the lightheadedness and tiredness that came with my poor diet, because those feelings meant that I was winning, that I was overcoming.

As the season progressed, things had become tense between my head volleyball coach, Coach Smith, and me. She was becoming suspicious. I felt like I was losing control. She confronted me about my eating and was angry that I wouldn't listen to her when she tried to make me eat. She knew I had a problem and yet she couldn't understand it. I was angry and hurt and she was suspicious and worried. We fought constantly. She just wanted me to eat, and I wanted to prove that I had control over this.

My malnourishment started to affect my performance. I was so tired that practice and games were becoming a struggle. I was still trying my best, but my best was slowly declining. Every practice, every game, I felt myself being watched. I hated it.

Then one day, with hurt in her eyes, Coach Smith approached me after a game.

"Why are you doing this to yourself? Do you want to lose weight?"

I felt like I had been slapped. I fumbled for an answer using my usual excuses, but I could tell that she didn't believe me. She felt sorry for me. This was something I didn't know how to handle. I could argue all day long, but it was the pity that I couldn't stand. I stood there and did my best to convince her I was fine. She asked me what I had eaten and I told her nothing yet, but I was going to. She looked at me, disappointment in her eyes, knowing she couldn't make me stop, and walked away. I didn't stop. By the time our last game of the season rolled around I had lost twenty pounds.

A couple of weeks later I attended the volleyball banquet. I didn't eat anything, but I sat and listened to the awards and laughed at the prank gifts. I even stood there as my coach managed to say something nice about me. I realized then that I had ruined my senior year by being disrespectful and hateful, and I had probably ruined hers as well. Volleyball was supposed to be fun and instead it had turned into a battle.

After the event ended, I approached her and apologized. I had to admit that I was the one who was wrong and that even though I wasn't going to change, I told her it wasn't the way I wanted the year to go. She just looked at me with tears in her eyes and gave me the biggest hug ever. I couldn't believe she was being so nice after all of the terrible things I had done. Then she said it. She gave it a name. "Eating disorders are hard," she told me trying not to cry. "If you ever want to talk let me know."

"Thanks, but I don't have one of those," I responded. She just looked at me with sympathy and heartache and nodded, knowing she couldn't change my mind. She thanked me for the apology and we went on with our lives.

Right before graduation I was thinking about all of the people who had influenced my life and I thought back to the volleyball season. I decided I had to let her know. So I wrote her a letter apologizing and thanking her. I gave her this letter on the last day of school, at the end of the day, and left thinking I would probably never see her again.

The summer after senior year was all about college. I had so much going on that the last year was almost forgotten for a while and I was glad to be getting away from it. Then one Saturday, I felt someone gently take my arm and say softly, "Lynne Jones... how are you doing?" And I looked up to see that familiar face. "Thanks for the letter," she said. "It meant a lot."

When I think of a coach, I think of someone above me, someone who gives instruction—not a friend. But Coach Smith refused to give up on me, and like any good friend, she confronted my problem even when I hated her for it at the time. I didn't deserve her kindness, but she gave it anyway. I will forever be grateful for her help, and now for her friendship.

~Lynne Jones

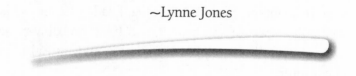

A Journey with Friends

Shared joy is a double joy; shared sorrow is half a sorrow.
~Swedish Proverb

"But Maggy, I'm all alone! I have no one left except my kids," I cried. "And they live far away, my parents are dead, and my sister too. I have no living relatives," I practically screamed at her. "I'm an orphan now!" I said bursting into tears.

It was my weekly therapy session. I had been seeing Maggy regularly for several months since my husband of forty-plus years left me a young widow. I was devastated when he died suddenly. Paul was my love and my rock. Now I was trying to cope with my life alone. I was truly terrified.

"Sallie, you are not alone. Your friends will come forward to support you," she consoled.

"Maggy, my friends are all still very busy. They're married with husbands, grown kids, and grandkids. They don't want me hanging around.

"Don't you get together with them now?" she asked.

"Sure. We go to lunches, book club, art club and I talk to them on the phone and text them a lot, but they have their own families; their own lives."

"Sallie, you'd be amazed at how friends step up when you need them. You'll see."

Well, I wasn't totally convinced. I had girlfriends who I'd known since grammar school but I also know how we all get wrapped up in our own stuff. My friends and I had all experienced the grief of our parents' deaths but I was the first widow in the group. I didn't think they'd know what to do with me, what to say to me.

As the months went by I would get so deep into my grief that I couldn't speak. I would cry until my eyes were almost swollen shut. That's when I would reach out to my girlfriends.

"Gerri, I can't live without him. How can I go on?" I sobbed into the receiver.

"I'll be right there," she replied. The next thing I knew there was a knock on my door. Gerri gave me a big hug and held me until I stopped crying. We sat in my kitchen having coffee as she offered words of comfort.

The next Sunday my doorbell rang at 10:00 a.m. I opened it to find my friend Eulalee standing there. I have known her since third grade and she cares very deeply but rarely shows her feelings outwardly.

"I'm on my way home from church and I just thought I'd stop by. Is it too early for tea?" she asked.

"Never, come on in," I replied, delighted to have some company and a welcome diversion from a long lonely weekend.

From then on, every Sunday morning my doorbell would ring and there would be Eulalee smiling and asking, "Got a few minutes?" I'd put on the teakettle and we'd sit for an hour or two. She'd listen to me talk about Paul and her eyes would glisten with tears. Sunday after Sunday she listened.

About this time I met a gal in my art class named T.J. We hit it off immediately and I found out that she was a mom with grown children, her husband was also named Paul, and she lived about a mile from me. She became my close friend and she would tell me what we came to call "bedtime stories."

Every night right after the ten o'clock news, the phone would ring.

"Hi there. Whad'ya do today?" T.J. would ask.

Just hearing her voice was very soothing. It settled and grounded me so I was able to sleep. She would listen to all the trivial events of my day. I felt safe and like I mattered to someone. She'd always end with "I love ya, sista!" If T.J. didn't hear from me for a day I'd get a text, "You okay?"

The culmination came when I got my first bout of the stomach flu while living alone. It was a particularly bad one. Lying on the bathroom floor, I wondered who would help me. I could die and no one would know.

I needn't have worried. When I didn't answer T.J.'s text message, she called. I answered weakly on her third try. I wouldn't let her come over since I was contagious so T.J. made an emergency run to the store. Pretty soon I had a care package of Jell-O, Gatorade, bananas, and chicken soup on my doorstep.

In so many ways these women friends have taught me a lot: that girlfriends care for each other through thick and thin; that there is nothing like another woman to soothe you; that they will go to any lengths to help and listen; that we're a sisterhood.

Maggy was right. How could I have doubted? I am not alone. It's been almost three years since Paul died and they still call, text and come by. We laugh and I still mention him but mostly we chat about their lives and my new life. They helped me move forward in a positive way. My recovery has been so much better because of my friends. When the time comes I will be there for them too, because that is what girlfriends do.

~Sallie A. Rodman

Chapter 8

Just Us Girls

Adventures with the Girls

A Day at the Beach

It is one of the blessings of old friends that you can afford to
be stupid with them.
~Ralph Waldo Emerson

I had always heard people say it was very hard for three people to be close friends—you know, the odd number problem. Two people can be close and so can four but three people... not so much. Obviously my two friends and I forgot to read the memo. We met in a class in high school and clicked from that very first day. We shared clothes, make-up, shoes, and most importantly, we shared our lives, hopes, and secrets. We were close.

We graduated, went to college, married, had kids, and stayed close as ever. Then two of us moved from Los Angeles to a beach town on the central coast of California, leaving our other friend behind. You have to make an effort to stay close when you don't live in the same city but we three made a pact before we moved that we would get together at least once a month. And we did just that. We would alternate—one time we would go to Los Angeles for the day and the next time our friend would come and spend the day with us. That worked.

The years flew by and now we three best girl friends had children in high school and college and it was even easier for us to get together. No young children at home to worry about. We still shared everything and we were looking forward to our friend coming to our central coast town one warm August day to spend some time at the beach with us. Rather than fix a picnic lunch we splurged and ordered lunches from a gourmet deli here in town. And we even decided to include a bottle of our favorite wine.

The day was perfect. Warm but not too hot, with a soft breeze blowing. We three spread out our blankets on the sand and got ready to eat. Eating has always been very important to us and we have shared some of our deepest secrets over meals. The lunch was delicious—why is it that things that you don't have to prepare yourself always taste better? And we enjoyed some of the wine too!

We had been sitting, eating, sipping, talking, sharing, and laughing for a few hours when we decided that, before we had our dessert, it would be really nice to stretch our legs and take a walk down the beach. This was the perfect beach to walk along as it was about a mile long and it had a nice wide sandy path to follow. When it got too warm we could just walk along in the water to cool off. Could things get any better?

Since it was a weekday, there were some people on the beach but it wasn't crowded. We walked for a while and the beachgoers thinned out to practically nothing. But way, way down the beach we saw a big group of people. They were far enough away from us that they looked like tiny ants. We thought we could walk to them, then turn around and walk back and have dessert. That would be enough exercise for us.

How could three friends talk as much as we did? How did we find so many things to talk about? We never seemed to run out of things to say. We were walking and talking and getting closer to that big group down the beach. We could tell now that some of them were playing in the water, some were playing beach volleyball, some were walking around, and some were relaxing on the sand. We were so engrossed in our conversation that we practically walked right through the volleyball court before we stopped short. And stop short we did.

Something was wrong with this picture. OMG! These people

didn't have any clothes on. Nothing. They were naked! We were in the middle of a nude beach! Okay, a few of them had hats on and one guy had on a pair of high-top tennis shoes but... that was it.

"Hello girls. Want to join in our volleyball game?"

Are you kidding me? We didn't know what to do. How to react. What to say. And excuse me but... where do you look? The three of us just stood there with our mouths open and our eyes popping out of our heads. We probably stood there for no longer than five seconds taking it all in but it felt like we stood there for hours. And then, at exactly the same time, we all reacted in a way that three adult women should when they find themselves among a group of naked people. We turned and ran like rabbits. No one said a word. We just ran. We hightailed it back down that beach so fast you would have thought we were running in a race — and we needed to win. After a few minutes I tripped and fell in the sand. That's also when we started laughing. Actually we got hysterical. You know the kind of laughter I'm talking about. The I-can't-catch-my-breath-because-I'm-laughing-too-hard kind. No wonder those people were way, way down the beach. Duh. They weren't wearing anything!

We finally made our way back to our beach blankets and were so glad to be back among people... who had bathing suits on. And we laughed. We ate dessert and we laughed. We finished our bottle of wine and we laughed harder. How had all three of us been so naive as to not realize why those people were so far down the beach, away from the usual beachgoers? Why couldn't we have walked in the other direction and looked at the seals and pelicans instead? Of course, if we had gone in the other direction, we would have missed out on a wonderful story to share with our families and friends. And we're still laughing about it today.

~Barbara LoMonaco

The Dance of the Deranged Caterpillar

You can always tell a real friend: when you've made a fool of yourself
he doesn't feel you've done a permanent job.
~Laurence J. Peter

My best friend Adrienne and I have been through it all together. The perils of dating, jobs, break-ups, engagements, marriage, kids, family matters, buying our first homes, moving out of town. You know, the usual life and death events that friends of twenty-two years would normally go through. We pride ourselves on always being there for each other.

I had the great privilege of being in the delivery room when she had her first son, my godson. She was the first one (after my husband) with whom I shared the news that I was pregnant. It's that kind of closeness that we share. But we shared a day even more intimate and close than most friends would ever admit to.

It started like any other typical girls day out. We had a quick lunch at our favorite Italian restaurant on State Street—our usual shared Brie cheese and pear appetizer, two Caesar salads, and iced teas. We had to eat fast, as we didn't have long before we had to relieve the babysitter of our combined four children.

We decided a quick trip to Macy's was in order, to peruse the women's department for some new clothes that would fit our post-baby bodies. After almost breaking into tears because of one too many too-tight pairs of jeans, I put my clothes back on, found Adrienne, and told her I was going to the lingerie section. She gave me a "that's brave" sort of look, and I headed over. I made my way past the push-up bras, teeny tiny lacy underwear, past the lacy, silky nighties, and over to the back wall. The dreaded Back Wall. It's where the "granny panties," girdles, and body shapers are. I had never stopped there before. But times had changed. I was a new mom. I had a new body. I needed a little help.

I reluctantly looked around, and when I was sure the size zero, twenty-something mom in the lacy undies section wasn't watching me, I grabbed an assortment of not-too-hideous-looking body shapers in an assortment of colors and sizes and dashed into the dressing room. Safe in the privacy of my own dressing room, I looked a little more carefully at the labels. Slimming, miracle lifting, tummy control, butt lifter... which shaper had all of these properties? Of course! The ugliest one of the bunch. A nude-colored contraption made of a rigid non-breathable nylon blend. The medium looked a little small, so I opted to try on the large.

I made a conscious decision not to look in the dressing room mirror until I had the shaper on. As I began to shed my clothes, I started picturing how this miracle shaper would transform my newly acquired mom body into a stunning re-creation of my former self. I would buy it on the spot. I wondered if they even had more colors.

I took the shaper off the hanger and debated for a moment if I should step into it or put it on over my head. I decide to step into it. Was it mismarked? The large seemed a little tight. I kept going. Shapers are supposed to be tight to hold your body in. I inched it up, a little at a time. It was getting hot. Did they turn on the heater in the dressing room? I started to sweat. After what seemed to be an extraordinary amount of time of tugging, tucking, pulling, and sucking it in,

I finally got it on. I looked like a stuffed sausage, fat bulging out in all the wrong places, body parts pushed in very strange directions. The heater must have been broken, because it was like a sauna in there. Suddenly, I realized I couldn't breathe. I had to get it off, and quick! Remembering how long it took to pull it on, I decided to take it off over my head. I crossed my arms, reached for the bottom of the shaper, and started to pull it up over my head. Houston, we have a problem! The shaper was so tight, and I so sweaty, that it had completely stuck to my body... and trapped me in it! My arms were straight up in the air, the shaper wound tightly around my arms, head, and upper torso. I looked like a fat caterpillar half out of her cocoon!

The flailing made me sweat even more, and I still couldn't breathe. How was I going to get out of this one? I moved and wriggled around trying to get my hands free so I could pull this thing back down. No luck. I didn't know what to do. New mom hormones still going strong, I started to cry. Just then, I heard Adrienne calling from the front of the dressing room.

"Cres? Are you in there?"

"Yes!" I screamed. "Help!"

She quickly made her way to my room. What a sight poor Adrienne had to endure. There I was, crying, naked from the waist down except for my mom underwear, and the upper half of my body trapped in a shaper! After a moment of silence, she started laughing hysterically! After two moments of silence... I was right there with her. Still trapped and now jumping around and doing the "dance of the deranged caterpillar," we both laughed until our sides hurt.

She helped me out of the absolutely-not-a-miracle body shaper and left me to get dressed.

We met by the escalator, and when I gave her an embarrassed look, she put her arms up in the air and began to hop around and do the "dance." I started laughing, and we headed down the escalator, thus putting an end to our not-so-successful shopping trip.

What Adrienne did for me that afternoon — finding me, coming

to my rescue, and turning my tears to laughter—is the true definition of a best friend.

~Crescent LoMonaco

The Friendship Tree

When friendships are real, they are not glass threads or frostwork,
but the solidest things we can know.
~Ralph Waldo Emerson

Only three weeks into our marriage, Richard and I disagreed on what kind of tree to get for our first Christmas. "How about an artificial one so we don't take the life of a living thing?" I said.

Richard, my traditional husband, wanted a big spruce like the ones from his childhood. Cuddled next to him, I whispered, "How about a live tree that will continue to grow, and grow old with us?"

Richard wasn't ready to give up his holiday custom and I couldn't bear to cut down a tree. We finally agreed that I could buy a small live tree (emphasis on "small") to put on our dining room table, decorated with red ornaments.

The next morning I visited several plant nurseries but couldn't find a tree small enough. At each nursery, I was informed that a spruce (Richard's choice) was meant to grow outside and wouldn't survive indoors. I couldn't give up the idea of having a live tree to enhance our future Christmases.

At a grocery store I found a small conifer-like tree, labeled "Norfolk Island Pine: does well indoors." I'd never heard of Norfolk Island but this tree was the right size, ten inches high with four branches. A slight bend in the trunk just above the first branch added personality, symbolizing hopes for itself and our marriage. I decorated it with tiny ornaments.

Three years later, Richard was offered a job in California. It gave us a chance to experience the West Coast. By this time, our little tree was eighteen inches high and had grown additional branches.

When the mover came to pack our belongings, he told me they couldn't take our tree. "Sorry, Miss, but it's against the law to bring plants into California."

Horrors! That tree was our marriage tree. How could we leave it behind? I called Marian, my best friend from college, and told her about the tree. "I don't know what to do!"

"Since you are driving across country, why don't you stop here first? David and I can take care of your tree while you are on the West Coast."

What a solution! We set off with our packed car for the cross-country adventure, the little tree cradled in my lap. I was elated that our special tree would be in good hands while we were away.

Marian and I spoke once a week by phone. I told her about the fabulous Southern California beaches, and she told me about her latest antique acquisition. I ended each call with a wish for the tree's happiness. She said it was doing very well. "It must be happy," she said. "The bend in the trunk has straightened."

After three years we returned east for Richard's new job in Washington, D.C. Marian and David were expecting their first child. When baby Jessica was born, Richard and I drove to Massachusetts to become godparents and retrieve our tree.

The tree looked great, now over three feet tall. The deep green waxy fronds spread wide and graceful. The bend had straightened, just as Marian described on the phone.

Within a couple of years, Richard and I separated. I moved back to New England to attend school. The tree came with me. At the same time, David and Marian separated. Marian and I continued our weekly phone calls. Our friendship deepened as we adjusted to our new lives. A conversation never closed without an inquiry from her about the tree and my proud response that it was doing well. "You should see how big it has grown. I'm so grateful you kept it for me."

The tree had become a third party to our calls. By now each branch jutted a yard from the trunk. It was taking up more room. In fact, the top reached my ceiling. Now it had no room to stretch to its full height. I was worried.

I received a new job offer and drove to Boston to look for an apartment. None had a tall enough ceiling for my tree, but I had to move in two weeks. "Marian, I don't know how I'm going to keep the tree in Boston. The moving company told me it was too cold outdoors to transport a tropical plant."

Even though it looked like a conifer, my tree was a tropical. After all these years, I had finally learned that Norfolk Island is in New Zealand. The tree would die if subjected to the cold. It was one of the few things that had not changed in my ever-changing life. It had grown old with me, but I couldn't take it to Boston.

"Why don't you find another home for it?" Marian suggested. "Your current location has many homes with cathedral ceilings. The tree would thrive if it had a good home."

"What are you saying? This is the tree that you nursed for me. It is part of our lives, our friendship for all these years."

"Precisely," she responded. "I guess it's time to tell you something about that tree—a long overdue confession."

What could she possibly have to confess?

"About a month after you left the little tree with me, it died." Marian continued. "I tried to keep it alive, but it just didn't make it."

"Oh?" I breathed.

"I didn't have the heart to tell you it had died, so I kept talking about it while you were in California. I knew what it meant to you!" She gulped.

I gulped.

Then she said, "When you and Richard came for Jessica's christening, I panicked. I knew I would have to tell you, but I couldn't. So, David and I found another Norfolk Island Pine." She rushed her words. "We were lucky that it was approximately the same size that your tree might have been after three more years of growth. None of the trees had the same kind of bend in the trunk. That's why I kept telling you it was so happy, its trunk had straightened out."

As I listened to her confession, my heart filled with gratitude and love for this friend and all she had gone through on my behalf.

Marian continued. "Oh dear Devika, even though it's a different tree, it is the one that we have known and loved all these years. Now it's time for you to give it a good new home."

The next week I found a home for the tree. I hired a U-Haul trailer, covered the tree with blankets against the cold, and drove down the parkway to a beautiful house with cathedral ceilings and tall broad windows. The house was full of light. It was also full of plants.

A young couple greeted me at the door and helped get the tree inside. "It's so beautiful," the young wife said. "I've always wanted a live tree in our house." Turning to her husband, she added: "See how tall it is? Perfect for our Christmas this year."

I handed her the box of ornaments my tree had worn through the years. "This tree has bound a friendship for twenty years. I know it will love living with you."

~Devika Jones

Two Girls and Their Dream

It's a lot like nuts and bolts — if the rider's nuts, the horse bolts!
~Nicholas Evans

Two little girls had a dream. But my friend Janelle and I were no longer "little girls." And even though we didn't live in the same place — she in Edmonton, Alberta, Canada, and I in neighbouring British Columbia on Vancouver Island — we still had dreams of things we wanted to do together, even if they were the dreams of little girls.

Despite the fact we were thirty-something with four kids between us, half the time we still acted like little girls — not the adults we were "supposed" to be. So when Janelle purchased a chestnut brown quarter horse named Kye and the owner assured her that Kye would be able to ride two people at the same time, I promptly packed up my kids and caught the next flight to Alberta. As the plane lifted off, I knew that we were about to fulfill our childhood dream. We were going to ride astride one horse together through the fields of Stony Plain, Alberta.

When my plane landed at the airport and we hugged in the terminal, with my two boys and her two girls between us, we knew we were going to have the time of our lives.

I arrived that summer's day to fields dried and charred by the sun. Although this was not the first time my kids had experienced the vastness of the Alberta plains, this was the first time they would be staying overnight with a horse "in residence." Our kids doubled up and took turns riding the horse, two astride. Kye hardly noticed their combined weights.

After a few days of becoming acquainted with Kye, we left the kids with Janelle's husband and set out on our adventure. With camera in hand I walked alongside my friend as she rode her horse, our anticipation building.

Finally we stopped. My partner-in-crime looked down at me from her mighty steed and with a glint in her eye said, "This is it!" I grabbed her outstretched hand, and with a swing of my camera and a flick of my hair, I hauled myself up onto the horse.

At that moment, a passing truck of real cowboys stopped to watch. Great! We would have an audience to bear witness to this momentous occasion!

But we barely had time to absorb the moment we longed for when it started. Though Janelle's blond curls blocked my vision, I quickly realized that I wasn't seeing the horse's ears because of his gait — he was trying to buck us off.

With every buck I rose higher and higher. Our audience in the truck must have had quite a view. I wish they had caught it on film and sent it to *America's Funniest Home Videos*. I would have liked to have seen us on a bucking bronco!

But there was no time for thoughts of television fame. Janelle didn't even finish shouting, "He's goin' — he's goin'!" when that poor horse bucked me right off his derriere, the soles of my feet paying homage to the never-ending blue above me.

For a second I lay stunned, looking into the cloudless sky. The once-lush grass was not as soft as I thought. I thanked every God available I was alive, while also promising I would never do anything stupid again if the camera wasn't broken.

Realizing I wasn't paralyzed, I bolted upright only to see my dear friend sitting (if you can call it that) sideways on the fiercely galloping horse, her hands in a death grip on the reins. I will always remember the sight of her blond curls bouncing in unison with the horse's every gallop.

She would later tell me that she hung on for as long as she could. She knew she risked being dragged if she let go and her foot got caught in a stirrup.

She eventually let go, only to fall you-know-what over teakettle, luckily without a foot stuck in the stirrup. Reins and stirrups flying, the horse's shoed feet mocked us with every gallop as he raced away, the metal shining back at us as if to say "Gotcha!" I ambled over to her and we stared wide-eyed at each other, confused as to what just actually happened.

Unsurprisingly, the cowboys in the truck had fled the scene.

We raced back to Janelle's house and hurried to gather oats and rope, then set out to find the mighty steed. We did catch him. I figure he must have resigned himself to the fact that he was not to be totally outdone. But he had already had his revenge in throwing us off.

We headed home, two limping women and one healthy horse. Shock set in, but with every sore step, laughter replaced shock. Despite our stupidity, we lived to tell the tale, had bruises to show for it, a limp to match, and were as proud as if we won the rodeo. And we had done it together!

We each "got back on the horse" the next day, but were saddened at our lost dream. We knew it would never become a reality—not with this horse, anyway.

But the experience was not only about riding the horse. It was about dreams shared with my friend. We will forever talk about the day we were thrown off a horse—together. I cherish the thought of us as two old ladies, rocking silently side by side, the clicking of our knitting needles the only sound, fondly remembering the days when we could actually climb up on a horse. And when my friend shifts uncomfortably in her rocker, wondering if that bad hip is a result of her not-so-soft landing, I will look at her and smile at how stupid we were.

So no, the horse never gave us the dream that we wanted, but he gave us a memory that we will never forget.

~Lisa McManus Lange

Angels and Cows

A true friend is one who thinks you are a good egg
even if you are half-cracked.
~Author Unknown

Her first wedding was a traditional church wedding. My girlfriend wore white and her father walked her down the aisle. I was there. For her second wedding she and her fiancé eloped. No one was there—not even her parents. Her third wedding was just weird. Really weird. And I was in it. She asked me to be a bridesmaid. I didn't want to do it, but how could I say no? She and I had been friends since junior high school. We had been through a lot together. She was sad I hadn't been in her other two weddings—she didn't have any bridesmaids for those—and she, for sure, wanted me in this wedding. I had to say yes. That's what girlfriends do for each other.

The wedding had a theme. A theme? Couldn't it just be a wedding? Oh no, it had to have a theme. "Angels and cows." What? The significance of the angels and cows theme was known only to the bride and groom. They wouldn't tell us why, but seated on a chair among the guests was a huge life-size stuffed cow... complete with cowbell. The looks on people's faces when they first saw the cow was priceless, and the lucky person who wound up sitting next to the cow during the ceremony had the strangest look on her face!

The bridesmaids took care of the angels part of the theme. Our dresses were a kind of dark, royal blue. The dresses were ankle length and each had a scarf that went with it. The dresses were gauzy so there was a full slip that went underneath. Oh, I forgot to mention one small detail... they had angel faces all over them. Angelic angel faces. And when you looked at them, they looked back at you. They were kind of scary, actually. It was like you were being watched no matter where you looked; someone was always looking back at you. And there was a headpiece that went with the dress. It had flowers like a crown and long cascading ribbons that went down the back. I was expected to wear this creation. The bride wore blue too—and these were the dresses she had chosen for her bridesmaids so we would blend in with her dress. Oh the things we do for our girl-friends! As a bridesmaid there was nothing I could say or do so I kept my mouth shut and wore the dress, and the slip, and the scarf, and the headpiece. But no shoes. We were all barefoot!

The wedding was held in a lovely old house—outside on the patio. Unfortunately it was on a busy street and the traffic was noisy. We dressed in a room right off the entry hall. People kept mistaking the room for a bathroom so while we were dressing a parade of people kept opening the door and coming in. The wedding was due to start at 3:00. The person officiating shall remain nameless because he is a well-known motivational speaker and he was late. 3:00 came but he wasn't there. 3:15 came and went. So did 3:30 and 3:45. Finally the bride and we four bridesmaids decided we would go out and mingle with the guests who, by this time, were quite restless.

We mingled and decided to have a glass of champagne. The only problem was that they had run out of champagne already. And nuts and cheese and crackers and soft drinks and... there was nothing to eat or drink and the wedding hadn't even started. The person in charge of the food kept running out to the store but would only come back with a small amount of food or one bottle of champagne. Never enough to keep the wedding guests happy. I think that was the last event she ever catered!

Finally the celebrity officiator arrived and it was time to start the ceremony. But there was another problem. The person who was supposed to play the didgeridoo for the ceremony flaked out. He was nowhere to be found. Probably went out for a hamburger because of the food situation! A few people finally rolled a piano out of the house onto the patio and someone started to play appropriate wedding music. Too bad the piano was out of tune!

First came the bridesmaids. There was no aisle this time. We approached from different directions. Each of us had been paired up with a friend of the groom. My guy was tall. Rather than stand, the bride had arranged for each couple to sit — in a corner of a square that surrounded the happy couple. Each corner represented one of the four directions... north, south, east and west. Then a person waving an incense burner walked around the square and chanted. The incense smelled like rotten cheese or a goat and I started to sneeze. And the ceremony hadn't even started yet.

Finally it started and I wiped the tears from my face with my angel scarf. Now the angelic angel was crying too. A soft breeze blew the ribbons from my hair into my eyes. I couldn't see and I was sneezing. Then we were all to hold hands and do that togetherness kind of thing. All touchy feely. Yuck. I hate that. The tall guy I was with held my hand and then... and then... he put his hand on my knee! Excuse me, but we were sitting in front of about fifty people including my husband, and he was trying to get fresh! If I had had shoes on I would have taken one off and hit him with it. I smiled and pinched his finger as hard as I could and moved as far away from him as possible. He moved his hand.

When it was time for the vows to be said, a group of about twenty-five motorcyclists drove by. Their motorcycles were loud. During the drive-by nobody could hear anything that was being said by the bride or groom. It was probably a good thing because they had written their own vows and I probably would have started to laugh if they had mentioned anything about the cow. I tend to laugh very easily and that would have been the end of me. I mean here I was, a vision of loveliness, wearing this particularly ugly dress, barefoot, with flowers and ribbons in my hair, sneezing with tears running down my face and being groped by some tall guy. If I had started to laugh that would have been the final straw.

Finally the ceremony was over. My friend was married and happy so I was happy for her. There was no reception after the wedding because we had mingled before the wedding and because there was no food left. There was no champagne toast either because... well you know why. Everyone just left. It was so strange. We had been asked to make sure the cow got home so we drove away with a huge cow taking up the whole back seat of our car. We went out to dinner because we were starving. We didn't even stop at home first so I could change my clothes, although I did put my shoes on. I got some strange looks from the people at the restaurant. I guess they had never seen a grown woman in such a lovely gown as the one I was wearing with wilted flowers and ribbons in my hair. I mean, we all have our terrible-bridesmaid's-dress-that-made-me-look-really-ugly story, but I think this one takes the cake. Hmm—come to think of it, they didn't have a cake at the wedding.

The saddest thing is the marriage didn't last more than a few months and I wore that stupid dress for nothing. And I guess the cow was put out to pasture. We never saw it again. But I love my friend and I see her on a regular basis. I have excused her temporary insanity, both for marrying that guy and for having that wedding.

Ah, the things we do for our girlfriends.

~Madison Thomas

72

Chicken Soup for the Soul

Time Out with a Friend

But if the while I think on thee, dear friend,
All losses are restored and sorrows end.
~William Shakespeare

y friend Ruth and I had talked about vacationing together at the beach for years. Every summer we'd declare this was the year. We took out our day planners, threw some dates back and forth, but nothing ever materialized. Other things always seemed more pressing.

But in the summer of 2004, I got serious about the matter. My daughter—my only child—had just graduated from high school and I had run around in circles like a wild woman, trying to do a million things in the months prior. The frantic pace had left me wrung out and done in.

And that was just the physical side. Emotionally, I was an even bigger mess. Not only was I facing an empty nest, I was about to turn fifty and, quite frankly, I was terrified. I just needed to get away from it all. I needed to hear myself think.

So, one afternoon I sent Ruth an e-mail and said, in essence, it's now or never, girlfriend. She must have sensed my desperation, because in a few weeks we had set a date.

"I'm buying my plane ticket tomorrow," I told her one evening. "No backing out now."

"I'll be there," she said. I knew she meant it. As youngsters, Ruth and I had spent summers together. She'd traveled with my family on vacations. We double dated as young women, and kept in touch after marrying, even though we lived hundreds of miles from each other. Distance kept us apart, yes, but Ruth and I were always there for each other in spirit. I couldn't wait to see her again.

Since we're both beach lovers, the plan was for me to fly to her hometown of Jackson, Mississippi. We'd drive a few hours to a beach condo in Orange Beach, Alabama, positioned right on the amazing emerald Gulf Shores, then spend six days doing whatever, whenever. No time restraints. No responsibilities.

It sounded like a fairy tale. The mere thought that I might actually rest while on vacation sent delighted chills up my spine. I wasn't sure I had ever done such a thing.

The days leading up to my departure seemed eternal, but finally, on a sunny Saturday morning, there I stood in baggage claim, waiting for my suitcase to appear, when I heard a familiar voice calling my name. I hadn't seen Ruth in ten years, but running toward each other, the time melted away.

Stuffing the luggage into the car, we headed southeast. By evening we stood on the balcony of our condo, gazing out at an ocean stretched like a shiny blue tray, as far as the eye could see. Almost paradise.

"Oh, my!" Ruth said, her voice taking on that giddy pitch that makes her so charming. "I can't believe we did this!"

I giggled like a schoolgirl. "Me neither. I keep thinking I'll feel guilty, but I don't. Isn't this fabulous?"

As I prepared for bed that evening, I wrote in my journal: "Vacationing with family is wonderful, but sometimes the heart needs to rest with a friend."

The next six days were filled with a simple richness that surpassed my expectations.

Mornings — defined as whenever we got up — found us drinking coffee at a sunny table on the balcony. Just below, an azure ocean stretched as far as the eye could see, while the waves splashed rhythmically to the shore, and back again, as if taking our worries with them.

Except for one day we'd flagged for shopping, our afternoons were unplanned and unhurried. We soaked up the sun. We took naps. We strolled along white beaches, looking for seashells. We stressed about nothing, barely keeping up with what day it was.

One afternoon found us reclined in beach chairs, kicking our feet in the sand, feeling the wind in our hair. It had been a difficult day for me. Ruth knew I had arrived with some concerns, one being that my daughter had announced she would not be attending college in the fall, but was going to get her own place and continue working full-time instead. She was barely eighteen, and I feared that she was making the wrong decision. I felt helpless and afraid.

As I sat there, pondering this, a sigh escaped my lips. Not a big sigh, but just enough to be heard.

"You have to let her go, Dayle." Ruth interrupted my thoughts. She has a unique way of knowing what I'm thinking, and exactly what to say. With her son close to graduating college, she and I had carried on this conversation before in e-mails and letters. "The hardest part for me with my son," she said, "was giving up control and understanding that he has to make his own choices... and his own mistakes."

"You're right, my friend," I said, "but why does it have to be so blooming hard?"

She had the audacity to laugh. "It really will get better. It really will."

Hearing her say so boosted my mood and affirmed, again, why I had come here.

Evening hours were perhaps my favorite of all. Ruth generally concocted some delicious sweet something—loaded with calories—I'd brew a pot of coffee, and we'd end the day on the balcony, much in the same way it had begun. Our conversations were comfortable and unforced. At times we laughed so hard it hurt, remembering funny stories of yesterday. Other times, we uncovered our souls, revealing old scars and some fresh wounds. Then there were times when we said nothing at all.

During those still moments, I recalled the words of Anne Morrow Lindbergh. "Here on the island," she wrote in *Gift from the Sea*, "I find I can sit with a friend without talking, sharing the day's last sliver of pale green light on the horizon."

One evening, we sat on the balcony, watching the sun set in a smear of red. While a slender candle flickered behind a hurricane glass, we talked of life and love, and then the subject turned to Lori.

I'll never forget the day in 1988 when Ruth called to say that her two-year-old daughter had been diagnosed with neuroblastoma, a common childhood cancer, with no known cure. I remember collapsing into a chair and weeping at the news. Lori had been born eleven days before my Anna Marie. I assumed our girls would grow up and become friends. But life takes tragic turns sometimes. Two years later—after a courageous fight for her life—Lori passed away.

In the difficult years following her daughter's death, Ruth and I talked often. We cried together. We prayed together. We talked about the hereafter.

"It's hard to believe that Lori would be Anna's age now," Ruth said. "Eighteen!"

"I know. It seems impossible she's been gone that long," I said. "Does it ever get easier?"

She thought a minute. "In time, you don't cry as much. You just learn to cope."

"I can't imagine your pain, Ruth."

"And I hope you never have to," she said, her voice filled with emotion.

The next day I received a call from home. Anna Marie had been involved in an accident, totaling her little yellow Mustang. Other than a few bruises, she was fine.

I wanted to fly home immediately, but my husband said no, things were all right, please don't worry.

I hung up the phone and let the tears fall. Ruth walked over and hugged me tight. "Thank God she's okay, Dayle."

I could only nod, thinking what Ruth knew so well already: Life is uncertain. There's no promise of tomorrow.

On our final night together, I was somewhat surprised by my feelings. Part of me felt sad to be leaving the seashore behind, saying goodbye to my dear friend, not knowing when we'd meet like this again, or if we'd ever get to. Yet part of me was ready to get back to the world of deadlines and demands. I felt energized, ready to resume my life.

As I mulled this over, the reason became clear. My goal had been accomplished! I had come here fragmented and worn out, but spending quality time with a friend had made me whole again. I was now equipped for the next stretch of the road.

Later I would write in my journal: "Every woman needs unhurried time in which to refuel and replenish her energies. Time out with a friend is the perfect solution."

~Dayle Allen Shockley

73

Camping 101

Camping: The art of getting closer to nature
while getting farther away from the nearest cold beverage,
hot shower and flush toilet.
~Author Unknown

Anyone who's known me for more than five seconds knows I'm not an outdoor person. I love the beauty of nature, but I prefer to see it from the comfort of a beautiful hotel window, or in a beach-facing restaurant while I'm eating brunch.

Somehow, however, I've always surrounded myself with girlfriends who are nature lovers. No... nature freaks! You know, those people who enjoy hiking, dirt trails, swimming in lakes—which I fondly refer to as "nature water"—and the like.

In college, I had a tireless group of girlfriends who begged me to experience the great outdoors with them. I finally relented and agreed to go (gulp) camping for the first time!

We decided to stick fairly close to home, in case I decided to chicken out and go home early. We drove the forty-five minutes up the mountain to Upper Oso Campground. It was a Friday night and almost dusk. My girlfriends immediately went to work. They scurried around unloading supplies, setting up tents, building a campfire, and whatever else nature freaks do to get ready for camping. What a lot of work!

I decided I'd better pitch in, so one by one, I asked my friends if there was something I could do to help. Knowing that I was not the outdoor type and that I didn't know Thing One about camping, each of my friends replied with a "we'll get this" attitude, and dismissed me. I wouldn't give up! I figured as long as I'd agreed to this adventure, I was going to do it whole-heartedly. I continued to offer my assistance until they finally caved and agreed to let me put the food away for the night.

Nightfall. Tents up, check. Campfire burning, check. Lanterns in place, check. Food put away, check! It was time to relax by the fire. There we stayed for hours—just us girls talking, laughing, and sharing our most intimate secrets. That's what girlfriends do when we are out in nature. Discussing very important things that college girls do, well into the night. We learned so much about each other. Lots of family stories, what we all planned to do after college, what inspired us, and what turned us off... which led back to the discussion of me not liking the outdoors. How, by the way, was I enjoying it so far? So far, so good.

One by one, we all turned in. I slept pretty well in my tent, complete with an air mattress and sleeping bag that had been wrapped around a rock that had been heated by the campfire (learning camping tricks already). Hmmm—maybe this wasn't so bad. I drifted off and thought of a delicious breakfast at the picnic table, under a canopy of oak trees. Really, this camping thing wasn't too bad after all.

The next morning, I woke to the sound of my friend Adrienne, yelling, "Hey! Where's all the food?" I quickly unzipped my tent and went over to the picnic area. By now, the others had gathered and were asking the same question. As I walked over, they all looked at me. "Crescent," they asked, "did you put away the food last night?" Of course I did! I put it all into the brown paper grocery bags, rolled the bags up tightly so no bugs could get in, and set the bags on the picnic table. They all stepped aside, giving me a clear view of the table, and there, amongst the shredded paper bags, was one lonely bagel with a single, tiny little bite taken out of it. Nothing else remained.

My girlfriends and I sat down around the picnic table, discussing which of us (me, of course) would drive back into town to get more food. As we were in the middle of our discussion, a tiny little squirrel ran past us, dragging an entire bagel through our campsite. We began laughing hysterically at what I'd done and it was at that moment that my nature freak friends and I decided I was hereby excused from any future nature trips. Thank goodness for that!

~Crescent LoMonaco

74

The Life of the Party

Lots of people want to ride with you in the limo, but what you want is someone who will take the bus with you when the limo breaks down.
~Oprah Winfrey

I didn't know what to do. So I cried. Hard. My housemates came into my room to find out what had caused my outburst. Liz and Stacey stood on either side of me, each with a hand on my shoulder or back.

"What's wrong?" Liz asked.

"I can't go to New Orleans," I said between sobs.

Looking back now, I realize I might've overreacted a bit. But, at twenty, the prospect of missing this once-in-a-lifetime experience with my friends was devastating. Our school's basketball team had just made it to the Final Four and all of my friends were going to the game. Up until that afternoon, so was I.

I had gone to nearly all of the home games, and a bunch of us traveled to follow the Orangemen during March Madness. After watching the team win the Elite Eight in Albany, New York, I was wicked excited to go to the Final Four. In New Orleans, of all places! It was going to be amazing.

We had the trip planned. Six of us would travel together — fly out Thursday to Mobile, Alabama, stay overnight, and catch a bus to New Orleans on Friday. We'd have all of Saturday to check out Bourbon Street and catch the semi-final games, tour around more on Sunday, see the championship game on Monday, and fly back Tuesday afternoon.

I had a brief presentation scheduled for that Tuesday at noon—part of a series of brief presentations each student had to make with only two scheduled for each class. So I figured I could reschedule mine, no problem. Wrong.

At class the Tuesday after the Elite Eight win—a week before my scheduled presentation—my professor announced no one could reschedule a presentation. No exceptions, no excuses.

I, of course, still tried. I had an extenuating circumstance. A once-in-a-lifetime opportunity. My professor would understand. I was a good student, always in class with my assignments done on time. Surely she'd let me change this arbitrarily chosen presentation date.

Nope. She didn't budge. I could come to class and present, or not and take a zero. At best, I'd get a B in the class. Not acceptable.

That's what landed me in my room, angry and crying.

I had calmed down enough to explain this all to Liz and Stacey.

"Okay, so you have to be back in time for class on Tuesday," Liz said. "Not a big deal, just leave Monday night."

"Good idea," I said. It wasn't ideal—I didn't love the idea of traveling by myself—but better than not going at all.

With that settled, Stacey left my room. Liz had taken charge of booking our trip, so she immediately went online to revise it for me.

"What time is your presentation again?" she asked.

"Noon."

"So if we leave right after the game Monday night, we can catch the bus to Mobile at 11 p.m., get on a 6 a.m. flight and be back in time for your class."

"We?" I asked.

"Yeah, of course," Liz said. "I'm going back with you."

That brought on more tears. Without a question or second

thought, she planned to travel through the night with me. We'd miss celebrating, or commiserating, with everyone on Bourbon Street.

"Are you sure? I don't want to ask you to do that."

"You're not making that trip by yourself. I'm going with you," she said matter-of-factly.

I hugged her, grateful beyond words. We had been friends since the end of freshmen year and had grown fairly close over the past year and a half. But still, I hadn't expected this. What a selfless act of friendship. And it turned into an even bigger deal when Syracuse won the championship. The minute the buzzer rang, we rushed out of the stadium, went to our hotel, picked up our stuff, and hauled butt through the partying streets of New Orleans to catch our bus.

As we waited to board, I turned to Liz, and from the bottom of my heart thanked her. I knew it wasn't easy to leave. All of our friends were either celebrating on Bourbon Street or back at school. Still in our Syracuse gear, even people on the bus looked at us oddly, obviously questioning why we were leaving early.

I fell asleep at some point on the ride to Mobile, and don't even remember the flight home. It all went smoothly, though, because I got back to school in time for class and I made my presentation.

We might've missed the party of a lifetime. But a decade later, that's not what matters. That night I realized I had a friend for life. And I still do.

~Kristiana Glavin Pastir

Chapter
9

Just Us Girls

Distant and Close

75

One of Us Has Breast Cancer

Some people go to priests; others to poetry; I to my friends.
~Virginia Woolf

I come from the South and grew up in a tight-knit circle of friends, so when something happens to one of us, it happens to us all. Louise, the larger than life, funny member of the group, now lives in Sun Valley, Idaho. Louise has a sense of humor that literally reduces her to tears and it tends to be contagious. She's also the organizer and plan maker who got it in her head one day to have Tama and me fly out to her home in the mountains for an extended weekend. Tama and I immediately fell in line, our husbands were alerted, our dates were set, and our plane tickets were secured. Tama and I were on our way, she from her home in Memphis and I from mine in L.A. Eight days before our scheduled departure, my phone rang. I looked at the display illuminating Louise's name and thought, "No doubt some sort of instruction is coming," but it turned out that wasn't the case. When I picked up the phone, Louise was crying.

"What is it?" I asked.

"Tama has breast cancer," Louise said, without preamble.

"What?" I asked again, only this time, with an entirely different inflection. This time, I meant two things: Did I hear you correctly? How in the world could this possibly be true?

I'll say this about all of us reared in the South: we know how to do. We know how to step up, we know the perfect gesture for everything no matter what you're talking about, and we know how to meet all of life's emergencies. We pretty much slide into an automated code of proper behavior because that's what our Southern mothers passed down to us.

"What should we do?" I asked Louise, because it was the first thing that came to mind.

"I think we should call off y'all coming out here," Louise said.

"Alright, is that what Tama wants to do?" I asked.

"Tama doesn't know what she wants to do. Her family is freaking out," Louise reported.

"I'm not going to call her today—when did she find out?"

"Yesterday," Louise interjected. "They called with her mammogram results, said they found a mass and wanted to do a biopsy, which Tama didn't bother to tell us, and now they're telling her it's cancer. Now she's telling us."

"I don't even know what to say," I exhaled.

"Call Tama tomorrow anyway," Louise directed.

You have to understand that Tama is a woman of few words. She's not one of those superfluous talkers; she simply contributes to a conversation with as few words as possible and leaves the floor to everybody else. She doesn't feel the need to position herself front and center, and this is exactly why Louise and I have always deferred to her.

The next day, I called Tama.

"God, it's always something," Tama said.

"Seriously, is there anything I can do?" I asked.

"Yes, come over here and tell my kids I'm not dead yet," Tama said, deflecting the gravity of the moment.

The three of us went on that way for days, back-and-forthing over the telephone, vacillating between drama and sarcasm, comparing thoughts and notes and ideas and stories of people who had gone through something similar and achieved a happy outcome until Tama's doctors presented her with a concrete, step-by-step agenda that would begin within the month. But I still didn't really know what to say—or do—for my friend.

Finally, one day, Louise came up with a plan. "I think y'all should still come out here," she said. "Tama says she may as well wait out here for the inevitable."

"Alright, let's airlift Tama on outta there; we may as well," I agreed.

I've found out that it's the little things you do in support of a friend who has breast cancer that end up truly mattering. For four unscheduled days, we followed Tama's lead, monitoring the understandable yet unpredictable fluidity of her emotions and finding the delicate balance between activity and restorative reprieve.

We had lunch with Louise's friends in Sun Valley, went shopping, and took long walks on the mountain trails. When Tama teared up, we teared up. ("Y'all let me cry now because I'm not going to cry in front of my husband or my kids when I get home," Tama said.) And when the look on her otherwise stoic face suggested she was overwhelmed, we simply retreated to Louise's house and took a nap no matter the time of day.

We spent a lot of time talking about our intertwined childhoods, our histories and our families, yet oddly enough, we didn't spend a lot of time dwelling on what was to come for Tama in the following months. For whatever reason, Tama just wanted to be, and Louise and I had the unspoken graciousness to just be right alongside her.

It's been a year and three months now and in that time, the harrowing, incremental progression of Tama's breast cancer has included multiple surgeries, chemotherapy, radiation, hair loss, ongoing hives, and reconstructive surgery. As friends in support, Louise and I keep vigil by demanding blow-by-blow details, sending presents, making phone calls and hanging on every twist and turn of her progress. It appears that the worst is behind her as there is no sign of the cancer's return. Tama's hair has grown back beautifully and she looks and feels like a glowing million dollars. In my heart of hearts, I believe that Tama will forever be one of the fortunate breast cancer survivors. Although there were times during her travails when I questioned whether anything I could do would ever help, I have realized that it is enough just to try and it is enough just to be there.

~Claire Fullerton

76

Good Night, Gracie

Can miles truly separate you from friends...
If you want to be with someone you love,
aren't you already there?
~Richard Bach

I t's not very often you meet someone who affords you the luxury of seeing life in a whole new light. The kind of friend that makes you wonder what you ever did without her.

Gracie and I have a friendship that defies explanation. I have always held the deepest belief that God works in mysterious ways. My friendship with Gracie is proof of that.

Our first conversation took place on a hot and muggy August afternoon. I received a call from a woman in Wyoming. She introduced herself as an advocate from a women's shelter. My sister had moved to Wyoming months before and Gracie's call was to inform me that she was helping my sister escape a potentially dangerous situation there. Gracie had helped my sister relocate to a safe house, and since my sister wasn't allowed contact with her family, Gracie would now be the go-between who kept me up to speed on how my sister was doing.

It wasn't easy since Wyoming was where the trouble was brewing and I was home in Chicago feeling helpless. But there was something about this soft-spoken woman that I liked. She brought a sense of calm to this volatile situation, which made it all the more devastating when, without warning, her phone calls stopped.

Even though her original reason for calling was traumatic, I found myself missing our long-distance interactions. And worst of all I had no explanation why the calls ended so abruptly.

Through some of our past conversations I had learned that we had much in common—the same stirrings, desires, and creative goals, and they were all tied together by a thread of Christian values.

Now, with the phone silent between us, I had no choice but to rationalize that maybe under different circumstances, Gracie and I could've possibly been the best of friends.

Little did I know the chance would come about a month later.

One night, out of the blue, the phone rang and it was Gracie. This time her reason for calling was strictly personal. Thankfully the problem that had originally brought us together was now safely resolved. This time she wasn't calling as an advocate for my sister. She was calling as a friend. The soft-spoken voice of a stranger became the familiar voice of someone special.

We soon went from dialing each other on the phone, to letting our fingers do the talking in e-mails after soaring phone bills caused my usually patient husband to bellow, "You called Wyoming HOW many times last month?"

We are two different women from two different worlds, connecting with the same spiritual and emotional hunger, quenched only by the bonding of our kindred hearts.

When our families are tucked into peaceful slumber, our cyberspace pajama parties convene, with the tap, tap, tapping on a computer keyboard that can be heard well into the night.

We are middle-aged women whose newfound friendship has brought out the kid in each of us. We are facing menopause with the vitality that's usually reserved for giggling teenagers. Together we are laughing our way through graying hair, expanding waistlines and wrinkles that are multiplying faster than candles on a birthday cake.

We are learning that you are never too old to be young at heart.

Under different circumstances it's doubtful our worlds would have ever collided.

Through the most tumultuous time of my life, Gracie helped me to ride out the darkness of a brutal storm and then returned to enjoy the beauty of its rainbow, a symbol of our deep and promising friendship.

It is sometimes hard to fathom how a woman I have never physically met has become the one friend I have been searching for all my life.

I begin each new day with a good morning e-mail to my dear friend in Wyoming. And each night, after all the doors are locked and the house is settled down in the quiet of sleep, I type in my final message of the evening. "Good night Gracie," and with those three little words I thank God for the blessing of this long-distance friend.

Her friendship fuels my soul with a deep contentment that no amount of miles can diminish. And I know that, with God's grace, we'll continue to weave a lifetime of memories into a tapestry of everlasting friendship and love.

~Kathy Whirity

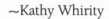

Chicken Soup for the *Soul*

New Friends, Faraway Friends, Forever Friends

Hold a true friend with both your hands.
~Nigerian Proverb

The tour guide stood at the front of our bus, microphone in hand. "You can visit the fantastic aquarium," she said, "or you can shop along Baltimore's harbor."

My choice was lunch and shopping, but I wasn't quite sure what my new friend would choose. Mavis looked at me and announced in her musical voice, "A fish is just a fish, but shopping...!" I nodded my head in agreement, and we both laughed. Dozens of women on the convention spouse tour left the bus and headed in various directions.

We had a wonderful afternoon eating crab bisque on a restaurant's outdoor deck, the special scent of the sea and sight of the boats bobbing in the harbor making it a memorable meal. We had a perfect view of one of the tall ships, sails furled. Both of us ate with relish and talked about our children, who were close in age, then browsed the quaint little shops. Mavis bought a small teddy bear for a grandchild soon to be born but was at a loss when it came time to pay. She held out a handful of American coins. "Nancy, find the ones I need to pay." We giggled like schoolgirls as I picked out the correct amount.

As the tour bus sped back to our nation's capital, I reflected on the past days. My husband, Ken, and I had gone to the huge cocktail party on the opening night of this weeklong bank convention. There had to be 300 or more people in the large ballroom. We didn't know a soul, so we slowly walked across the room, holding our drinks. Another couple was doing the same from the opposite side. He was tall and slim, and she was short, blond, and a bit on the round side. We met in the center, smiled at one another and introduced ourselves.

We could not have been more opposite. My husband headed a small trust department in a bank in a mid-sized college community in Kansas. Mike headed the trust department of a very large British bank in Johannesburg, South Africa. Despite the thousands of miles between our homes and different cultures, we hit it off immediately. Ken and I had been invited to a party later that evening given by an investment company. Ken asked our new acquaintances to accompany us. "Is it alright to crash a party in America?" Mike asked. Ken assured him it was okay if they were with us. I rolled my eyes at my husband but seconded the invitation.

The pattern was set for the remainder of the week. Mike and Ken attended meetings all day while Mavis and I headed for the spouse tours. The four of us had dinner together each evening at various restaurants near our hotel. We traded information about our towns, our families, and our backgrounds. We ate and laughed and soaked in the atmosphere of Washington, D.C. The bond between us became stronger with each day. It pleased me that the men got along as well as Mavis and I did.

Finally, the last day arrived. As we'd done each morning, Mavis and I met in the hotel coffee shop for breakfast. Ken and Mike had eaten earlier before their final meeting. For the first time, I was not enjoying myself with my new friend. Only because I knew I would never see this witty, warm woman again.

I felt as if I'd known her for twenty years, not a mere week. I pushed my scrambled eggs round and round on my plate, my appetite suddenly gone.

"We must write one another, Nancy," Mavis said as she poured each of us a second cup of coffee. We exchanged addresses and lingered as long as possible. When we could delay no longer, the two of us walked to the elevator and I pushed the button a bit harder than necessary.

I told Mavis how very much I'd enjoyed the week, but my voice quavered as I did so.

She put her arms around me and we gave one another the warmest of hugs. Sometimes, a hug can convey so much more than words. This dear woman stepped back and in her British accent said, "I know we will see each other again."

As I looked into her blue eyes, part of me believed her while another piece of me thought, "Fat chance of that!" The lump in my throat was so big that all I could do was nod, give her another quick hug, and flee inside the elevator. The tears flowed as I walked down the hall to our room. How awful, I thought, to have such a wonderful new friend only to lose her at the end of a week.

It turned out that Mavis was right and I was wrong. We sent letters across the ocean, then faxed messages, and finally started chatting via e-mail. Now, we even Skype one another.

In the twenty-four years since we met, Mike and Mavis have visited our home three times. On each of those visits, we have taken them to parts of the States they haven't seen before. We have gone to South Africa to visit them twice, where they squired us from one end of their beautiful country to the other. We have met in England, Ireland, and Germany to travel together, spending three weeks each time in one another's company. I am always sad for our time together to end.

We have been warmly welcomed by Mike and Mavis's children whenever we have visited their homes in South Africa and England. Our children have graciously hosted our dear friends when they have visited here in our country. Over the years, the circle of friendship grew to include our extended families.

We clicked that first night in Washington, D.C. and our friend-ship strengthened more and more through the years. We have shared our hopes and concerns for our children. We have heralded the arrival of each other's grandchildren, one by one. We have laughed together, we have held deep discussions about our individual countries. We've chuckled over the senior moments we all seem to have now, and we have savored this unusual friendship. We are two couples from dif-ferent parts of the world who found they had a great deal in common. Once we were new friends, then faraway friends and finally, forever friends.

~Nancy Julien Kopp

78

No One Is a Stranger

Everyone has a gift for something,
even if it is the gift of being a good friend.
~Marian Anderson

I'm a military brat. My father was a marine officer before my birth and until I started high school. We moved twelve times in fourteen years. When people learn this, they ask, "How did you ever make friends with anyone? That must have been hard on you."

I know my parents worried about my three brothers and me every time we changed schools. Military transfers happened often and they happened fast—usually within a few weeks of orders. If my family wasn't in transition, then someone we knew was moving.

But I don't think it was difficult. Quite the opposite is true. Each move was an opportunity to grow and a chance for adventure.

About once a year my parents announced, "We're being transferred." Then the map came out and we'd huddle.

"This is where we are. This is where we're going." My father's fingers landed on our current home, and with the other hand, he pinpointed our final destination.

My mother reminded us, "You may be sad about leaving your best friend here, but you will make a new one where we're going."

I learned she was right.

Even though I left behind best buddies, I never dreaded the moves or shed tears when we left one military base for another. I can't say we enjoyed goodbyes as we waved to friends out the car window, but military families learn to adjust and even anticipate the journey.

At every base, there was a mass of children to befriend. And each military child was connected. We each knew the angst of leaving behind friends and the eagerness to make new ones. We felt the sadness of leaving behind a favorite hiding place mingled with the thrill of finding a new one at the next locale. We discovered the East had true changes of season that were completely different from the short autumns and winters of the West. We were exposed to each state's history and these experiences were a common thread among military children.

Military transfers taught me the meaning of acceptance. Diversity was something to be embraced, not shunned. I heard the twang of Louisianans, the slow drawl of Texans, and the "far out" of laidback Californians. I learned Northerners and Southerners have opposite demeanors. I learned no matter where someone came from, or how different we were, we had something in common that could be the foundation of a friendship.

As an adult, the moves we made have served me well. Meeting folks from different backgrounds gave me the ability to mingle in a crowd of strangers. As a military child, I didn't wait for someone to befriend me; I stepped up and introduced myself. A kid is just a kid, no matter their birthplace. And there was always the chance of another transfer looming around the corner. Like a sprinter near the finish line, when I made friends, each second counted.

Knowing we're all on the busy racetrack of life, I still rely on this trait. If I see someone standing alone at a party, I'll head towards them with a smile. If I see someone sitting alone at the doctor's office, I'll strike up a conversation. Yes, at times the other person may not be receptive, but there's always the chance the first hello will become a forever friend.

I stay in touch with several from my childhood. Karen gives me accommodations when I'm in California. Elizabeth opens her doors when I'm in Virginia. We don't live close to one another or see each other often, but we value our friendship and reminisce about the adventure our military upbringing provided.

Because of my military experience, my adult friends are varied and numerous. They keep my life dynamic. They challenge me to be a better person, give me support during down times, and grant forgiveness for my flaws.

As a military brat I can't say, "I've lived in this house for twenty years." But I'm blessed to have gained lifelong friendships and characteristics that move my life in a positive direction every day.

~Gail Molsbee Morris

79

Women of Letters

*To send a letter is a good way to go somewhere without moving anything
but your heart.*
~Phyllis Theroux

My one-week suitcase bulged with two weeks of clothing. Fifty-four years old, I was filled with the excitement of a ten-year-old when faced with the prospect of meeting my pen pal—someone I only knew through the scores of e-mails Pamela and I had shot back and forth through cyberspace over the last couple of years.

Ours had been an unlikely pairing. I was a lifetime Midwesterner, married, with two almost-grown kids. Pamela was a New Yorker, single, a French teacher who had spent most of her life living with and later caring for her mom, a first-generation immigrant.

I live in a house surrounded by Iowa farmland, and Pamela lives in an apartment in Queens. The 1,100 miles between us were erased by our common love of writing, a discovery we both made in our fifties.

Our first correspondence occurred in 2005 after we'd submitted essays to an AARP publication. Total strangers, we were both coming to terms with our new calling as writers and were wondering if we had anything of value to say to the world. After we'd submitted 400-word essays on AARP's topic of the month, "What I Really Know About Letter Writing," Pamela reached out to me with an e-mail:

You don't know me, but I noticed we were both on the list that was not chosen for the hard copy magazine. It looks like AARP wants to use our essays on a website. That was three weeks ago and I've not heard a thing. Have you found out when our stories might appear?

I'll admit I was a bit reluctant to answer her note. At my age, I really wasn't interested in collecting new friends, especially ones I'd never see. But I'd been wondering about my essay, feeling like a failure with a rejection letter in hand, and I found comfort in Pamela's words. Maybe we weren't failures if, instead of hard copy, our work could appear on a website. And at least I would not fail alone.

"No. I haven't heard anything either, but I'll watch the website," I wrote back. We made a pact to let each other know as soon as we heard from AARP.

Our friendship sprouted. Our stories did appear several weeks later, accompanied by beautiful artwork—a very nice look, we decided. Both of us were nostalgic about the lost art of pen-on-paper communication, and we'd approached "letter writing" from two unique perspectives. Via e-mail discussion, Pamela and I decided that we'd done a pretty darn good job, and maybe we could support each other on our quest to publish. So we continued a series of e-mails back and forth between Iowa and New York, forging our writing skills and our friendship one word at a time.

Pamela and I made a habit of trading our essays and asking for input. We constructed a friendship built of carefully chosen words and mutual respect. Pamela's work was brainy and well thought out. Mine was gritty and random, but we enjoyed our differences and gleaned writing tips and submission opportunities from one another.

As destiny is inclined to do, it finally brought two keyboard tappers together geographically in the summer of 2007. My family thought I was nuts to choose to meet a total stranger (probably an axe murderer) in the largest city in the United States. But my college-aged daughter was spending the summer in New York, providing me with a perfect excuse to meet my pen pal.

We agreed to rendezvous at Le Pain Quotidien, a bustling Midtown Manhattan hangout where Pamela said we could share a light lunch. But the evening before our date, I panicked. How would I find one stranger in a city of eight million? We had not exchanged photos or planned secret gestures—tools that could identify either one of us in a crowd. I went to the keyboard and zapped Pamela a frantic e-mail.

"How will we find one another?" I asked. "I am middle aged and short. I have freckles and brown hair."

Pamela too must have wondered how we would connect. "I am African American with medium length hair," she typed. I smiled, thinking how we might look together, a pale rural tourist and a suave city sophisticate, strangers seeking common ground.

To my eager eyes, every person who hurried through the door at Le Pain the next day was African American with medium length hair. I must have lurched toward at least six women, my mouth half open with a nervous unspoken greeting, when I felt a tap on my shoulder. "I'm Pamela," she said and led me to a table. We chatted non-stop like reunited girlfriends. Our virtual friendship took on a verbal dimension.

Loud New York conversation was a prelude to resumed silent e-mail back home; Pamela and I became connected in more personal ways. Over the next few years, at our keyboards, we met our respective friends, traded travel tales and confessed our food weaknesses. We swapped fitness frustrations and shared our holiday traditions. Gingerly, we stepped out of cyberspace to exchange travel postcards, favorite books and finally, irresistible holiday goodies.

Now, when planning infrequent New York trips, I reserve a "Pamela afternoon," and she always finds time for me in her busy schedule. When she learned that I had majored in art, we added museums to our list of places to visit together. Pamela, the best personal tour guide in New York, is in tune with her city and in touch with the art world in a way I deeply admire. She's uncovered great local food spots for us, and we always leave each other regretfully, mid-sentence, vowing to reserve more time for our next meeting.

Back home in front of my laptop, I happily pluck Pamela's messages from an inbox infested with advertisements, forwarded jokes, and chain letter threats. I eagerly devour her witty essays and encouraging messages. She seems to know the writer I hope to be, and I try to reciprocate her sincerity across miles of thin air.

Ignoring my initial inclination to run from a new friendship was a blessing. I'm thankful she found me, honored to call Pamela a loyal, cherished friend. A kindred spirit. As time adds layers of meaning to our messages, I'm always excited to find where our words will take us, both as writers and as friends.

~Kristi Paxton

80

Fraternity Sisters

Friendship improves happiness, and abates misery,
by doubling our joys, and dividing our grief.
~Marcus Tullius Cicero

e met at a Rutgers University Homecoming Game when I was a twenty-one-year-old bride. I was anxious because I was the new kid on the block—I'd married my Rutgers alumnus that summer.

Just being married felt weird. The prospect of meeting all of my husband's old college friends and their wives—it was even more daunting than I'd expected.

The other women I was being introduced to were a bit older, and more connected already. I'd heard their names, and I'd met some in the blur of our wedding reception.

I remember fussing over what to wear and finally settling on the wrong choice: a plaid wool dress that itched and was far too warm in the blast of October sun.

Besides, I couldn't keep the women's names straight, and felt like an idiot.

But I can still remember how warmly I was welcomed, and how my instant feeling was one of relief. These women were new in my life, but lovely and warm.

I exhaled—and by the end of the day, I finally learned who was who.

That was back in 1960.

I can tell you with certainty that not one of us, back then, could have imagined how this sisterhood of women would bond. Or that we would still be together more than five decades later.

But here we are, women who married crew-cut college guys whose bond was a past we didn't even share—New Jersey's state college, Rutgers, was an all-male school when our husbands started there as freshmen in 1950.

No one could have imagined that in so many ways we would grow up together, we Rutgers wives, and share every imaginable milestone.

Nor could we have foreseen, in our youthful naïveté back then, that bad things happen to good people.

By the time we were in our early forties, Don and Dick were tragically gone. One heart attack, one terrible car accident.

The losses only drew us closer.

And yes, their widows (such a strange word, back then) remarried, but stayed with us. We women all recognized that while our guys were the core, we had something that was growing as special as what they had. The "ZBT Group," as it is still affectionately known in tribute to the fraternity the boys had loved, bonded us, their wives, as surely as it had bonded them.

So together, we wives built our own foundation. Together, we survived early marriage, kids, mortgages—the station wagon years—and then a torrent of change.

The world had changed from our coming-of-age days when marriage was the finish line, the happily-ever-after. Suddenly, some of us were back in school, some were entering the world of work, and all of us held fast to each other as social revolutions were changing the earth under our feet.

It was an amazing, interesting, challenging time. And we were ever grateful that we had each other as life support in the murky waters of change.

Officially, our gatherings were spaced out to about five times a year. But the ties that bound us didn't depend on the calendar, we learned. A phone call for reassurance, a note hastily scribbled before e-mails, a visit and a hug when the going got really tough—these things meant that the miles separating us didn't matter so much.

We marched through the inexorable toll of losses and sadness—and celebrated the triumphant times—together.

We buried our parents, wept at the weddings of each other's children, greeted one another's grandchildren with love and awe.

We still do.

All of us can still sing the words to the Rutgers alma mater, and we women feel like honorary members of the Class of 1954 at reunions.

We no longer race up the stadium steps for the Homecoming Game. But we still go with our Rutgers alums.

And like seventh graders at the school dance, by halftime, we women have shifted the seating so that we can be close to one another, and what's happening on the field is, well, secondary to our rich and textured conversations.

I love these women. I know they are there for me, and always will be.

No—we're not childhood friends. We're not sorority sisters. We're not family, although sometimes, that's hard to remember. What we are is both simpler—and more complex—than any of those.

We are wives of husbands who promised to stay close—and kept that promise.

We're friends. Such good friends.

How blessed we are.

~Sally Friedman

81

Kylie's Scar

Because nobody goes through life without a scar.
~Carol Burnett

"Oh my gosh, Kylie, I—I don't know what to say. I mean... open-heart surgery? You're barely twenty-three!" I said.

I looked at Sam for help. She too was stunned by the news.

"Are you sure you've talked through all the options with your doctor?" Sam asked.

"Yeah, I'm sure," Kylie said. "The first surgery attempt only made the hole bigger. We've gone through all the options. There's no guarantee, of course, and I'll have a scar, but I decided this is the only way to fix the problem for good. So for the rest of my life I don't have to worry about there being a hole in my heart, you know?"

At that moment I felt like I was the one with a hole in my heart. Open-heart surgery? Isn't that for older people who need to bypass clogged arteries? Certainly not for young, fit, healthy, and super active young people like Kylie! My mind reeled with possible bad endings, and it took all I had to fake a smile for Kylie. This was her life, after all, and right now she needed a shoulder to lean on, an ear to listen, and most of all, our unconditional support.... I had to swallow my terror and doubts.

It had been five years since the three of us met during our first year at the Naval Academy. We bonded in an unforgiving, predominantly male environment. Together we found outlets from the stress and discipline — we laughed, ran, wrote countless e-mails and messages, made crafts, and enjoyed endless adventures around town and even overseas.

We all chose to major in oceanography, and our friendship blossomed in the rocky soil of life at the Academy. We went to class together alongside our fellow uniformed future Naval and Marine Corps officers. Kylie sat in the front row, I took the middle, and Sam preferred the back. Sitting together was not an option. We had to separate ourselves or we'd cause a ruckus. We found that the more boring the teacher and the more tedious the subject, the closer we grew. We composed witty notes and crafted intricate doodles — and sent them soaring through the air from one end of the classroom to the other. Hijinks aside, we studied hard, helped each other, and earned good grades.

After four hard years, we graduated and left Annapolis. Sam went to The Basic School for Marine officers in Virginia; Kylie went to Rhode Island to earn her master's degree; and I went to San Diego to serve aboard a ship. We always found time to visit each other, and every time we did we were still the same giggly, mischievous girls we were in college.

Two months before Kylie told us the news, the three of us competed in a Half Ironman triathlon relay. Kylie swam 1.2 miles, Sam cycled 56 miles, and I ran 13.1 miles. Kylie knew then that she needed surgery, but true to her character, she waited until after the race to break the news. She always puts others before herself.

The weekend before Kylie's surgery, we kept her mind off the topic by going for runs, bundled up against the harsh wintry wind, telling stories and laughing the whole way. We visited art stores in Cambridge and sipped hot buttered rum at an Irish tavern in Harvard Square, something Kylie rarely did. She showed me the city she'd come to know through her visits to see her boyfriend, who was getting his master's at MIT. After a long weekend of pure, uninterrupted girl time, she saw me off at Central Station. When I said goodbye, I gripped my red roller bag as tightly as I could, blew her a kiss, and tried not to cry. I had to be strong for Kylie. It wasn't until the train was out of sight that my tears came falling down.

Before the surgery, Kylie told me that her biggest fear was that she'd be bedridden for a month afterward. Then it would be another month before she'd be allowed to do any sort of physical activity. I imagine she had deeper fears, but her focused concern over the recovery period reflected her character—she was such a positive thinker and getting back on her feet was already at the forefront of her mind.

She went under the knife the next day at seven in the morning Boston time, four in the morning my time. The surgery lasted five long hours. Kylie's mother sent updates whenever she could. I couldn't focus at work. I prayed for Kylie and her family. I pleaded with God to pull her through the surgery. I kept thinking that Kylie was far too strong, far too sweet, and far too giving to deserve this!

After the surgery, Kylie slept for ten hours. When she finally awoke, her mom sent me a text message saying that she was stable and well. My heart felt ten pounds lighter and surged with joy and relief that my best friend was going to be okay!

For three months after the surgery, she attended physical therapy. Day by day, Kylie gathered her strength. A few days later, we spoke on the phone for ten minutes—she didn't have the strength to stay awake any longer. I'd never seen Kylie too tired for anything! She was the most energetic girl in the world. But her body needed time to recover, and she was coming along well—that's all that mattered. Kylie was the type to sneak in a few pushups and sit-ups in the hospital room, and I have no doubt that she did. Within two and a half months, Kylie was back on the treadmill, working her way back toward her natural, super-active self. I was so proud. I am so proud.

Kylie motivates me to be the best version of myself, to never give up, and to be brave above all else. She is the most inspiring person I know. I am truly blessed to have her in my life.

This past April I got married, and Kylie and Sam served as bridesmaids in the wedding. They and the other four bridesmaids wore handmade flowered scarves with their strapless pink and orange dresses. Kylie's scar was nowhere to be seen, and I had the very best looking, and certainly unique, bridal party of anyone I know!

~Katie Cash

Owed to Joy

Humor does not diminish the pain—it makes the space around it get bigger.
~Allen Klein

I slid the argyle sock over Mary's delicate toes and worked it over her heel. Her husband poked his head into the bedroom. "Thanks for doing that. I can finish dressing her just as soon as I put away breakfast."

Mary rolled her eyes. "That man! He simply can't keep his hands off me."

"With a looker like you, who can blame me?" He pursed his lips into a low wolf whistle, winked, and tossed the kitchen towel over his shoulder.

I grinned into my lap as I knelt at Mary's feet and started on the other sock. That was simply another in an ever-growing list of things that I admired about my friend. Her sense of humor. Her determination to always choose joy.

Rheumatoid arthritis had struck Mary nine years into her marriage. Over time, the dreadful disease ravaged her body until she now relied on others for nearly everything. Dressing. Bathing. Meals. Yet she maintained a positive outlook, full of love and laughter and life.

I'd once accused my quick-witted friend of having a prepared arsenal of one-liners. "What do you do, Mary, stay awake at night to think up these quirky quips?"

"You know," she admitted, "I'm awake anyway." She avoided talking about the pain that caused her restless nights. "And I decided years ago that no one wanted to be around a person who complained all the time."

"Complain? You? Why I've never heard you complain at all!"

Mary looked out the window. "Let's hope you never do."

When it came to the complaint department, we both knew she qualified for more than her share. Twenty-four surgeries in forty-five years of marriage. And the last hip replacement came at a high price: a permanently oozing infection that added a new element to her daily routine.

Mary and I had met over two decades earlier, me a new mother, her with a brood of teenagers and a married daughter. We'd quickly found common ground—church, writing, hobbies—and forged an easy friendship. Already using crutches, Mary knew what was coming; even so, I watched as she opted to wring all the pleasure she could out of life—and she swept her friends along with her.

For me, personally, she filled whatever role was most pressing at the moment: friend, confidante, sister, mother. She sanded my life's rough edges and I loved her for it.

No wonder I was upset when she and her husband decided to move to another state, where their oldest daughter would oversee their health during their declining years.

"You will call, won't you?" Mary's frail hand found mine. "And come west to visit us? Utah or bust!" Her smile was watery and weak.

I could only nod.

Thank goodness for phone calls. They were our lifeline as her health declined further. Even when she could no longer move and her daughter had to hold the phone to Mary's ear.

"You'll be glad to know I've decided to face death with humor," she immediately quipped. "Then it's less of a grave matter."

I groaned into the phone. "And hello to you, too. How are you today?"

"I'm skinny, weak, as helpless as a baby—and not nearly as cute," Mary admitted.

"Are you looking for excuses?" I tossed back at her. I swear I could hear her grin.

"No." Her tone sobered. "But I am looking for wings."

"Wings?" I blinked in confusion, still waiting for a comic comeback.

"Wings," she half-whispered. After a short pause, her humor returned. "After all these years, I figure I've probably forgotten how to walk. And, anyway, I'd rather fly. So I'm thinking God better have a spare pair of wings waiting for me."

Mary died one week later.

When you lose someone you love with all your heart—even when you know it's time—it is still possible to feel selfish in your own need. Your private loss. Your penetrating pain. The day passed in a fog as I tried to process life without Mary. I remembered that last phone call with regret. Did I tell her I loved her? My thoughts spiraled. Why hadn't I made an effort to visit last month? Did she know how much she meant to me? Why hadn't I told her goodbye? Had I ever really thanked her for her counsel, her friendship, her grace, her example? Her very presence? What would I do without her?

Exhausted with grief, I tumbled into bed. But even in the dark of night, I couldn't put my heart and mind at ease. I lay on my back, staring at the moon shadows on the ceiling. The tears dammed up in me wouldn't wait anymore.

"I miss you already," I whispered. "I love you so much."

And that's when I felt it: a quiver. No, no. A kind of tickle. A ticklish flutter somewhere in my chest. Light. Airy. Ethereal. Like a silent, gossamer giggle or like... like...

Wings!

"Oh, Mary," I breathed. "You did it. You found your wings!"

At that very moment I knew that—like Mary—I, too, could choose joy. That's what I would do with her—and without her. I would choose joy.

What a legacy!

~Carol McAdoo Rehme

83

Chicken Soup for the Soul

When Our Hearts Meet

There is magic in long-distance friendships.
They let you relate to other human beings in a way that goes beyond
being physically together and is often more profound.
~Diana Cortes

I've had a best friend for thirty-one years... and we've never met. We're pen pals. I live in Seattle and Denise lives in Texas. For thirty-one years we've written hundreds of letters, sent thousands of e-mails and exchanged countless gifts but we've never spoken on the phone and we've never met face to face.

In 1982, Denise read a story in a magazine I'd written and she wrote to me. I answered her letter and we became instant friends.

We went from being pen pals, to being "forever" friends and one soul living in two bodies.

We have become mirrors of each other's emotions. If she's sad then I'm sad, if I'm happy then she is happy for me. When I'm right, she cheers me on. When I'm wrong, she still cheers me on. It's easy to have a friend who sticks by you when you are right; it's harder to find a friend who sticks by you when you are wrong and who tries, with love and encouragement, to get you back on the right track.

Three times we've given each other the same Christmas gifts, the packages crossing in the mail.

We both know we can share any secret, voice any opinion, reveal any heartache, or cry a thousand tears and there is one person who will listen, understand, sympathize, and try to help if possible. If there is nothing we can do to help, then we are just "there."

We like the same books, the same movies, the same music, but we don't always agree on everything, and that is okay. The years have seen us go from being young mothers to being grandmothers. We brag about our children when they do well, and we weep over our children when they have problems. We've shared a dozen diets, none of which have worked for us.

Family members, our children, and other friends might not "get us," and might be quick to criticize, but Denise and I are so fortunate—we can reach out any time of the day or night and pour out our hearts and know there is someone out there who will understand.

Big traumas like divorce and death are treated with compassion and sympathy and encouragement. Small traumas like weight gain and bad haircuts are also treated with a proper amount of sympathy and a great deal of humor.

We can spend days laughing over nothing, exchanging dozens of e-mails filled with what would be utter nonsense to anyone but us. People ask us what we could possibly think of to talk about that often, but we never seem to run out of things to say. We only run out of time to say them.

Our children have grown, Denise is divorced, and I lost my husband several years ago. She lives alone in Texas and I live alone in Seattle.

We've talked about trying to meet and maybe even taking a vacation together but she's taking care of her mother who has Alzheimer's and I have my own obligations. In some ways it is disappointing to think we'll never meet each other or spend time together, but maybe we don't need to. I don't know how we could be any closer or love each other more. The odds are against us meeting—distance, health, finances, and duty keep us from just jumping on a plane and flying across the country.

Every morning I have the same routine. I get up, get dressed, walk into the living room and turn on the computer. I go into the kitchen and turn on the coffee pot, then return to my computer to see if Denise is there yet. Most of the time she's there to say good morning, and she often has a joke or something funny to share that will start my day with a smile.

I wish we lived in the same town. I wish we were neighbors. I get tired of living alone and especially during the holidays it is hard to have a best friend who is a thousand miles away.

Almost every night I go for a walk and look at the moon.

I watch the moon change shape from crescent to full and change color from silver to gold and I am in awe of the beauty of God's handiwork. My family never understood my love and fascination with the moon. They spend their evenings watching TV or sitting at their computers.

Last night I looked at the moon and felt melancholy and lonely. Before I went to bed, I checked my e-mail and my friend had written, "I saw the moon tonight and it looked like a pale, crooked pearl."

A thousand miles away, my friend had looked at the moon and thought about me, and suddenly the thousand miles between us vanished and we were together.

Denise and I may never meet face to face, but our hearts meet every day.

~April Knight

84

Feel Better

Happiness is an attitude. We either make ourselves miserable,
or happy and strong. The amount of work is the same.
~Francesca Reigler

When I first met Beth, she was limping. I saw her for the first time at a Mother-Daughter night in third grade. She was dragging herself across the floor with a sprained ankle, pathetically trying to shoot a basketball into the hoop. She never was very athletic, but I can say that, because she's my best friend now.

I didn't like Beth much when I first saw her in that elementary school gym. As a hopelessly romantic drama queen, all I saw was a damsel in need of saving, and I was convinced all the boys I loved in secret adored her. I was a little stout and awkward, so boyfriends were few and far between. But when we found ourselves in the same class in fourth grade, it was clear that I was about as wrong as I would ever be. We clicked immediately. We wrote a stellar script for a class project about glass blowing in colonial America, and the rest was history. We were destined to make each other laugh until we cried for the rest of our lives.

We grew up together. Beth became a self-assured brunette stunner, and boys mercifully started developing crushes on both of us, but one thing about Beth never changed. She was always injured... and I mean always. One summer, I helped her limp through camp, holding races on her crutches (the perpetually healthy girl, of course, thinks crutches are awesome). I used the coveted middle school elevator key so that Beth and I could leave early from class and I could wheel her or carry her backpack to the next class. Freshman year of high school she convinced me to join cross-country with her, only to sprain her ankle the first week of practice. She became the student manager of the team, and I became a pretty poor excuse for a middle distance runner.

Even with an injury history that belongs on an NFL roster, Beth is one of the strongest people I know. I lost count of her ankle sprains long ago, but that didn't stop Beth from moving to Michigan for college and heading to California as soon as she graduated. She has since become a successful communications and sales expert, traveled all over the world, and made new friends everywhere she goes. Sadly, since we left our hometown, we've never lived in the same place. We can't do the stupid things we used to do, like call the oldies radio station requesting songs until they actually tell us to stop calling (true story). But our friendship has never been stronger.

When I graduated from college, I was determined to take New York City by storm and become an actor. I never thought it would be easy—I'm not an idiot. But I didn't know it would be quite so hard. After long days auditioning, I felt every insecurity I had ever had resurface. "I'm not talented," I would say to myself. "I'm fat... I'm not working hard enough... I'll never make it." On days like those, I knew exactly who to call.

"Mad," Beth would say to me. "You are amazing. You're attempting to do something you absolutely love. What's better or braver than that?"

Last year, while Beth was living in Washington, D.C. and I was in New York City, I hopped on a bus and spent a girls' weekend in her studio apartment. We hadn't seen each other in almost a year, and the reunion was a nonstop giggle fest. I tried on all her clothes, we sang an embarrassing duet together while we got ready for a night on the town, and we even snuck a water bottle filled with wine to tour the monuments in the middle of the night. (Shh, please don't tell the president!)

But there was a snag in our fun. Beth had been suffering from a mystery illness, one that was so severe she had been forced to take disability leave from her job at the age of twenty-four. She was in constant back pain and feared that maybe all of her bad luck throughout the years was actually adding up—to a chronic pain condition. Her doctors were testing her for fibromyalgia and she was in the torturous stage of waiting for results. On the one hand, she wanted to know, finally, why her body didn't ever seem to work properly. On the other hand, the thought of being diagnosed with a pain condition that would never go away was terrifying.

The second night of our girls' weekend, we stayed up late talking. Teary-eyed, she confessed her fear, and how she was really feeling. Beth, the perpetual optimist, was not feeling so optimistic. My friend who always told me not to worry, always convinced me that things would get better and fall into place, was unsure of her own future.

"I just feel like I'm not good enough. I'll never be strong or healthy. I can't do my job right now and I'm losing money. What am I going to do?" she asked me.

I looked at her, and I just knew she would land on her feet. "Beth," I said, "you are the strongest, bravest person I know. And if you need someone to run races for fibromyalgia or carry your crutches... whatever it is, I'll be there. You know I will."

Crying and laughing at the same time, we snuggled in for a sleepover. Both of us knew, underneath it all, that everything would be okay. It was, of course. It turned out that Beth does have fibromyalgia, but with a change of job and scenery—an opportunity in San Francisco—her positive outlook has never been sunnier. Even though she's physically farther away than she was before, I know she's still close, just a phone call away when I need her most. And that's the beauty of my friendship with Beth. Whether she's limping or I'm down on my luck, the world is a better place when you have a friend who will always—always—make you feel better.

~Madeline Clapps

Just Us Girls

The Write Stuff

Wild Women Wielding Pens

The reluctance to put away childish things
may be a requirement of genius.
~Rebecca Pepper Sinkler

We haven't been BFFs since kindergarten, and the only thing we had in common when we met was a desire to write and publish our work. Our girlhoods are thirty to fifty years in our pasts, but the five of us will always be girls at heart. We don't wear hats or a particular color when we are together; we don't need a uniform to confirm our affiliation. We have collectively mopped our foreheads and mouths as we've sweated out an essay, dealt with an ex-husband, had a hot flash, shared personal details, or devoured delectable cuisine.

When the five of us gathered for our initial meeting at a bookstore, we presented ourselves as friendly freelance writers with hopes of striking it rich. We did just that! We hit the mother lode when we banded together for biweekly Wednesday evening meetings. Not only have we made a little spending money on our individual publications, but we've discovered a gold mine of greatness and a chunk of hilarity worth a million bucks. Each week one of us discovers a nugget to add to our coffers.

Sioux, the rebel, admitted she was born Susan. Her sharp tongue matched her wit and we soon discovered that she could reduce us to gasping laughter with her observations and perceptions.

Tammy, soft-spoken, wrote powerful prose. Her professionalism and editing ability resulted in a nickname: "Grammar Girl."

Lynn, quiet and shy, graciously opened her home to us after our third meeting at the bookstore. The patrons who distracted us at our first meeting didn't compare to the incredible characters Lynn created in her stories.

Beth, the youngest of our group, resembled long-legged actress, Julia Roberts. She flipped her long hair in a similar fashion. She had more action in her life than Julia's stunt double, and she cracked us up with her true confessions.

I, a seasoned teacher, writer, wife and grandma, have seen it all and may have done it all. I am willing to share it all with "my girls," a unified group of gals with a serious side of sass.

When we first met, some of us wrapped our necks in scarves, hid our feet in socks and Crocs, kept our posture perfect and acted prim and proper. We didn't reveal too much skin or personal details. After a few months we were not only fleshing out phrases, we were baring our arms and souls, exposing crooked toes and teeth, slouching in a living room and letting it all hang out. Toes that is. We love our flip-flops, and although we are old enough to know that the original name for these freeing shoes is "thongs," we're wise enough never to refer to them as such. We gab, guffaw, and snort about escapades. We eat, drink, brag, and complain. Our meetings are as rejuvenating as expensive face cream, a chunk of dark chocolate, or a vacation from reality.

It was only natural that one of us, the wildest of course, would suggest a girls' weekend at the lake. We packed our bags and piled into the car, promising not to look at anyone's swimsuited flab. Beth opened the door to her father's breathtaking lake house and welcomed us in. She didn't know that our bags were packed with birthday gifts for her. As she set about preparing a buffet of food, we laid out a table for her in the living room.

As she unwrapped an abundance of chocolate and gag gifts, she started giggling, her laughter slowly escalating. She startled us when she jumped up from the couch and darted to the bookcase.

"Oh my gosh, oh my gosh!" She squealed as she grabbed for what appeared to be a decorative air freshener globe. "ARGGGH! I can't believe this. I'm dead! This is my dad's live feed motion detector camera."

Beth turned the device around. I was all for burying it. We laughed ourselves into near convulsions. Then we selected individual bathrooms and bedrooms to undress in and put on our swimwear.

"Don't peek," someone said.

Peek? I was afraid there was a nanny cam in each room! It was bad enough my friends would see my cellulite. I didn't want Beth's dad to get a glimpse. I flipped off the light, and in the dark I got my foot hung up in the Spandex and nearly knocked my head into the wall.

We wrapped ourselves in towels and followed Beth down a long staircase built into the hillside that led to the lake. There is something freeing about floating, being in over your head and knowing you have someone to rely on, to buoy you. We relaxed, unwound, and left all of our cares behind. We dangled our legs, treaded water, and divulged details of our lives.

We returned to the daily grind renewed and refreshed. That one weekend had a longer-lasting effect. When we Wild Women Wielding Pens gather together, we feel exactly the same way we did when we were at the lake. For three hours, twice a month, we are adrift, our worries lifted, our lungs expanded from hearty laughter. We indulge in food for our bodies, intellectual stimulation for our minds, and inspiration for our souls. We cross our "T's" and dot our "I's", but we don't have to mind our "P's" and "Q's" and act our ages. When we're together, we're just us girls.

~Linda O'Connell

Sister Friends

*It is not often that someone comes along
who is a true friend and a good writer.*
~E.B. White, Charlotte's Web

My chest tightened and my heart ached a little as I tried to become accustomed to the view from my new kitchen window in the Nevada desert. I saw unfamiliar mountains looming in the distance and cacti and shrubs growing in the yard. I couldn't choke back the tears. I missed the ocean and lush greenery of my former home on the central coast of California. Also, I missed my life there and my friends.

"You're very lucky to be a freelance writer and able to write from anywhere on the planet," my husband said when he left for work that morning.

It had taken two weeks to unpack and get settled into our new house. I didn't feel settled, but my husband did and he was happy with his new job.

I knew my husband was right. Indeed, I, too, had to settle in. After all, I was a writer and most writers lead reclusive lifestyles, but we do need an occasional break to rejuvenate our senses. For me, that entails having lunch with a writer friend or hobnobbing with fellow writers. I'd left those fellow writers behind and even though I was grateful for being able to stay in touch with them by phone, e-mail, and social media, it wasn't enough. I needed up close and personal to fill the void in my life. An Internet search located a writer's group that met every Tuesday evening at a local bookstore.

On Tuesday evening, after I signed up for the writer's group, the bookstore clerk at the front counter directed me to a long rectangular table adjacent to the coffee shop in the back of the store.

My knees shook as I approached the table of ten people with laptops, yellow lined tablets, and pens. "Is this the writer's group?" I asked.

I relaxed as a smiling face welcomed me, "Sister friend, my name is Mimi. You've come to the right place. Have a seat."

A sandy-haired gentleman pulled out a chair for me, "Hi, I'm Mike. Please join us. We need some new blood in this group."

Once introductions, genres, and writing information were shared, a fellow author read the first three pages of his new novel.

My stomach churned... I didn't know these people... I was new. Surely, I couldn't be truthful. His story needed work... a lot of work. As I pondered what to say, my thoughts were interrupted.

"It's boring," Mimi said. "Your story needs dialogue."

I was stunned by Mimi's directness, then amazed at the camaraderie between the two writers. No offense was taken. He admitted he needed help in writing dialogue and Mimi offered to help him.

At the end of the evening, Mimi and I lingered over coffee and blueberry scones. Mimi clinked my mug, "Sister friend, we're meant to be friends."

In between sipping coffee, nibbling scones, talking, laughing, and swapping stories about our lives, we bonded. We became best friends that very evening.

As we left the bookstore coffee shop, we discovered we were not only going in the same direction, we lived four blocks away from one another.

We have so much in common. In college, Mimi majored in psychology and minored in journalism. I, too, took courses in journalism. Our love for writing began when we were both eight years old. We have empty nests—her four children and my two children are launched into adulthood.

Mimi writes fiction—both short stories and medical thriller novels. I write inspirational non-fiction stories and essays. We're published authors. We love words. We encourage and support each other's writing. The letters on our keyboards are worn, because we write for long hours each day, even toiling during the wee hours when our creative juices are overflowing. We each submit our work and anxiously await a reply. We celebrate with a glass of chardonnay whether it's an acceptance or a rejection.

Sometimes Mimi and I finish each other's sentences. We look alike. People who don't know us think we're sisters. We know each other's secrets. All but one... Mimi would never disclose her age. I never pried, but I'd come to the conclusion we were the same age.

Recently, Mimi asked me to tag along with her to her favorite eyewear shop to have the frames for her reading glasses repaired. After the eye specialist typed Mimi's name into the computer, she needed to verify the year of her birth. Mimi hesitated for a moment, then whispered her birth date.

"You're the same age as me," I giggled.

"I knew you were sisters, the specialist remarked, "but I didn't know you were twins."

"No, just sister friends," we said in unison.

~Georgia A. Hubley

Road Trip to Friendship

No road is long with good company.
~Turkish Proverb

We met through an online writing/critique group for women. Since the group members were spread out across the world, I wasn't looking for a friend. I just wanted to exchange critiques with other writers to improve my writing.

Within a couple of weeks I noticed that one of the writers, Mavis, tended to have the same opinions as I did. When she liked a piece, so did I. Even more importantly, when she didn't like a piece, neither did I—even if everybody else thought the piece was great.

I began to look for her name and read each of her critiques carefully, no matter whom she was critiquing, applying many of her suggestions to my own writing. Word by word, sentence by sentence, my writing improved.

After one particularly thorough critique of a piece of mine that had me alternately smiling and cringing, I e-mailed her privately. She responded. Soon we were e-mailing each other every couple of days, but always about writing. At some point, the e-mails turned into long-distance phone calls, still with a writing bent. To this day I'm still not sure who made the first call.

Then, about six months later, the writing group decided to hold a face-to-face conference down in Virginia. Since I prefer to spend my days behind a computer screen rather than with people, I was nervous about spending four or five days with a group of women I barely knew. To be honest, I wasn't even sure if I wanted to spend that much time with women I did know.

However, with some arm-twisting by the moderator, I agreed to attend. About a week later Mavis decided she would come, too.

I was about to book my flight from Toronto to Dulles when Mavis, who lives in Victoria, British Columbia, called. "I have a problem," she said. "When I went to renew my passport, the clerk wouldn't process my application. Apparently there's a mistake on my birth certificate and there's not enough time to fix it and get a new passport, so I can't fly into the States."

"What will you do?" I asked.

"I suppose I could take the ferry to Seattle and show other ID at the border. It'll be a few months before we need passports to travel by land. Then I could just fly from Seattle."

"Or," I said, "you could fly to Toronto and we could drive down together." As soon as the words were out of my mouth I wanted to stuff them back in. A week before I had been worried about sharing a cabin with women I didn't know and here I was suggesting I spend two days in a car with someone I only knew through e-mails and phone calls.

There was a pause on her side as she thought about it. "We could do that. I have some friends and ex-family in Toronto I haven't seen in a while. I'd come down a couple of days early, stay with them until the night before we leave, and then we'd drive down. If we split the driving, it shouldn't be too bad."

"Slight problem. I don't drive. But I can read a map and I'll print out Google directions. How lost can we get?"

"So, you want to do this?"

"Sure," I said, gulping a little. Before I could change my mind, we made our arrangements and set a date for her to appear on my doorstep.

The moment I got off the phone, anxiety set in. I called my best friend. "Susan, I've done something really stupid. Remember that woman I was telling you about? Mavis. The one in my writers' group. Well, I suggested we drive down to the conference in Virginia."

Susan laughed. "Why is that stupid?"

"Why?" I said. "Because it's a two-day drive, so we'll be sharing a motel room on the way down and again on the way back."

"I repeat: Why is that stupid?"

"What if Mavis is an axe murderer? Or she snores? Or worse, she's one of those drivers who picks her nose while she drives." I'd barely gotten the last word out when I realized what I sound like. "I'm being an idiot, right?"

Susan said what all best friends would say in this situation. "Yes, a complete idiot."

Three weeks later, a tall woman with gray hair rang my doorbell. I opened the door and we stared at each other for a moment. Then she said, "You're going to think I'm nuts but I just have to ask you one question. You're not by any chance an axe murderer, are you?"

I grinned. "Nope. I was going to ask you the same thing."

She shook her head and grinned back at me. Suddenly, the trip really did seem like a good idea.

The next day we picked up our rental car, drove back to my place and loaded it with suitcases, a cooler stuffed with hardboiled eggs, milk, juice, cheese, and dips, plus bags of fruit, crackers, chips, nuts, and other munchies.

"You know," Mavis said, nibbling on a cracker, "calories you eat on the road don't count. Oh, and I'm not sure if I told you, but I can only drive for about two hours before I need to rest my wrists." She held them. "Carpal tunnel."

"Perfect," I said. "I'll need to go to the bathroom about then. Middle-aged bladder."

We both laughed. The good idea turned into a great one.

For the next two days, Mavis drove and I navigated—mostly correctly. We began by talking about our writing, but within a couple of hours we were laughing and talking about friends, family, pets, and our lives in general. It was hard to believe that we had only officially met the day before.

As we pulled up at the conference site, I turned to her. "I don't care how the conference goes. This has been the best road trip of my life."

"I know what you mean," she said. "And we still have the trip back home. I can think of at least a dozen stories I haven't told you yet."

At the end of the conference, we filled out evaluation sheets. One of the questions was: What was the most important thing you got out of the conference? I thought about the information I had learned about marketing, about writing personal essays, about making a pitch to an agent. I thought about all the notes I'd taken. I thought about putting faces and voices to the names I'd seen online for a couple of years.

But in the end, I wrote three words: A new friend.

~Harriet Cooper

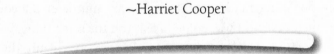

My Ohio Friends

The language of friendship is not words but meanings.
~Henry David Thoreau

It was a humid July morning and I was somewhere in the middle of Ohio. I had left Connecticut questioning my judgment in signing up for the Antioch Writers' Workshop in Yellow Springs, Ohio. Back in March I'd eagerly signed up for this conference where there'd be nothing else to do but focus on my writing. Now it seemed audacious to think I could stand alongside these confident writers. I wanted to stay in my boxed-in room at the Days Inn. Instead I got in the car, looked at a map, took a breath and headed for the conference.

That first morning, back roads led me by fields of swaying corn, like gentle arms pointing me in the right direction. Down a long hill, then up another, and quite suddenly I was in an oasis of thick oak trees. Though lush and green, it didn't keep me from feeling as if I was still the little girl entering fifth grade midyear. I even think my hands were shaking.

Our conference was held in the forest preserve of Glen Helen, where a bike and walking path allowed for an easy stroll into town. The morning consisted of four lectures on various forms of writing as well as a three-hour workshop in the afternoon. One could sign up, with about twenty others, for lunch with one of the lecturers, an opportunity for some casual time with a writer of merit. Timidly I wrote my name down, though what I would say to an accomplished writer eluded me. I started off by myself into town.

"What do you write?" A voice on my right startled me.

"Fiction," I blurted out, though the truth was I'd never written fiction before. This conference was a testing ground for my first story. Saying the word, though, ever so slightly empowered me.

"What about you?" I inquired.

"Young adult. Well, I try. It's something I've been working on." She laughed. "I'm Pam, who are you lunching with?"

And just like that we began nonstop chatter about writing.

Me: "How long have you been writing?"

Pam: "Forever."

"Are you taking a workshop?"

"How many words are you turning in?"

"I was fascinated with the lecture on poetry this morning."

"Oh, didn't you love the one about avoiding writing? How great to hear that."

"Do you talk out loud when you write dialog?"

"How did you know? My family thinks I'm crazy."

No talk of last names, no "where are you from?" or "what do you do for a living?" No husband or children talk. This was all about something we couldn't really speak about to anyone else. There's such joy in being able to share an energy that usually takes place in solitude. This person I'd only met four minutes ago knew instinctively the fears and aspirations I thought only I harbored. And off we went to lunch.

Pam is a woman at ease with the earth. Her close-cropped sun blond hair, shorts and sleeveless shirts, and tanned arms spoke of days spent outdoors. Her story, an intricate thriller, made me want to shout out, "What's next?"

Yellow Springs is a village of shops, galleries, and more than one bookstore. Wildflowers seemed to be everywhere. After lunch Pam and I walked the small streets with dripping ice cream cones. We also ended up walking back to Glen Helen with two other women.

"I dread reading my work out loud today." That was Mary, still in her twenties with an open, inviting smile. We discovered we were in the same workshop.

"We'll sit on either side of you, not to worry." That was Ann, also in our workshop, neatly pulled together, so proper looking, but with quick humor and lofty, dark writing.

Twenty-four hours after landing in this serene little town, the four of us went for burgers where a sign outside the restaurant proclaimed: "Every Visit Is Special." By now I'd heard Mary's story of a burdened immigrant family and Ann's of a dark, stormy love. Writing is personal. We share reluctantly and with misgivings. Handing over our private thoughts is a decisive move. Though that's what the four of us did that evening. We began to reveal our creativity and in doing so we solidified our friendship.

We continued each day as we sat on the steps at Glen Helen with coffee in the morning. We did it with a reassuring hand on an arm when we read our stories out loud for others. We did it with a deliberate voice when commenting on each other's writing. We did it, here in this special village, at this conference of like-minded people, together for only a week, forging friendships to last much longer.

We have a little online chat room now where we join up for an hour or so every few weeks. It's been going on for years. We start with talk of families and eventually end up speaking about our writing. We read each other's work and we're honest in our critique. We encourage, offer suggestions, and in between make jokes unique to us. When we sign off, we know we've been someplace special, as only good friends can understand.

I look back on my first day of the conference but I don't regret my apprehension. I learned from it. Dare to step out of your comfort zone. Fly off to Dayton, Ohio or wherever. Take a chance and seek out others whose interests are yours. Look what happened to me. Here's to my Ohio friends.

~Priscilla Whitley

Fiber-optic Friendship

The talent of writing agreeable letters is peculiarly female.
~Henry Tilney

"Hello, Sara?" drawled an unfamiliar Southern voice on my answering machine. "This is Amy. I just had to call to congratulate you...."

"Who was that?" my ten-year-old twin daughters, Leah and Chloe, asked when the message ended.

"My writer friend," I said.

They knew who Amy was; I talked about her almost every day. They knew where she lived (Kentucky), they knew she had three daughters (Mara, Kassidy, and Delaney). They even knew the names of her two pet goats (Elvis and Gracie). But like me, they hadn't initially recognized her voice on the machine. Although Amy and I had been friends for two years, I had never seen her in person or even spoken with her. We met on the Internet.

Back in March of 2009, I was feeling lonely. My daughters, then eight, kept life busy, and any time left over went to maintaining my marriage, keeping up with household chores, and following my dream of becoming a children's writer. Even though I felt the lack of a close woman friend, I didn't have the energy—or the time—to go out there and find one.

Then, one day, scrolling through my favorite website for children's writers, I saw this posting on the virtual bulletin boards:

"I'm looking for someone to swap critiques with. Not to sound too picky, but I'd like to work with someone who has similar writing interests."

The poster, who went by the name of "Writermutt," went on to mention authors she liked and magazines she'd been published in. Because my stories had appeared in the same magazines, I thought we might be a good fit. So I answered the post.

Amy replied with a long e-mail. In it, she shared more about her writing interests—she liked humorous stories and had started three novels—and told me she had married her high school sweetheart, lived on a farm, and had a whole bunch of animals, including four dogs, six cats, and twenty-seven chickens! I wrote back, telling her about my writing goals and admitting that my family—with only one dog—couldn't compete with her on the pet front. We agreed to swap manuscripts twice a month.

As the weeks went on, I learned that Amy and I had more in common besides writing. Both of us were homebodies, had daughters who were afraid of tornadoes, and loved chocolate. I found out deeper things as well: both of us struggled with perfectionism, considered our husbands our best friends, and practiced a similar spiritual faith. Amy revealed some of her childhood struggles with me, and I did the same with her. And over time, she became more than a writing buddy; she became a friend.

Amy and I had a lot of long-distance fun together. At Christmas, we sent each other packages, in the process finding out what kinds of cookies were traditional in the other's home. In January, we entered the same magazine fiction contest and spent the week before the deadline bombarding each other with e-mails—up to ten a day—asking each other to look over the latest revision. In February, Amy and her daughter Kassidy (who had become pen pal to my Chloe) sent a box full of Valentine surprises for the whole family. We continued to share writing news, of course, and even that was fun. We reported rejections to each other immediately, and the sympathy e-mail that followed took some of the sting out of it. And when a story was accepted, the happiness was increased because we rejoiced together. Once, she even sent me a card and a celebratory baggie of confetti!

Then one morning, about two years after we'd started corresponding, I received some exciting news. I had won first prize in a well-known children's magazine fiction contest. My immediate reaction, after sharing the news with my husband and daughters, was to tell Amy. But although I knew she'd celebrate with me, I debated whether or not this was a good time to announce it. In the previous weeks, a relative of hers had been seriously ill in the hospital, and I knew the situation was taking up most of her energy. After thinking it through, I decided to send her a more subdued e-mail than I normally would.

Her immediate reply was full of capital letters and exclamation marks, and her words full of true happiness for my good fortune, even though she'd entered the same contest. And then, two days later, when I returned from an errand, there was that message on my answering machine: "Hello, Sara? This is Amy..."

Rather unexpectedly, the thought of calling her back made me nervous. What would it be like to talk to someone I'd known for two years, but had never spoken with? With my heart pounding, I punched her number into the phone.

At first, our conversation felt awkward to me. As we kept talking, though, Amy on the phone and E-mail Amy began to come together. We chatted about the contest, about writing, about our kids. We laughed and joked around. Before ending the conversation, we allowed Kassidy and Chloe to spend a few minutes talking, too. As I hung up, I was smiling. I felt like we'd just connected over coffee.

It's been almost three years since I answered Amy's post. I often wonder if—or when—we'll ever meet in person. Somehow, in spite of the 800 miles that separate us, I believe we will. Because even though our connection may be a product of the modern age, in the ways that count, it's still good old-fashioned friendship.

~Sara Matson

Amies, On and Offline

Let us be grateful to people who make us happy,
they are the charming gardeners who make our souls blossom.
~Marcel Proust

"Are you Crystal Goes to Europe?" asks a smiling blond woman who has come up to me on the sidewalk. I smile back and nod my head. "Travelling Amber?" We laugh and embrace like old friends, when in reality, this is the first time I've ever seen her face to face. Until now, Amber has been "Travelling Amber," one of my expatriate online friends who "met" me thanks to my blog—a blog I began on a whim almost eight years ago, in 2005, just before moving from Ontario, Canada to a small town in the north of France to teach English at a high school.

I had just graduated from university with an Honors English Literature and French Linguistics degree and was ready for some real life experience. I left the comfort of my parents' house and my tight-knit circle of friends with a suitcase, a plane ticket, and a work visa valid for eight months. I initially started my blog, "Crystal Goes to Europe," as a way to keep in touch with my friends and family back in Canada while I was away in France. I wanted a way to share my experiences and feel connected to them despite the distance. What

I hadn't planned on were all the new connections I'd make, or just how my silly little travel blog would impact my life for the better in the years to come.

Amber and I take a seat at a *terrasse*, one of France's charming sidewalk cafés with solid wicker chairs and checkered tablecloths. There's no need for introductions—we've been reading each other's blogs for years and she knows just about everything about me already. Like me, American Amber came to France temporarily and then stayed permanently for a "Frenchie"—the nickname many expats give their French boyfriends and husbands. In a lot of ways, our personal and professional lives are strangely parallel, and it is friends like her who have kept me grounded, kept me sane, and at times, convinced me not to give up on my marriage and return to Canada when the homesickness got really bad. I know that when I write about the hardships of being in a multicultural couple, or not always understanding why the French do things the way they do, Amber and the others get it. Most of them have been there and offer up valuable advice and support when I feel like I'm losing my mind.

"How long will you continue to blog, do you think?" Amber wants to know as the waiter sets down our kirs. We both love the white wine and crème de cassis drink.

"Who knows?" I answer honestly because I realize now I'm not just writing for myself and my family anymore; I'm writing for the all the other expat women who read my blog and find comfort and connection in a girl living a life much like their own. I may not be able to sit down with all of them at a café, but we have woven tight bonds of friendship through the comments left on each other's blogs as we navigate the world of French men, French bureaucracy, and French idiosyncrasies. Eight years ago, I started making new friends without really even knowing it.

"I thought this might be weird, but it isn't!" Amber laughs as we order another kir. It may be our first time meeting from out behind our computer screens, but we chat as though we've known each other forever, and we both don't want the moment to end. Here we are, two young expat women far from home, giggling like teenagers as we compare our thoughts on the French and the challenges we face as immigrants. She may be a "new friend" in the sense that I'm just now meeting her in person, but she's been a treasured old friend for some time now.

The bill comes and Amber snatches it up. She's pulled out her French bankcard to pay even before I can get to my wallet. I know all about her giving, yet take-no-nonsense personality, so I let her. A sudden wave of sadness rushes over me as I realize we are saying goodbye. I'm not sure when I'll be able to see her again because I'm moving 200 kilometers away for my husband's job.

"So are you going to blog about meeting up with me?" she asks with a twinkle in her hazel eyes. "Of course!" I laugh and snap a photo of us together with my mobile phone. The sun is shining in the north of France for once and our lips part into toothy grins as we press our cheeks together and capture the moment on film.

Since meeting Amber in person, we have continued to grow as friends despite living further and further apart. She's welcomed a Franco-American baby into her life, which has made for some interesting posts on her blog, and I've been able to move all around France thanks to my Frenchie's military job. When a few days go by without a blog post, we shake figurative fingers at each other, and when something really good or really bad happens, I know one of my first blog comments will be from her.

I can't really explain how happy I am that I started a blog. I'm making new online friends all the time, and with each new comment or follower, I get the same thrill of connecting with someone through my words and photos. Each time I have to move to follow my husband, I'm often lucky enough to have some blogging friends ready and waiting to meet me in person. My "new old friends" as I like to call them.

As Amber walks away and I head to the train station, I realize I can't wait to get home and write all about our day together. I can't wait to tell all my friends.

~Crystal Gibson

Amies, On and Offline: The Write Stuff 321

Friends for a Season

Some people come into our lives and quickly go. Some stay for a while,
leave footprints on our hearts, and we are never, ever the same.
~Flavia Weedn

When Beth left her husband, she left me too. Unforeseen, our friendship of sixteen years came to an abrupt end when she walked out with no explanation, no forwarding address, no phone message. Just left.

I struggled with my questions: What did I do wrong? She may have had problems with her husband, but what were her problems with me? I assumed we'd be friends for the rest of our lives, since I thought we'd been so close.

I loved Beth's outrageous sense of humor, her dramatic way of spinning a story, the way we made each other laugh. We shared our deepest feelings, about our siblings and aging parents, our joy and frustration in raising our sons, both of us with two boys. We had a common interest in art and decorating, spending Saturdays hunting for treasures for our homes. Not only were we friends, our husbands and sons were close as well, sharing in church and Boy Scouting activities. Our families enjoyed summer vacations at the beach and cozy Christmas Eve dinners.

Pictures and memories were all that were left of our once thriving friendship.

Like children of divorce, left wondering when their parents' love had become a lie, I wondered when our friendship had become a fake. Wouldn't a real friend have confided what she was about to do? Not that she should have told me anything about their private struggle, but weren't we close enough that Beth should have at least said goodbye?

My questions were never answered. Restless and sad, I coped in the way I had years earlier when my father died suddenly; I wrote. I put my questions into my journal and during the time I used to spend with Beth I developed my short stories and essays. Feeling more confident in my writing, I decided to attend a writers' conference in Greensboro, an hour from my home. I felt a little hesitant, since I didn't know anyone going to the conference, but then I reasoned that we all shared the same love of writing and with that common bond they wouldn't really be strangers.

The morning was packed with sessions that allowed for little time to get to know one another. At lunch we were instructed to sit anywhere in the café area. I joined a table with a teenage girl and a man around forty. A woman who appeared to be in her mid-fifties, like me, joined us. Her name was Erika and she lived within ten miles of me. We talked about how we started writing.

"I had to write to keep from going crazy!" Erika confided. "My dad came to live with us when he was diagnosed with dementia. I quit my job teaching English in a middle school to take care of him, and as it turned out I finally had time to write.

"My mother has dementia too. It's so sad to see her changing. A lot of my essays are about Mama," I told her. Not only did we talk about our parents having dementia, I was a middle school nurse and that garnered immediate empathy from Erika.

The man and girl finished eating and left. Erika and I talked on and exchanged e-mail addresses. We rushed back to the session that had just started as we took our seats.

Over the weeks after the conference, we sent regular e-mails, talking about our writing and our parents. Eventually we added comments about our husbands and children. Erika had four and both of us were dealing with how to parent children who were now in their twenties and living out of state. Within a couple of months we decided to meet at a coffee shop.

"Jeez, I didn't think I was going to make it. Dad kept asking me over and over where I was going," she said, breathless and running her hand through her hair as she sat down at the table. "I really needed to get out this afternoon."

"Me too. Another crazy Friday in middle school!" I said as we stood in line to order our lattes.

We sat for two hours talking about everything: changes in our parents' mental status, the disappointment of infrequent phone calls from our children, the way we coped with husbands who were in professions that were very demanding and kept them away from home. Eventually we got to our writing.

"I brought you these," Erika said, and gave me several magazines and a list of websites. "I think you should submit that essay you were telling me about to this anthology," she pointed to one of the web addresses. I could see the teacher in her as she challenged me. "Heck, I just write things quickly and send them off. That slap-dash method works for me. I don't worry about it being perfect!" she said and laughed, her casual and assured attitude the opposite of my careful perfectionism. She had published a lot in a short amount of time and now she was generously sharing these resources with me.

"Thanks. I'll do that," I promised her.

And I did send it off. When I got the news that it was selected for publication, my first, I couldn't tell Erika fast enough. She was delighted, even with my essay beating hers out from the finalists to make it into the anthology! In the months that followed, we e-mailed and met at the coffee shop regularly and attended writing conferences together. We met to celebrate birthdays and Christmas and the pictures from my older son's wedding. We agonized over the next steps in taking care of our parents, the pain being easier when shared with a friend.

Now I think of the song I learned as a child: "Make new friends but keep the old, one is silver and the other's gold." While I no longer have my friendship with Beth, I still have all I learned from her, and all the memories that remain. I don't know how long Erika and I will be friends. But whatever time we have, whether it's for a season or the rest of my life, I'll cherish each moment as both silver and gold.

~Connie Rosser Riddle

Fabulous Forty

If you have lived, take thankfully the past.
~John Dryden

"Women come into their own when they turn thirty," an acquaintance told me as my thirtieth birthday approached. "That's when they redecorate the house the way they want and take control of their own lives."

I have to say that I think she got it wrong. My thirties were a blur of child-rearing years. Who had time, money, or energy to even look at the house and picture it differently? Just having it clean was a lofty enough goal.

Upon turning thirty-nine, I decided that every decade was a milestone worth celebrating and informed my family that I expected a big celebration when I reached the big four-oh. But as time went on, I changed my mind. I just couldn't see blowing a ton of money on a party.

"You always were tight with your money," my mom said.

She was right. But it didn't bother me one bit. Maybe the difference between thirty and forty isn't deciding to do what you want; it's having a better idea of what it is you want to do.

My birthday was on a Saturday — a Saturday of one of my Sixteen Thumbs writing group meetings. I was glad. I couldn't think of a better way to celebrate making it to forty than with these incredible women who understood the passion to write and who had been by my side for eight years as we cheered each other on and held each other up.

And then I hit upon the perfect plan, a far cheaper alternative to a ridiculous party. Who, I wondered, made the rule that people are supposed to receive things on their birthday just for making it around the sun another year? In my gratitude for being here, I decided that it was I who would be giving gifts as a thank you to the important people in my life for making the journey with me.

I took the interactive workbook for writing conferences that I had written and revised it into a special form so that each member of my writing group could have her own copy to use the next time she attended a conference. Best of all, I searched my computer, disks, and stray CDs for photos of the group. I also spent hours poring through quotation books and notes from writing meetings to develop a personalized cover page for the workbook.

Finally, the day arrived. I was so excited that I could hardly wait for nine o'clock to roll around. I will never forget making an unintended "grand" entrance. There they all sat around the dining room table, one empty space waiting for me.

"Here I am, and I've got gifts for you all," I interrupted whatever conversation they'd been having.

"What?"

"Why?"

"It's my fortieth birthday and I can do whatever I want. So, I am giving you all gifts in honor of my birthday."

It was such fun watching their faces and hearing their oohs and ahs as they read the front cover, admired the photo, and perused the workbook.

I don't know yet how I'll choose to celebrate turning fifty, but I do know that in the meantime, I'll savor memories of that fabulous day on my fortieth birthday, when I brought joy to my cherished friends.

~D. B. Zane

93

Fiftieth Reunion

I am no bird; and no net ensnares me:
I am a free human being with an independent will.
~Charlotte Brontë

On the day I finally stopped waffling and sent in my check for my fiftieth reunion at the University of Pennsylvania, I felt something akin to panic. My memories of college—and of myself—go back to the 1950s, the era when America liked Ike, and when caution and conformity were our twin gods. They called us "The Silent Generation" for a reason.

Like so many women of that era, my dreams were of marriage, kids, and a home straight out of a Doris Day/Rock Hudson romp. So I followed the rituals of the mating game, wearing the uniform: a straight skirt with demure kick pleats, boring sweaters, and a hairstyle called a pageboy fluff, loosely modeled on a blond goddess in a shampoo ad.

I accepted without question that I could not write for Penn's daily newspaper, nor could I enter the best room in the student union, the one with the grand piano and Oriental rugs, which was for men only. Why did I never ask why? I got my diploma from Penn's School of Education that sometimes felt like a nunnery—I can't remember a single male in my classes there, and I planned to be a teacher because all of our mothers told us, back then, that teaching was something you could always "fall back on."

I married an older man of twenty-seven three days after my graduation from Penn. I had made it to the finish line at twenty-one. And I've had a wonderful life, but one that turned out to be quite different from the one I'd been groomed to expect.

So I went to my fiftieth reunion not just to ransack the closet of memory, but also to find out how my Penn "sisters" had fared in these fifty years.

The answers came during a spirited session called "Womenspeak," planned by a few of us who yearned for the real scoop. It was open to any and all female class members, but men were barred at the door.

The goal: to share our thoughts about the way we were, the way we are, and how it all feels.

The big topic of the day: achieving independence!

We could have gone on for a week.

In the manner of women who know that time is fleeting, and that chances like this are rare, we dug in.

It ultimately boiled down to this: when it came to independence, we were the "astonished generation." We'd left college just as the 1960s began exploding around us, and so much had changed in a blink. Like dazed wanderers in a parallel universe, we had learned one set of rules, and then they were swept away in the women's movement and the sexual revolution.

"Pre-consciousness," one of our classmates observed.

For some of us, the learning had been painful.

There were plenty of divorces in the Class of 1960. There was the shattering of Camelot with the assassination of our gallant young knight, JFK. Our "brief shining moment" had ended. Then Betty Friedan alerted us that the world was larger than a baked potato, and we heard her.

For most of us, there were baby steps, then giant steps. We had no road maps, and few mentors, to guide us. Yet we somehow soldiered on, crashing our way into courtrooms and boardrooms and yes, even newsrooms.

Among us now were psychologists and law professors, artists and chemists, pianists and financial advisers—scrappy women groomed to be teachers, nurses and wives who had reinvented ourselves out of desire—and necessity.

I became a freelance writer. It's been high-risk, high-tension, low-security, but infinitely better than trying to force-feed the rudiments of grammar to eighth graders who didn't care much about the predicate nominative.

Like my classmates, I had created this marvel called a "career," along with marriage and motherhood. Who knew that a woman could do that?

The game plan we had learned so perfectly—marry a solid guy, present him with clean, happy babies, and wait to be taken care of—that landscape had vanished.

With my evolving independence—and a career—I had to renegotiate the marriage contract with my husband who learned to change plenty of diapers, yield a mean vacuum and not just grocery shop, but make the list, too.

We may have been the first generation of women to experience this miracle.

I have my own credit cards. So predictable now. So unexpected for 1950s women.

Occasionally, I travel alone. Another astonishment.

I've learned to lean on... myself. Being taken care of was no longer a vital, critical part of the marriage contract. While I adore my husband, I am not joined to him at the hip. There's a "we" and an "I."

As dusk settled around the campus on that reunion day, we fifty-year veterans agreed that the rewards had been as mighty as the challenges. Most of us felt a certain peace, serenity, and yes, contentment.

Along with the bittersweet memories and jolting insights, there were, of course, still a few questions without answers. That's because we are still works in progress.

But we women of the Class of 1960 had written and rewritten our own Declarations of Independence.

And that, we understood, was a reflection of our timeless, endless ascent toward enlightenment.

~Sally Friedman

94

Waltzing Matilda

Friends can be said to "fall in like" with as profound a thud
as romantic partners fall in love.
~Letty Cottin Pogrebin

"What's this?" I asked, as my next-door neighbor handed me five days of accumulated mail.

A puzzled look crossed his face. "Your mail?"

The white lumpy mailer among the envelopes intrigued me. Had I ordered something and forgotten it? Like a little kid at Christmas I tore into it as soon as he left. Then I began to laugh. Not a tiny giggle, but a great big belly laugh that echoed off the walls of my empty house.

A fuzzy brown bear emerged from the mailer, sporting personalized accessories. I named her Matilda the moment I saw the pink net tutu encircling her tummy. But instead of dancing shoes, she wore black and yellow "bumble bee" shoes that mimicked the tennies on my own feet. Seashell jewelry decorated her ears and wrist. And a zebra-striped bra topped her heart of gold. Suddenly I understood just how intimately my new friend, Dawn, knew me. After only two face-to-face meetings, she understood my love for the sand, the sea, and even the absurd.

Matilda watched over me as I struggled to write, edit, and rework short inspirational stories for submission. She watched over me as I prayed, cried, and slept. Sitting on my dresser, she acted as a visible reminder of a friend who encouraged me from her home 200 miles away.

I thought back to our initial meeting. Neither of us expected to make a new friend that day. Dawn joined several of us at a round table at the writing conference in Salem, Oregon. We introduced ourselves with the usual information, but when Dawn's turn came she blurted out, "I'm from the Seattle area and I came because I needed to run away from home." She filled in a few details. How her husband was out of town on business. How her roof had sprouted a leak. And how her out-of-work son had just moved in, along with his pregnant wife, toddler, and hairy dog. Having a married out-of-work son of my own, I sympathized with her.

As we all adjourned to separate workshops, she thrust her business card into my hand. "Sorry. I don't usually spill my guts to strangers."

At the end of the daylong conference we met again and hugged like the friends we were destined to become. As I held Dawn close, I prayed into her ear. "God, protect Dawn as she travels home. Give her the strength and wisdom to deal with what's on the other end."

When my husband and I returned to our home in Newberg, Oregon, I pulled out her business card and shot her a quick e-mail. As she shared her deep feelings I responded openly with my own. Her wisdom, humor, and writing skills captivated me, as well as her honest walk with the Lord. Thus our friendship began, built on a foundation of prayer, compassion, and our love of writing. Checking in with each other by e-mail at the beginning and end of our days became as routine as taking a shower or brushing our teeth.

A few months later we met halfway for lunch. Dawn brought fresh cut flowers from her garden. I gave her homemade red currant jam and purple grape juice, harvested from the fruit in my yard. On another occasion we met for coffee. Time stood still as we shared the luxury of a face-to-face meeting, complete with hugs and laughter.

Although she warned me that she didn't understand poetry, I sent her glimpses of my private world of poetry, something that I seldom shared with people. Little by little, like a timid swimmer testing the water's temperature, I sent her poems reflecting my ups, my downs, my questions, my musings. I sent them all. She understood my inner world!

Dawn challenged me in my writing. While she liked my poetry, she believed I could write in other genres too. She rejoiced when I received letters of acceptance. She encouraged me to move on when a rejection came instead. By editing each other's work, we sharpened our skills, all the while creating a refuge of friendship few people have the opportunity to experience.

But Dawn challenged me as a person, too. While I preferred the comfort of my cocoon, straying out of our small town only to see my grandkids, or to journey the hour and a half to the Oregon Coast, she traveled with an ease I envied. Being the wife of a former Air Force pilot, Dawn was not intimidated by the intricacies of hotels, airlines, strange cities, or different cultures. She enlarged my vision of the world and I traveled vicariously through her as she e-mailed from writing conferences or as she traveled with her husband. But I struggled emotionally through the enforced "fasting period" from our friendship when she visited places that disrupted our daily Internet correspondence. I missed my encourager, my sounding board, my virtual next-door neighbor. Days felt like an eternity.

Recently we celebrated the two-year anniversary of our meeting by attending the same writing workshop in Salem, Oregon. This time Dawn spent the nights before and after at my house instead of in a hotel. It's funny to think all this came from a decision to sit at the same table at a writing workshop! We thought we went to hone our writing skills. But it turns out we both needed something much deeper.

~Linda Jett

Chapter
11

Just Us Girls

Relative Friends

95

Fifty Ways I Love His Mother

To know when to go away and when to come closer is the key
to any lasting relationship.
~Doménico Cieri Estrada

She was a writer. They all were—journalists, novelists, corporate writers, poets, playwrights, and pamphlet writers. The entire family loved the written word, producing it, reading it, talking about it.

I fell in love with their son first, and then with all of them. They embraced me as family and we were all pleased that, when I married their son, I'd have official family status.

When I had married for the first time, as a young Sicilian-American woman, my then-husband and I were integrated instantly into each other's families and called both sets of parents Mom and Dad. But by the time I got engaged this time around and met his family, I was too many marriages and in-laws down the road to call her Mom, though we grew so close, I might as well have.

I loved her.

Words weren't my own mother's thing—numbers were. She had quit banking to raise a family and when she was alive our conversations revolved around our family's latest crisis, our vacations, and the mundane minutia of everyday life.

But this? This was different. His mother and I could talk about plot and words. Books and craft. Turning life into theatre. Creativity.

Together, we strolled purposefully through art galleries and museums. Like me, she knew what she liked and could move quickly past what she didn't. Our comments were brief, a few pointed words or a "what do you think of that?" Then, lunch and more talk about books or plays or movies. Once, we even talked about our first loves, in ways a potential mother- and daughter-in-law usually don't, but writers can.

Letta didn't look girly, but secretly she was. Her vibe was casual, but dressed up in suit and boots, blunt-cut gray hair, glasses on her nose. She was every inch the playwright.

We liked off-beat, heady movies, the kind her husband and son, both poets, didn't enjoy, like *Rabbit Hole*, and I'd sometimes take the ninety-minute train ride up to San Francisco just to see a matinee with her.

At bookstores we'd split up and browse, every so often seeking the other out, an interesting book in hand, asking, "Have you read this?" I'd always follow her recommendations.

This is the family I should have been born into, I thought.

Everything in Letta's life was fodder for her plays, and sometimes, sitting in the audience I recognized dialogue and family situations that had really happened. Marriages that had ended. Sibling relationships. Her son's marriage proposal to me.

She could be indirect, sly, even manipulative, and not just in her writing. She had a tweaked sort of mother-energy, different but familiar. Since she hadn't raised me and our relationship wasn't fraught with history, her motherly manipulations made me laugh.

And then, one day, four years after we'd met, it was clear that her son and I weren't going to get married. That I'd have to give him up.

The thought of giving her up, too, was too much to bear.

In my life before then, deaths both literal and figurative had taken husbands, lovers, family. There were only so many loves I could face leaving behind and hers was not among them.

We managed to remain friends, still spending time together. We never really discussed it; we just continued to see each other. Some of her family didn't approve, thinking our continuing contact, and how much we both seemed to enjoy the connection, made her son feel bad.

She asked him if he minded. He gave his blessing.

Several years passed. She got me involved with a theatre group she co-founded. I remarried. She met and liked my new husband. My friends met and liked her. People who had just been names in conversations became faces, too, and personalities. Our relationship grew even stronger.

Then one day, both of us leaning against the wall in the sunshine outside a small theater in San Francisco where we'd just seen a play, she asked, apropos of nothing, "Do you love me just because of my son?" Her tone was plaintive and maybe a little uncertain, but her meaning hit me like a punch to my solar plexus.

"Oh my God, no! Do you really think that?" I was shocked to the core.

She shook her head. "No. No." She quickly demurred. "We have a really special relationship."

On the train home that evening her question was all I could think about. Did she really think that my love for her was all about her son? Had she always thought that way?

Houses along the train track rushed by in a blur and my Kindle lay idle on my lap. Then I had another thought, this one more disturbing. Could she be right? What was our friendship really all about? Why did I love her?

And then, improbably, I heard a Paul Simon song play in my head and I knew.

The moment I got home I began to write. Cut, paste, and inserted it into an e-mail addressed to her.

Into the subject line I typed: Fifty Ways I Love His Mother.
SEND.

The next morning, a reply.

"Thank you."

Later, she told me she'd printed it out, read it and re-read it.

I was relieved. She was almost twenty-five years older than I. One day, in all probability, I'd survive her.

But right now? I wasn't ready to give her up.

Even if, one day, I see a play she's written in which an older woman asks someone like me, "Is my son the reason you love me?"

Because, I realized later, it was entirely possible and even plausible that she'd asked the question to generate dialogue she might later use.

Like I said, sly. Number forty-nine of the fifty ways I love his mother.

~Carol A. Cassara

96

Common Ground

There is one friend in the life of each of us who seems not a separate person,
however dear and beloved, but an expansion, an interpretation, of one's self,
the very meaning of one's soul.
~Edith Wharton

I have a dear friend named Barbara. We share a lot. We have so much in common—our love of sewing, our large families, the common bond of single motherhood. Our birthdays are close and we even have the same favorite color—any shade of purple! Last year we gave each other the very same gift for Christmas. Sometimes being so much alike is alarming.

At lunch last Wednesday I said, "I have come to the conclusion that in this life, God wants me to learn one thing. And that is..."

"Patience." Barb finished my sentence.

That is how it is with Barb and me. We finish each other's sentences, laugh at the same jokes, and pick up the same items on any shopping excursion. On one occasion, she said, "It's kinda scary to find a blond version of myself!"

There is one other thing that we have in common. We have the same ex-husband. I was married to him for fifteen years; she was married seventeen. So, with this in mind, our children remain stepbrothers. Her daughter is a stepsister to my sons. And although I don't know her children that well, I've followed every step of their growth through Barb and our weekly lunches.

Barb and I are sisters of the heart. And I must confess that she is the one that started it.

I was supposed to have my sons on Christmas morning in 1985. However, Barb called me about ten days prior. She explained that her family was going to have a big reunion on Christmas and she was wondering if I would allow the boys to go with them. The reunion was later in the day and wouldn't interfere with our Christmas morning festivities. So the boys went.

When they returned home, my son, Curtis, gave me a wrapped gift from Barb. The card had a small note:

Thank you for sharing the boys with us.

Love, Barb

I can't tell you what was in the package. But nearly thirty years later I can remember every word in that note. We both recognize that you can't put "sharing" and "love" in the same note and not have common ground.

~Linda A. Lohman

My Dearest Friends

A daughter is a little girl who grows up to be a friend.
~Author Unknown

I've watched two of my dearest friends grow up. I've laughed and cried at their antics. I caught them when they stumbled, taught them that rolling their eyes was rude, and shared my love of books with them.

My daughters, Lacey and Carina, have become my daughter-friends.

This new relationship wasn't planned. It's blossomed over the years.

I think it started during a shopping trip. I edged out of the dressing room, tugging uncomfortably at a shirt that should have fit me. Carina, my eighteen-year-old fashionista, wasn't very subtle. She yawned.

Lacey, three years older and more sensitive, said, "Mom, it looks like everything else you own. Why not try something different?"

Carina put her hands on her hips. Her Old Navy checked shorts and coordinated top were perfect. "Mom. Definitely not. Next."

I slunk back into the dressing room. I heard Lace whispering something to her sister. I caught the words "be gentle."

They rejected all of my choices and picked a much more trendy outfit than I was used to wearing. The message was clear. Mom's taste was boring. Theirs wasn't.

That was the beginning of the change.

From clothes to relationships, the girls aired their opinions, advised me about dating, and stepped all into my business. Our roles had expanded. Friendship means being honest, loving, and loyal. My girls embodied all those characteristics and more.

One fall, my best friend, Sharon, and her husband invited me to Ohio for a long weekend, but all I could think of were bills. We were all caught up, but single moms always worry. I didn't think we could afford it.

Lacey watched me mope around the apartment all day. She and Carina disappeared into their small bedroom. I wanted to call Sharon, but I couldn't bear her disappointment. Tomorrow, I'd call.

"Mom," Lacey stood in my doorway. Arms crossed in front of her, mustering her fiercest frown. "Tomorrow morning, you're going to be on the 8:00 a.m. bus. You'll be in Pittsburg by 2:30. Rina's packing your bag. No arguments."

"Honey, what are you talking about?" I put down the book that I'd been pretending to read. "I told you that I wasn't going. We can't afford it. Who's going keep an eye on you?"

Rina nudged her sister aside. She rarely wasted time arguing. She operated with the motto, "Make your point and move on."

"Mom. Tough love time. You deserve a break, and you're getting one. Bus tickets are cheap, so we bought you one. We asked Dad to help. He owes you big time 'cause we turned out so well." Her grin softened the words.

"Yeah," Lacey said. "We're over eighteen. We're grown-ups, even if we still act like kids sometimes. So, we'll be alright by ourselves."

She and Carina exchanged that mysterious sister look that I'd intercepted over the years.

It meant they had a plan.

"Listen, this is very sweet, but you're college students. You need to save your money for books and things." I couldn't believe they'd engineered all this. I was the mom. I decided who got vacations and how money was spent, right?

"Since you've always given us rules to live by, we made a list of rules for you." The two giggled, just like they were little kids about to get into mischief.

Lace cleared her throat: "Rules for Mom's *How Stella Got Her Groove Back* Weekend. One. Call us when you get there and when you're about to leave, just like we have to."

Rina read the next rule. "Two. Don't do anything you'll regret in the morning. Remember, you'll have to tell us everything, 'cause we'll find out the truth."

"Three. No bringing back a guy as young as us. You're not really Stella."

"Four. Have fun. When was the last time you had fun, Mom?" That question floored me. Maybe I'd thought they wouldn't notice my lack of social life.

To say that I was in awe would be an understatement. I hugged these two young women whom I'd raised and worried over, realizing that they were worried about me. I loved them more every single day.

I visited Sharon, lived by the rules, and had a great time. My daughters continue to fascinate and delight me, and their friendship means everything.

Having daughter-friends is an unexpected perk to being a mom. I'm very fortunate.

~Karla Brown

98

The Dance

A friend is someone who dances with you in the sunlight,
And walks with you in the shadows.
~Author Unknown

I t doesn't always turn out well. There's that little dance where I say, "Hi, glad to finally meet you, I've heard so much about you." And she counters with, "It's nice to meet you too." Polite conversation, hesitant, careful steps. I try to multitask by keeping the lips moving while my brain processes the image. Gee, I didn't think she'd be this tall and skinny. She does have a pretty smile though and that hair, wow, like a shimmering shawl wrapped around her shoulders. Her deep brown eyes sparkle. She's lively, she's fun, she's full of life.

A couple of meetings later and things are still cool and breezy. I can see she's here to stay. Sometimes I feel old and stodgy in her presence. My clothes don't fit like they used to, despite buying a larger size. Her clothes float around her, accentuating her lovely curves. How does she stay so thin? Is she really that thin, or am I just that fat? Oh, it's difficult being the older model! We do have a bit in common and we can build on that. We do the minuet by daintily presenting a foot and lightly pulling it back. She loves animals, so do I. She loves kids, so do I. She's a klutz, so am I! These little things add up.

Another chance meeting. I like her style. Do I dare admit that to her? She can wear anything and look great! Even in her welding outfit she's a charmer. She actually complimented my au gratin potatoes. Maybe this could actually work. She has a brother, no sisters, and her mother—well, they have their "issues." I have two sisters and we three are so different. My mother—well, we had our "issues" too. How do we get to know someone? Listening, sharing, caring.

Let's do a foxtrot today, a sly, sneaky step here and there. I love how she grasps the humor in any situation. Her wit, warmth, and winning smile fill the room. She tells me how she messed up at work. "Luckily for me they finally hired me full-time instead of temporary. And what do I do? My first day of permanent employment I drilled holes into 400 parts in the wrong place." She gets my impossible moments too. "And there I was with three little kids and a car frozen shut at midnight. Funny now, not so much at the time."

Now we're into a tango. Our families are not perfect, downright crazy, and who would want any part of that? Sometimes the steps we are asked to take are too difficult. We've shared too much too fast. I don't want to know about the drugs and alcohol. Can't you just stay perfect? I can't deal with how you lost custody of your children. She on the other hand doesn't "get" the struggles I've had with my son. Our steps retreat, fade away. We take a break, and the dance floor clears.

It's exciting to be part of this younger crowd, visiting the apple orchard. We run from the hay wagon to the crafts area, the smell of apple pie and cider permeating the air. The apples are hard, smooth, and shiny. We can't wait to taste them! We buy some and head to the café where we can relax and sample the wares. As I crunch into my first Macintosh I feel the drizzle of juice dribble down my chin and know that this is a good day, a day of memories. Who better to share it with than my best friends? Yes, this is my favorite group of people. And yes, this would not be nearly as much fun if she were not a part of it. The guys think this whole apple orchard thing is idiotic. But they have forgotten the little boys who ran up and down the hills, apples in hand, yelling with excitement. My friend and I give each other a tiny, smirky glance behind the guys' backs. We understand each other and we know we'll remember this day fondly.

Has it been a year already? I like the way the visits have become comfortable, like doing a slow waltz, both parties understanding where the steps are leading. We are comfortable with the arrangement. I don't see her as skinny now, but rather as slender and elegant. Her smile still radiates warmth. I never expected to share so much so freely. I never expected a daughter-in-law to be a friend. I never expected my life to be so enriched. We dance on.

~Linda Bartlett

99

Chicken Soup for the Soul

Kory

*A sister is a gift to the heart, a friend to the spirit,
a golden thread to the meaning of life.*
~Isadora James

It's never been easy having a "Peter Pan" father—someone who never grew up and never cared about anyone but himself. His presents were never things I wanted, and his phone calls were few and far between. After thirteen years of pain and suffering, I finally gave up on him. I didn't need him.

But when I was nine, I found out about another daughter of his, an older half-sister of mine, named Kory. For eight years, I wondered about her. What was her favorite color? Did she like country music? What kind of person was she? Was there any way she could be anything like me? I imagined some rocker chick, with a black pixie cut and intense green eyes. Sometimes, I'd wish I could ask her things, something any girl would ask their big sister. "How do you do your make-up?" and "What do I wear to homecoming?" She became like a fairy tale for me. Some untouchable, make-believe being. Until a few months ago.

I had recently turned seventeen and started junior year of high school. I was painting my nails when my mom came into my room. "Hey Kenzi?"

"Hmmm?"

"I have something to show you."

I groaned and followed her to the computer. She clicked on something called "Planters Princesses" and showed me a picture of a tall, brown-eyed, beautiful girl in a light green dress. I somehow immediately knew who it was. "Is that... is that Kory?"

"Yeah," Mom whispered. She showed me a few pictures and then highlighted something in the e-mail between her and Kory's mom, Joy.

"Kory will be eighteen soon and very much wants to start talking to Kenzi," the e-mail read. "She knows she has a sister out there and wants to know her."

This can't be real, I thought. I couldn't even form a complete sentence. "She... she wants to talk to... to me?"

Mom looked at me. "Do you want to talk to her? Are you ready?"

It was a big choice for me. Was I ready to accept this new person in my life? I was having a hard time finding out who I was anyway, without a new sister in the mix. But after a long time of thinking, I finally said yes. I wanted to know Kory. I wanted to finally see who she was.

Mom "friended" her on Facebook and I read over her shoulder as she talked to Joy. I was still trying to let the reality of this sink in.

Mom finally plopped me down in her chair and I stared at the computer screen. My life was about to change. Suddenly, a message popped up.

"Hey..."

I don't think there was a full thought in my head, at the time.

"Hey."

And then we were both typing at once, trying to type faster and trying to soak up any amount of knowledge we could.

We agreed on a love of theater and her favorite animal was an owl. She was a cheerleader but was also a bit clumsy. We both kept typing, "I can't believe this," over and over and over. Finally, at 10 p.m. we realized we had to get to bed. Both of us had school the next day.

School was another story though. I could hardly focus! I remember sitting in Spanish and all I could think about was Kory.

Throughout lunch I talked my poor boyfriend's ear off about her. "Does she like fruit snacks? Does she have a boyfriend? Does she have any other brothers or sisters? Is she thinking about me? What's her voice sound like? What's her laugh like? What does she smell like? Is she thinking about me? Why does she do cheerleading? What music does she listen to? Does she like texting? What about the *Twilight* series? Is she thinking about me?" I literally could not stop thinking about her. I was finally going to have all my questions answered!

Soon, we started texting each other. The question and answer sessions lasted all day, every day. She'd never read my favorite play, *Cyrano de Bergerac*, but also hated coconut. She'd seen *Footloose*, liked it, but wasn't obsessed like I am. She also loved chocolate. She'd taken Spanish, and our opinion of it was the same — "Ew." We both obsessed over our phones, and both of us had a longtime boyfriend. Our first kisses were both during freshman year of high school. Her favorite show was *Grey's Anatomy* while mine remained undecided. We were sisters, there was no doubt about it.

Currently, I'm lying on my bed, texting Kory and writing this. She told me I should do it, so I did. She's getting ready for a game she has to cheer at way off in Washington while I sit here in Oregon. And guess what? Distance doesn't matter. It doesn't matter that I didn't talk to her until last year. She's my sister. And I love her more than you can imagine. She recently got a scholarship award and I'm so proud of her. She's not the rocker chick I dreamed up, but she's better.

And yeah, all those silly little sister questions? I ask them all the time. She helped me pick out my homecoming dress via text. She's helped me with my relationship with God. She's the best big sister I could have ever asked for. She's beautiful, smart, talented, and the kindest person I know.

She was worth waiting for.

~McKenzi Seggerman

Sister-Friends, Then and Now

Our brothers and sisters are there with us from the dawn of our personal stories to the inevitable dusk.

~Susan Scarf Merrell

They arrived at noon bearing a perfectly arranged fruit salad. Joycie would have liked a much earlier start, perhaps 7 a.m., because Joycie is a morning person. But her sister Nancy talked some sense into her.

"Will we have enough time?" Joycie, our unofficial timekeeper, fussed. And this time, for good reasons.

These periodic reunions of two sets of sisters who lived next door to one another as Philadelphia children are rare. Joycie lives in Portland now. She's a widow. So visits back East don't happen often.

Nancy is in the Philadelphia suburbs, but still works full-time.

My sister is not as footloose and fancy-free as she used to be because her significant other is ailing.

And I am the wild card—the unscheduled, often overwhelmed freelance writer.

But we managed it this time, and I was hosting. My husband graciously—and I think gratefully—removed himself for the day. Our common denominators, our private jokes, our kaleidoscopic memories, are not really his—or anybody else's—to share.

Lunch for this group meant figuring out food for four dieters. But talking was clearly our sacred mission.

We have been talking for years. Since early childhood.

We grew up together, smoked our first forbidden cigarettes together, learned the intricacies of applying mascara without blinding ourselves as a quartet, and have been through every imaginable milestone, loss, triumph, and test together.

Sitting at our dining room table, time stood still.

So many of our sentences began with the words "Remember when?"

Remembering, now, is both wonderful and awful. Coming of age has yielded to just plain aging, and one of us noted that we'd spent as much time talking about aches, pains, and insurance plans as we used to spend talking about boys.

Joycie, Nancy, and of course, my sister, listened patiently to stories about my dates with awful guys, promising guys, and ultimately, an older man named Victor who would turn out to be The One. I think they all knew it before I did.

Nobody knows me better. I like to think that few people care about me more.

And there are no others in my life who would tolerate my musing over whether I should level with one of my daughters about her new frumpy look.

We talked about regrets, about the roads not taken, about Nancy's career issues, Ruthie's situation with her guy, Joycie's coping skills as a new widow in a new place.

I told my beloved lunch companions how it feels to be the group's only first-marriage survivor. And I listened to them reflect on what they'd learned from some difficult times in the holy state of matrimony department.

We drank decaffeinated coffee and herbal tea and argued about what constitutes joy at our stage of life.

And as the afternoon wound down, we remembered our parents. With love, delight, and regret.

Joycie and Nancy recognized the paintings, now in our bedroom and living room, which had once hung in my parents' Philadelphia home. Nobody else would ever have that sense-memory.

Nancy, with her no-nonsense, common sense approach to life, listened to a couple of my family issues and issued her crisp observations. In minutes, she had helped me clear my mind of several problems.

Sitting around our dining room table were women "of a certain age," women who love one another, like one another, and have the common bond of shared memory.

I wanted the three of them to stay forever. Of course they couldn't and didn't.

But as we said goodbye in the driveway, the hugs were a bit tighter than they used to be. The promises to do it all again, sooner rather than later, had more urgency.

We are old friends, dear friends, sister sets. We are women joined at the soul.

And oh my, how much that matters.

~Sally Friedman

Starbuck

A journey is best measured in friends,
rather than miles.
~Tim Cahill

It had been several months since I had seen my friend Lauren. We had worked together at a local farm for several years and had shared more than a few unexpected and unconventional times.

I spent the better half of my day making chicken Parmigiana, garlic and oil pasta, a tossed salad and garlic bread. For dessert, a lovely cheesecake. It had been way too long since I had seen my friend.

Minutes before she was due to arrive I quickly set the table and opened the wine—always a staple at our dinners. My husband Jack and daughter Emma would be joining us. When we all got together there was never any shortage of laughter, or wine!

The doorbell rang and in came Lauren with yet another bottle. She was greeted by our nine-year-old, 135-pound Mastiff, Max, who approached her with the outward appearance of a junkyard dog but the inner gentleness of a nine-month-old pup. After accepting the customary kisses from Max, she came to me for our long overdue embrace.

Emma and Jack came down from the upstairs office and the three of them gathered in the living room while I transferred the food from the kitchen to the dining room. It was already almost nine so we sat down to eat right away.

Halfway through our meal I noticed that Lauren had not touched her wine.

"Lauren, would you rather have white?" I asked.

"No, I won't be drinking this evening."

I blurted out the first thing that came to mind.

"Are you pregnant?"

"No, no, no," she answered, with a surprised smile. "No! It's just that after dinner I have to drive and pick up something for the farm," she explained.

"What do you have to pick up at ten at night?"

"A goat."

"A goat? Where do you pick up a goat in suburban Connecticut?"

"He's not in Connecticut. He's in Virginia."

I waited, trying to process what my crazy friend had just said.

"So let me get this straight. You are going to leave here after ten and drive to Virginia? With whom?"

"Just me," she replied matter-of-factly.

At the same moment Emma and I looked at each other and both screamed, "Road trip!"

I looked over at my husband, who enthusiastically said, "Go for it!"

Like two little kids just invited for an impromptu sleepover, we left the table, ran upstairs, packed a quick overnight bag and met back downstairs within minutes. Jack was in the kitchen preparing a snack bag because, after all, no road trip is complete without Twizzlers, Cracker Jacks and other assorted munchies.

Before I knew it we were in the truck, Emma in the backseat and me as sidekick. Despite being direction-challenged, I would serve as navigator. I estimated it would take us approximately five hours to get to the little town in Virginia, an hour south of Washington, D.C.

Adrenaline flowed throughout the ride. Emma was home for summer break. She had countless tales of classes and roommates.

She shared her dreams of saving the world. For her, the world was a blank canvas and she was going to use as many colors as she could.

Lauren and I chimed in with our thoughts and before you knew it, we were thinking of things that could help Emma as well as ourselves accomplish things that had been on our to-do lists.

Soon the conversation turned towards Lauren. She had just broken up with someone after many years. Actually, as the conversation developed, we learned that her boyfriend had abruptly broken it off. Emma and I were shocked. As upbeat as Lauren was, as she described the breakup, Emma and I knew she was broken-hearted. As the conversation developed, Emma and I started the customary bashing of the ex-beau and before you knew it we were all laughing through her tears.

It was good for Lauren to be able to talk to us about this unexpected turn in her life. And to help her realize that in all actuality she had outgrown that relationship a long time ago. Her life had been heading in a different direction for some time and now she could explore her own dreams.

Along the way we learned that the goat farm that Lauren ran was looking to expand their herd and needed an additional buck to mate with the current does. We were on a mating mission! We laughed at that thought as Emma and I made mental notes of guys we knew who would be a good fit with our newly single girlfriend.

Before we knew it, four hours had passed. We decided to stop for the night at a small motel about an hour away from the farm where we were to pick up the buck the next morning.

We awoke well rested to a crystal clear sky. There was a small diner renowned for its pies down the road, so we all had pie for breakfast. To make it well balanced we ordered our pies à la mode.

The last leg of our trip had us traveling down a long winding road towards the farm. I was so in awe of the landscape, with miles and miles of undeveloped land. It was breathtaking. At the end of the road we found ourselves in front of the most majestic farmhouse.

We sat reflecting for a few minutes and then I broke the silence. "Great trip, Lauren! Thanks for letting us invite ourselves."

She just smiled that gorgeous, dimpled smile back at me.

Getting out of the truck, we all took time to stretch. I was happy to see that a nineteen-year-old, a thirty-year-old and a forty-nine-year-old shared the same symptoms after sitting in a car for so long.

A woman in her early forties appeared from the house and asked if we had any problems finding them and whether she could get us anything.

"We're fine. Thanks."

Her young son, who had been hidden from view, suddenly jumped out from behind her. "Please Mom, can I take them to the stall? Please?"

"Go ahead, Joe. You can say your goodbyes to Starbuck and help the ladies get him in the truck."

"Starbuck?" I repeated. "Is that the name of your goat?"

"Yes," the little boy answered. "He is a star! He is so handsome and all the does love him."

Joe located Starbuck in his stall, attached a lead to him and guided him into Lauren's truck. Then, quite nonchalantly, he said goodbye, sending Starbuck on his way to Connecticut.

Driving with Starbuck in the back cab, we noticed a strange, unpleasant odor. Emma and I asked Lauren what it was. With a sly smile, she announced that Starbuck was ready to meet the does of Connecticut. He was in heat.

Five hours and several stops later we were back in Connecticut. We pulled into the farm, taking the service road to the goat pens.

Through the darkness we heard the restless sounds of the female goats pacing in their stalls. We realized that Starbuck's arrival had been confirmed. The does were looking forward to their visitor.

Starbuck settled into his new home. Emma and I got back in

the truck and Lauren drove us back to our house. When we arrived, Lauren looked at us with a devilish smile.

"Now that we got Starbuck a few dates," she said, "you wouldn't have anyone in mind for me, would you?"

Emma and I laughed. "Of course!"

We were ready for another mating mission.

~Jeanne Blandford

Meet Our Contributors

Georgia Alderink and her husband Fred lived in Takoma Park, MD from 1982 to 1994. After retirement they moved to Arkansas. Georgia has had two children's novels published, *Who's Been Soaking in My Hot Tub?* and *Pea Brain and Wheelchair Willie*, plus two non-fiction stories for adults. E-mail her at georgia.alderink@gmail.com.

Diana M. Amadeo is an award-winning author whose byline has been seen in hundreds of publications including books, magazines, anthologies, newspapers and online. This is her ninth published story in a *Chicken Soup for the Soul* book.

Monica A. Andermann lives on Long Island where she shares her home with her husband Bill and their cat Marlo DeCarlo. Her work has been included in such publications as *Angels on Earth*, *The Secret Place*, *Woman's World*, and several other titles in the *Chicken Soup for the Soul* series.

Linda Bartlett received her BS degree from the University of Wisconsin-Superior and a master's degree from Bethel College in St. Paul, MN. She taught school for thirty-one years and then became a flight attendant for Delta Connection. She is now retired, traveling the world and writing for fun.

Jeanne Blandford is a writer/editor who, along with her husband Jack, is currently producing documentaries and creating children's books. When not in their Airstream looking for new material, they can be found running SafePet, a partnership between Outreach for Pets in Need (OPIN) and Domestic Violence Crisis Center (DVCC).

Marcy Blesy is the author of a picture book in the grief genre entitled *Am I Like My Daddy?* as well as a young adult short story trilogy and a middle grade novel available on Amazon. She blogs about books at www.marcyblesy.com. Marcy and her family reside in Southwest Michigan.

Lil Blosfield is the Chief Financial Officer for Child and Adolescent Behavioral Health in Canton, OH. She enjoys time spent with her family and friends, hot summer days by the pool and cozy winter evenings by the fire. She plays the piano and sometimes attempts karaoke with her husband, Ted. E-mail her at LBlosfield40@msn.com.

Grand prize winner in the Coast Weekend's serial mystery chapter contest, **Jan Bono** is writing a cozy mystery series set on the southwest Washington coast. She has written four short story collections, numerous one-act plays, two poetry chapbooks and over 700 blog entries. Check out her work at www.JanBonoBooks.com.

Cynthia Briggs celebrates her love of cooking and writing through her heartwarming cookbooks, *Pork Chops & Applesauce* and *Sweet Apple Temptations*. She's written two e-books and writes for newspapers, magazines and publishers. Other than writing, Briggs enjoys speaking to women's groups and coaching budding authors. E-mail her at cynthiabriggsbook@yahoo.com.

Karla Brown is a writer of non-fiction short stories, fantasy adventure and children's manuscripts. She is a flight attendant with US Airways Express. Karla adores her husband and daughters who, along with her impish grandson, make her smile every day! She enjoys children, books, swimming, and gardening. E-mail her at karlab612@yahoo. com.

Katie Cash earned her Bachelor's of Science with Honors degree in Oceanography from the United States Naval Academy in 2011. She is a Surface Warfare Officer currently stationed in San Diego, CA, where she enjoys surfing, hiking, and triathlons. She is also an aspiring novelist and loves to travel the world.

Carol A. Cassara is a writer who lives life out loud in the San Francisco Bay area. She loves books, travel, blue skies, her dogs and coming up with essay ideas. Her memoir about reconciling with her husband twenty-seven years after their divorce is in progress. E-mail her at ccassara@aol.com.

Beth Cato is an active member of the Science Fiction & Fantasy Writers of America, and a frequent contributor to the *Chicken Soup for the Soul* series. She's originally from Hanford, CA, but now resides in Buckeye, AZ, with her husband and son. Learn more at www. bethcato.com.

Writing is both **Jane M. Choate's** avocation and vocation. Being able to touch another with her words is her greatest thrill.

Madeline Clapps lives in Brooklyn with her boyfriend and her cat Vanilla Bean. She went to New York University and is a singer, writer, and editor, with many stories published in *Chicken Soup for the Soul* books.

Lisa Ricard Claro is an award-winning short story author, Pushcart Prize nominee, and freelance commercial copywriter. Published across multiple media, Lisa is affiliated with RWA/GRW and SCBWI. She resides in Georgia with her husband and loves to hear from readers! E-mail her at lisa.r.claro@gmail.com and read her at blog www.WritingintheBuff.net.

Carol Commons-Brosowske is a native Texan. She's been married to her best friend Jim for thirty-nine years. They have three grown children. She enjoys quilting, her four dogs and of course writing. She's a weekly columnist for *Frank Talk* magazine and has been published in several anthologies. E-mail her at cab2821@verizon. net.

Harriet Cooper is a freelance writer and has published personal essays, humor and creative nonfiction in newspapers, newsletters, anthologies and magazines. She is a frequent contributor to the *Chicken Soup for the Soul* series. She writes about family, relationships, health, food, cats, writing and daily life. E-mail her at shewrites@ live.ca.

Candyce Deal, Ed.S, a writer based in Georgia, is a former schoolteacher and administrator. She has written curriculum and designed thematic units for numerous educational publications. The mother of three, she often writes about parenting and child development. Other topics of interest include balanced living, fitness, wellness, and creativity.

Mary Dempsey, a former teacher and bookstore owner, resides in Bluffton, SC. Her writing has appeared in newspapers, magazines and three *Chicken Soup for the Soul* anthologies. She is a freelance writer for a local newspaper and recently published a book of her short stories. E-mail her at Marydemp27@yahoo.com.

Laurie Carnright Edwards received her BA degree from Berkshire Christian College and an MATS from Gordon-Conwell Theological Seminary. She is a pastor's wife and the mother of two wonderful grown children. She enjoys working with children and teens, and writing to honor God. E-mail her at laurieedwards@myfairpoint.net.

Shawnelle Eliasen and her husband Lonny raise their brood of boys in Illinois. Her stories have been published in *Guideposts*, *MomSense* magazine, *Marriage Partnership*, *Thriving Family*, *Cup of Comfort* books, numerous *Chicken Soup for the Soul* books, and more. Visit her blog, Family Grace with My Five Sons, at Shawnellewrites.blogspot.com.

Holly English is a freelance writer. She enjoys playing the banjo and piano badly. She has four mostly perfect children.

Melissa Face teaches high school English and devotes her free time to writing. Melissa's stories and essays have appeared in numerous magazines and anthologies. She lives in Virginia with her husband and son. E-mail Melissa at writermsface@yahoo.com.

Andrea Farrier has been a teacher, lobbyist, writer, and home-schooling mom. Soon, however, the Farrier family is getting ready to embark on their greatest adventure yet—sharing the gospel as missionaries in Guatemala. If you want to follow their adventures, e-mail them at farriersoffaith@yahoo.com.

A longtime contributor to the *Chicken Soup for the Soul* series, **Sally Friedman**, a Moorestown, NJ writer, has been writing about family and generational issues for decades. Her work has appeared in the *New York Times*, *Philadelphia Inquirer*, *Huffington Post* and other national and regional publications. E-mail her at pinegander@aol.com.

Claire Fullerton is an award-winning essayist whose first novel, *A Portal in Time*, will be published in early 2014. She is a contributor to numerous newspapers and magazines, and is an avid ballerina who divides her time between Northern and Southern California with her husband and two German Shepherds.

Crystal Gibson is a Canadian expat in France who graduated from the University of Western Ontario with a degree in English and French Linguistics. She is a freelance writer and teaches business

English. She can be found blogging about her pets and expat life at www.crystalgoestoeurope.blogspot.com.

Robin Gwozdz is a semi-retired registered nurse, grandma of the world's most adorable twins, and lifelong desert rat. After a long career caring for the elderly and disabled, nowadays she loves family time, working out, writing, sports, laughing with friends, and above all, her husband Mike. E-mail her at robinsmytucson@yahoo.com.

Deanne Haines is a Wisconsin-based freelance writer and frequent contributor to parenting magazines across the country. She feels blessed to have a wonderful husband, three children and amazing friends—old and new. In her spare time Deanne enjoys running and traveling to exciting locales. Find out more at DeanneHaines.com.

Nancy Hatten returned to her native Illinois two years ago, after twenty years in Texas. She enjoys walking, yoga, gardening, and photography. Nancy hopes to live long enough to see the Chicago Cubs win the World Series.

Miriam Hill is a frequent contributor to *Chicken Soup for the Soul* books and has been published in *Writer's Digest*, *The Christian Science Monitor*, *Grit*, *St. Petersburg Times*, *The Sacramento Bee* and Poynter Online. Miriam's manuscript received Honorable Mention for Inspirational Writing in a Writer's Digest Writing Competition.

"The Inncrowd" is a group of women who work at the Channel Road Inn and the Inn at Playa del Rey in Los Angeles, CA. As a member of this sisterhood, writer **Rebecca Hill** considers it an honor and a privilege to work in the hospitality industry as an innkeeper.

Georgia A. Hubley retired after twenty years in financial management to write full-time. Her work has been published in *Woman's World*, the *Chicken Soup for the Soul* series, Hallmark book series and various anthologies and magazines. She resides with her husband of thirty-five years in Henderson, NV. E-mail her at geohub@aol.com.

Jodi Icenoggle is a native Montanan with a degree in sports medicine. She is raising three horse-crazy, rodeo-loving boys in the Big Sky State. Jodi enjoys hiking, horses, books, and just about anything outdoors. E-mail her at jodi@jodiicenoggle.com.

Jennie Ivey lives in Tennessee. She is the author of numerous works of fiction and nonfiction, including several stories in the *Chicken Soup for the Soul* anthology. Learn more at www.jennieivey.com.

When she's not walking on the beach with her husband, former librarian and teacher **Linda Jett** writes, practices massage, and grandparents from her home in Newberg, OR. As an active member of Oregon Christian Writers, she has published true inspirational stories, devotions, and poems in a variety of collections.

Linda Jewell, a home-front mom, supports our nation's troops, their families, and military veterans. She writes, speaks, and interfaces with the media on the topics of patriotism, parenting, and prayer. Linda provides practical tips, resources, inspiration, and encouragement to help moms be courageous in tough times. E-mail her at LJewell@ npgcable.com.

Devika Jones received her B.F.A. degree from Massachusetts College of Arts and M.S. degree from MIT. She is a Life Coach in Arizona. Devika loves to inspire and assist her clients fulfill their potential. When not writing a short story, she loves to paint. E-mail her at target@earthlink.net.

After joining several different writing associations, fellow writers and "girlfriends" encouraged **Alice Klies** to publish. Her stories have appeared in *Angels on Earth*, *Wordsmith Journal* and anthology books;

God Meets Needs; *Grandmother, Mother and Me*; *Grandfather, Father and Me* and *Friends of Inspire Faith*.

April Knight is a profession artist and a freelance writer. Her favorite pastimes are riding horses and traveling. She recently visited Australia and Alaska. Her most recent novel is *Sweet Dreams: 50 Romantic Bedtime Stories for Big Girls*. E-mail her at aknightscribe@gmail.com.

Zoe Knightly will receive her Bachelor of Arts degree in Chemistry from the University of Richmond in December of 2013. She plans to pursue her career interests in health and medicine. Zoe loves cats, running, joggling (juggling while running), triathlons and creating unique art projects. She aspires to write motivational books.

Nancy Julien Kopp lives in Manhattan, KS, but is originally from Chicago. She began writing late in life, but has been published in thirteen *Chicken Soup for the Soul* books, other anthologies, ezines, newspapers and magazines. Once a classroom teacher, she now teaches through the written word.

Lisa McManus Lange, a multi-published author of humorous and inspirational slice-of-life articles, is from Victoria, BC, Canada. This is her third publication in the *Chicken Soup for the Soul* anthology. Learn more at www.lisamcmanuslange.blogspot.com or e-mail her at lisamc2010@yahoo.ca. This one is dedicated to Janelle.

Karen E. Lewis was born in Scotland and has served as a missionary in Mexico. She currently lives in England with her husband who pastors a local church. She enjoys traveling, the company of good friends and laughing until her belly hurts. E-mail her at karenhaveafantasticday@gmail.com.

A frequent contributor to the *Chicken Soup for the Soul* series, **Linda Lohman** lives in Sacramento, CA. Retired from two separate careers she writes for pleasure, extensively for grieving widows. Family, friends, and her Yorkie, Lucy, give her a plethora of stories and memories. E-mail her at lindaalohman@yahoo.com.

Barbara LoMonaco has worked for Chicken Soup for the Soul as an editor since 1998. She has co-authored two *Chicken Soup for the Soul* book titles and has had stories published in numerous other titles. Barbara is a graduate of the University of Southern California and has a teaching credential.

Crescent LoMonaco used her knowledge from years of working behind the chair and owning a hair salon to write the "Ask a Stylist" column for the *Santa Barbara Independent*. She is a frequent contributor to the *Chicken Soup for the Soul* series. She lives on the South Coast with her husband and son.

Patricia Lorenz is an art-of-living writer and speaker. She's the author of thirteen books including *Life's Too Short to Fold Your Underwear* and *Positive Quotes for Every Day*. She has over sixty stories in fifty books in the *Chicken Soup for the Soul* anthology. To have her speak to your group, visit her website www.PatriciaLorenz.com.

Lauren Magliaro lives in New Jersey with her husband and their six-year-old son. Lauren loves reading, hockey, Bruce Springsteen, the Yankees, planning events with her "survivor sisters" and being a stay-at-home mom. Being published was on her bucket list, so she's thrilled to be part of this book! E-mail her at LaurenMags19@aol.com.

Sara Matson lives with her family in Minnesota, where she home-schools her twin daughters and spends her free time reading, writing, and chatting with her friend Amy by e-mail. You can reach Sara through her website at www.saramatson.com.

Dayna Mazzuca is working as a poet, writer and creative workshop leader in Victoria, BC, Canada. She has a background in philosophy and spiritual formation, and loves to lead writing groups through her church. She home-schools her children and enjoys hiking, biking and swimming in lakes. E-mail her at 2dayna@telus.net.

Cynthia Mendenhall writes in Phoenix. She has completed her memoir, and two other books—all yet to be published. She enjoys swimming, coffee, small adventures and bubbles. Cynthia is a Certified Life Coach available to speak to groups of women. E-mail her at rcmendy@hotmail.com.

When **Gail Molsbee Morris** isn't chasing after God's heart, she chases rare birds across America. She can be reached through her nature blog godgirlgail.com or Twitter @godgirlgail.

Lava Mueller jumps for joy when her stories are accepted by the *Chicken Soup for the Soul* series; she does the Happy Dance and her children get very embarrassed. Lava and Marion are closer than ever and this is why Lava's arms are constantly bruised. E-mail Lava at lavamueller@yahoo.com.

Nell Musolf lives with her family in Minnesota where she likes to read, write and visit with her neighbors. She writes a "blog opera" that can be viewed at schuylersquaredailydrama.blogspot.com.

Linda O'Connell is a multi-published writer from St. Louis, MO who finds humor in everyday experiences. She enjoys a good laugh, a great book and beach vacations with her husband Bill. Linda blogs at lindaoconnell.blogspot.com.

Chicken Soup for the Soul editor **Kristiana Glavin Pastir** earned a journalism degree from Syracuse University in 2004. When she's not reading, writing, or editing for Chicken Soup for the Soul, Kristiana enjoys reading, yoga, and adventures with her husband—especially their scuba diving trips around the world.

Kristi Paxton majored in art at Iowa State University. For fun, Kristi travels, cooks, kayaks, walks and writes. Her features and photos—from ice fishing to flower farming—appear in a regional newspaper. She lives with her husband and dog. E-mail her at kristi.a.paxton@gmail.com or read her blog at kristipaxton.tumblr.com.

Allison Potter is a wife, mother, volunteer, and aspiring writer from Michigan. She is a graduate of Hope College in Holland, MI. Allison's favorite place is any beach on Lake Michigan with a good book.

Veteran editor, active ghostwriter and award-winning author, **Carol McAdoo Rehme** spins stories from a window-banked office nestled in her historic Victorian home. Her newest releases include *Fundamentally Female* (placed in the swag bags at the 2013 Oscars) and *Finding the Pearl: Unstoppable passion, unbridled success*, both award-winning books.

Lydia Gomez Reyes is a published writer and poet. Her love for God is the driving force behind her writing. Several of her devotionals and poems have appeared in *The Secret Place*. Lydia lives in Colorado Springs, CO with her husband, Rey, of thirty-five years. Learn more at www.lydiareyes.com.

Connie Rosser Riddle lives in Apex, NC with her husband, David. She recently completed an inspirational memoir about her yearly solo journeys that followed her struggle with cancer and being fired from a job. Visit her blog at ConnieRosserRiddle.blogspot.com. E-mail her at ConnieRosserRiddle@gmail.com.

Nan Rockey graduated from Taylor University in 2012 with a BA degree in Media Communications with a writing emphasis. She married a fellow writer, Jordan Rockey, in February 2013 and enjoys creating stories and spending time with her husband and pet tortoise in Bloomington, IN. E-mail her at nanleajohnson@gmail.com.

Sallie A. Rodman received her Certificate in Professional Writing from CSULB. Her stories have appeared in numerous *Chicken Soup for the Soul* anthologies. She loves creating art, writing and being with her friends. Sallie is planning an inspirational book on finding your way back to a happy life after widowhood. E-mail her at sa.rodman@verizon.net.

Sioux Roslawski is a third grade teacher in St. Louis, a teacher-consultant for the Gateway Writing Project and is also a member of the WWWPs, a writing critique group. Currently she's working on a variety of projects, including a novel. Visit her at siouxroslawski.com.

Mona Rottinghaus enjoys creating things. Her hobbies include sewing, embroidering, writing, music, and gardening. She is currently writing a family love storybook and plans to write an inspirational book documenting her journey into the world of mental illness, and the lessons she learned. E-mail her at mona@monasoriginals.com or visit monatheoriginal.blogspot.com.

Carolyn Roy-Bornstein is a mother, a doctor and the author of *Crash: A Mother, A Son, and the Journey from Grief to Gratitude* and the upcoming *Chicken Soup for the Soul: Recovering from Traumatic Brain Injuries*. Her non-fiction stories have appeared in *The Boston Globe*, *The Writer* magazine, *JAMA* and several *Chicken Soup for the Soul* anthologies. Read more at www.carolynroybornstein.com.

Mitali Ruths lives and knits in Montreal, Canada. Her story "Liftoff" was published in *Chicken Soup for the Soul: Here Comes the Bride*. E-mail her at mitali.ruths@gmail.com.

McKenzi Seggerman graduated from Marshfield High School and will be attending the International Air and Hospitality Academy. She met her sister, Kory, on July 8th of 2012. McKenzi plans to become a flight attendant. E-mail her at kenzi-elaine@hotmail.com.

Dana Sexton is a freelance author who has recently moved from Houston, TX to Nebraska. In 2012, she received the Susanne M. Glasscock award from Rice University in both poetry and fiction. Long ago and far away she earned a BA degree in English Literature from San Diego State University.

Dayle Shockley is an award-winning writer whose byline has appeared in dozens of publications. She is the author of three books and a contributor to many other works. She and her husband (a retired fire captain) enjoy traveling RV-style, enjoying God's handiwork. Dayle blogs at www.alittleofthisandthat2.blogspot.com.

Diane Stark is a former teacher turned stay-at-home mom and freelance writer. She is a wife and mother of five. She loves to write about the important things in life: her family and her faith. Learn more at www.DianeStark.blogspot.com.

Noelle Sterne publishes essays, writes craft articles, and spiritual pieces in many venues. With a PhD (Columbia University), Noelle coaches doctoral candidates to dissertation completion. Her book, *Trust Your Life: Forgive Yourself and Go After Your Dreams* (Unity Books), helps readers release regrets, re-label their pasts, and reach lifelong yearnings.

Loni Swensen and Lindsay are still dear friends who keep in touch between their current residences in Wyoming and Florida, respectively. Lindsay has two beautiful children and Loni had her first in February 2013. You can read about Loni's daily adventures on her blog at www.thingstowritedown.blogspot.com.

Beverly F. Walker resides in Greenbrier, TN and spends most of her time taking photographs and scrapbooking pictures of her grandchildren. She also is caregiver for her husband who is battling cancer and is thankful for the forty-seven years they have had together. She is published in nineteen *Chicken Soup for the Soul* books.

Sally Walls loves to encourage people. Sharing her experiences through storytelling has been a great platform to accomplish that. She shares life with her husband and son in the Canadian Rockies. She is a certified public speaker and can be contacted at sallywalls@ shaw.ca.

Kathy Whirity is a newspaper columnist who shares her sentimental musings on family life. Kathy is the author of *Life Is a Kaleidoscope*. She is also a contributor to the *Chicken Soup for the Soul* series. Learn more at www.kathywhirity.com or e-mail Kathy at kathywhirity@ yahoo.com.

Priscilla Whitley attended the University of Missouri as well as Fordham University majoring in Creative Writing. She has worked at Simon & Schuster and as a contributing feature writer for Hersam Acorn Newspapers. As facilitator of the Candlewood Writer's Group, Priscilla runs workshops for writers in Fairfield County, Connecticut.

Crysta Windsor has retreated to her journals to find release, through writing, since she was small. Her other hobbies include painting and baking. She is currently finishing a Bachelor of Arts (Honours) degree at Mount Royal University. She is an English major and plans to continue onto a master's degree in 2014.

Julie Winn is a musician and freelance writer/editor living in the Toronto area with her husband and three children. Her hobbies include singing with the Amadeus Choir, composing music, studying French and German, and working on her blog, found at winnwords1. wordpress.com.

Ferida Wolff is the author of books for both children and adults. Her essays and poems appear in anthologies, newspapers, magazines, and online at www.seniorwomen.com. Read her nature blog at www.

feridasbackyard.blogspot.com or e-mail her at feridawolff@msn. com.

Melissa Wootan enjoys refurbishing old furniture but is most passionate about writing. She has created a Facebook page to showcase both. ChIC vInTiQuE was designed to provide "Inspiration for the Heart and Home." Contact Melissa at www.facebook.com/ chicvintique. She'd also like to invite you to visit Tesi's website at www.trialsandtestimonies.com.

Linda C. Wright lives on the Space Coast of Florida with her husband Richard and her four-legged friend Ginger. Several of her personal essays have been anthologized in the *Chicken Soup for the Soul* series. In her spare time, Linda teaches creative writing to at-risk teens and enjoys traveling, photography and bike riding. E-mail her at lindacwright@ymail.com.

D. B. Zane teaches middle school history, is the mother of three, and always makes time to spend with just the girls. Her stories have appeared in other *Chicken Soup for the Soul* books and elsewhere. E-mail her at dbzanewriter@gmail.com.

Sheri Zeck enjoys writing creative nonfiction stories that encourage, inspire and entertain others. She lives in Milan, IL with her husband and three daughters. She has contributed stories to the *Chicken Soup for the Soul* series, *Guideposts*, *Angels on Earth*, *Farm & Ranch Living* and other magazines. Learn more at www.sherizeck.com.

Lori Zenker lives in a small town in Ontario, Canada. She is a frazzled pastor's wife and mom of three teenagers. She collects and sells old toys and junk, and spends all her extra time and money renovating her old house. This is her third story published by Chicken Soup for the Soul. E-mail her at lori@zenker.ca.

Melissa Zifzal worked in newspaper and public relations as a writer, designer, and editor before becoming a stay-at-home mom. She enjoys volunteering at her children's school and serving as a 4-H advisor. Melissa and her husband, Dwayne, live in Bloomingdale, OH with their sons, Ethan and Caleb, and daughter, Lindsey.

Meet Our Authors

Jack Canfield is the co-creator of the *Chicken Soup for the Soul* series, which *Time* magazine has called "the publishing phenomenon of the decade." Jack is also the coauthor of many other bestselling books.

Jack is the CEO of the Canfield Training Group in Santa Barbara, California, and founder of the Foundation for Self-Esteem in Culver City, California. He has conducted intensive personal and professional development seminars on the principles of success for more than a million people in 23 countries, has spoken to hundreds of thousands of people at more than 1,000 corporations, universities, professional conferences and conventions, and has been seen by millions more on national television shows.

Jack has received many awards and honors, including three honorary doctorates and a Guinness World Records Certificate for having seven books from the *Chicken Soup for the Soul* series appearing on the New York Times bestseller list on May 24, 1998.

You can reach Jack at www.jackcanfield.com.

Mark Victor Hansen is the co-founder of Chicken Soup for the Soul, along with Jack Canfield. He is a sought-after keynote speaker, bestselling author, and marketing maven. Mark's powerful messages of possibility, opportunity, and action have created powerful change in thousands of organizations and millions of individuals worldwide.

Mark is a prolific writer with many bestselling books in addition to the *Chicken Soup for the Soul* series. Mark has had a profound influence in the field of human potential through his library of audios, videos, and articles in the areas of big thinking, sales achievement, wealth building, publishing success, and personal and professional development. He is also the founder of the MEGA Seminar Series.

Mark has received numerous awards that honor his entrepreneurial spirit, philanthropic heart, and business acumen. He is a lifetime member of the Horatio Alger Association of Distinguished Americans.

You can reach Mark at www.markvictorhansen.com.

Amy Newmark has been Chicken Soup for the Soul's publisher, coauthor, and editor-in-chief for the last five years, after a 30-year career as a writer, speaker, financial analyst, and business executive in the worlds of finance and telecommunications. Amy is a *magna cum laude* graduate of Harvard College, where she majored in Portuguese, minored in French, and traveled extensively. She and her husband have four grown children.

After a long career writing books on telecommunications, voluminous financial reports, business plans, and corporate press releases, Chicken Soup for the Soul is a breath of fresh air for Amy. She has fallen in love with Chicken Soup for the Soul and its life-changing books, and really enjoys putting these books together for Chicken Soup for the Soul's wonderful readers. She has coauthored more than six dozen *Chicken Soup for the Soul* books and has edited another three dozen.

You can reach Amy with any questions or comments through webmaster@chickensoupforthesoul.com and you can follow her on Twitter @amynewmark or @chickensoupsoul.

Thank You

We owe huge thanks to all of our contributors. We know that you poured your hearts and souls into the thousands of stories that you shared with us, and ultimately with each other. As we read and edited these stories, we were truly amazed by your experiences. We appreciate your willingness to share these inspiring and encouraging stories with our readers.

We could only publish a small percentage of the stories that were submitted, but we read every single one and even the ones that do not appear in the book had an influence on us and on the final manuscript. We owe special thanks to our editor Barbara LoMonaco, who read the stories that were submitted for this book and narrowed the list down to a more manageable number of finalists. Our assistant publisher D'ette Corona did her normal masterful job of working with the contributors to approve our edits and answer any questions they had. Editor Madeline Clapps helped create the final manuscript and proofread the stories along with our editor Kristiana Pastir.

We also owe a special thanks to our creative director and book producer, Brian Taylor at Pneuma Books, for his brilliant vision for our covers and interiors.

~Amy Newmark

Chicken Soup for the Soul

Improving Your Life Every Day

Real people sharing real stories—for twenty years. Now, Chicken Soup for the Soul has gone beyond the bookstore to become a world leader in life improvement. Through books, movies, DVDs, online resources and other partnerships, we bring hope, courage, inspiration and love to hundreds of millions of people around the world. Chicken Soup for the Soul's writers and readers belong to a one-of-a-kind global community, sharing advice, support, guidance, comfort, and knowledge.

Chicken Soup for the Soul stories have been translated into more than forty languages and can be found in more than one hundred countries. Every day, millions of people experience a Chicken Soup for the Soul story in a book, magazine, newspaper or online. As we share our life experiences through these stories, we offer hope, comfort and inspiration to one another. The stories travel from person to person, and from country to country, helping to improve lives everywhere.

Chicken Soup for the Soul

Share with Us

We all have had Chicken Soup for the Soul moments in our lives. If you would like to share your story or poem with millions of people around the world, go to chickensoup.com and click on "Submit Your Story." You may be able to help another reader, and become a published author at the same time. Some of our past contributors have launched writing and speaking careers from the publication of their stories in our books!

Our submission volume has been increasing steadily—the quality and quantity of your submissions has been fabulous. We only accept story submissions via our website. They are no longer accepted via mail or fax.

To contact us regarding other matters, please send us an e-mail through webmaster@chickensoupforthesoul.com, or fax or write us at:

Chicken Soup for the Soul
P.O. Box 700
Cos Cob, CT 06807-0700
Fax: 203-861-7194

One more note from your friends at Chicken Soup for the Soul: Occasionally, we receive an unsolicited book manuscript from one of our readers, and we would like to respectfully inform you that we do not accept unsolicited manuscripts and we must discard the ones that appear.

Women have always been wonderful sources of inspiration and support for each other. They are willing to lay bare their souls, even to perfect strangers. Put two random women together in a waiting room, on an airplane, in a line at the supermarket, and the sharing begins, often at the deepest level. Women share hope, humor, and inspiration with each other in these 101 favorite stories from Chicken Soup for the Soul's library.

978-1-935096-04-7

More Fur